Silenced Sextet

Silenced Sextet

*Six Nineteenth-Century
Canadian Women Novelists*

CARRIE MacMILLAN

LORRAINE McMULLEN

ELIZABETH WATERSTON

McGill-Queen's University Press
Montreal & Kingston • London • Buffalo

© McGill-Queen's University Press 1992
ISBN 0-7735-0945-3

Legal deposit 2nd quarter 1993
Bibliothèque nationale du Québec

Printed in Canada on acid-free paper

This book has been published with the help of a grant
from the Canadian Federation for the Humanities,
using funds provided by the Social Sciences and
Humanities Research Council of Canada. Publication
has also been supported by grants from the University
of Ottawa, Mount Allison University, and the Canada
Council through its block grant program.

Canadian Cataloguing in Publication Data

MacMillan, Carrie, 1945–
  Silenced sextet: six nineteenth-century Canadian
  women novelists
  Includes bibliographical references.
  ISBN 0-7735-0945-3
  1. Canadian literature – Women authors – History and
  criticism. 2. Women authors, Canadian (English) –
  Biography. 3. Canadian literature – 19th century –
  History and criticism. I. McMullen, Lorraine, 1926–.
  II. Waterston, Elizabeth, 1922–. III. Title.
  PS8089.W6M33 1993   C810.9'9287   C92-090725-3
  PR9197.33.W65M33 1993

Illustrations, except for that of Robertson, are taken
from Henry J. Morgan, ed., *Types of Canadian Women
Past and Present*, 2 vols. (Toronto: Walham Briggs 1903).
Robertson photo courtesy of McCord Museum of
Canadian History, Notman Photographic Archives.

Typeset in Palatino 10/12 by
Caractéra production graphique inc., Quebec City.

Contents

Illustrations follow page x

Preface / ix

Introduction / 3

Rosanna Mullins Leprohon: At Home in Many
Worlds / 14
LORRAINE McMULLEN and ELIZABETH
WATERSTON

May Agnes Fleming: "I did nothing but write" / 52
LORRAINE McMULLEN

Margaret Murray Robertson: Domestic Power / 82
LORRAINE McMULLEN

Susan Frances Harrison ("Seranus"): Paths through the
Ancient Forest / 107
CARRIE MacMILLAN

Margaret Marshall Saunders: A Voice for the Silent / 137
ELIZABETH WATERSTON

Joanna E. Wood: Incendiary Women / 169
CARRIE MacMILLAN

Conclusion / 201

Notes / 209

For

Mona Wandless Gardner
Bertha Smith Hillman
Anna Foley McMullen

Preface

This book is the result of a collaborative effort over time and distance. Five years ago we discussed the phenomenon of Canadian women in the nineteenth century who achieved great popularity as writers of fiction but subsequently disappeared from view. In the regions and archives we knew best – Ontario, Quebec, New Brunswick, and Nova Scotia – we began tracing the lives and careers of six of these women; then we followed their literary and life-paths to Scotland, England, New York, Boston, California. At every stage we exchanged manuscripts, worked out a common approach, and agreed on the surprising diversity in these women's life-patterns, choice of literary modes, and fictional strategies. The final outcome is a book in which collaboration ranges from direct co-authorship in one chapter to general infusion of ideas from one another in every part of our book.

We conceived this joint project because we share three interests. We are all Canadianists (though two of us originally trained in other fields) with a special interest in fiction. Our studies in fiction have involved us individually in publications on nineteenth-century developments in the United States, France, England, and Scotland, but our focus has been on Canada. Second, we all read, teach, and write with feminist interests in mind. We are all particularly interested in the changing roles and opportunities of women in the late nineteenth century. Our third common interest is in archival work. We all savour the search in manuscripts and forgotten publications for new light on literary creation.

The six authors we study are interesting not only because they were women but also because they were widely read writers who, in their successive development of plot motifs, character studies, and stylistic mannerisms, reveal publishing conditions, readers' demands, and critics' influence over a century of Canadian life. In their letters and journals as well as their fiction these six authors also faced and reported on Canadian particularities in religious norms, political currents, regional preoccupations, and family life. We hope our examination of these writers and their works will be of broad value in cultural and feminist as well as literary studies.

We are grateful to the Social Sciences and Humanities Council of Canada for individual grants in support of our work, and to the Canadian Federation for the Humanities for a grant in aid of publication. At McGill-Queen's University Press, Philip Cercone encouraged our collaboration from the outset, Peter Blaney sustained this encouragement through the publication process, and Susan Kent Davidson suggested graceful ways of doing fuller justice to our authors. We thank the people in our own home libraries, at Mount Allison University, the University of Ottawa, and the University of Guelph, and all the other archivists who have helped us to rediscover facts about our authors and their work. Each of us also acknowledges a personal network of support. Unlike the women we studied, who wrote in virtual isolation from like-minded people, we have all worked with the sustaining help of supportive family and sympathetic colleagues.

Carrie MacMillan
Lorraine McMullen
Elizabeth Waterston

Joanna E. Wood

Margaret Murray Robertson

May Agnes Fleming

Susan Frances Harrison
(Seranus)

Margaret Marshall Saunders

Rosanna Mullins Leprohon

Silenced Sextet

Introduction

In the late nineteenth century, numbers of women deliberately sought a place in the public sphere, and the world of literature provided for many a compatible milieu. Six Canadian women were among the most successful and popular writers of this vital, expansive period.

Rosanna Leprohon, appearing first in English Canadian journals of the mid-century such as the *Literary Garland* and the *Family Herald*, became in the 1860s and 1870s even more popular in Quebec in French translation than in her original English. During the same period Margaret Robertson was published and widely read not only in Canada but also in Britain and the United States; May Agnes Fleming became Canada's first international best-selling author. As "Seranus," Susan Frances Harrison was publishing in prestigious American and British magazines such as the *Atlantic Monthly* and *Pall Mall Magazine* at the turn of the century. In 1894 Joanna Wood's *The Untempered Wind* was called "the strongest and best American novel of the year"; in 1896 Marshall Saunders' *Beautiful Joe* became a world-wide bestseller, translated into more than seventeen languages. Besides being extraordinarily popular, these six writers all developed impressive literary skills – strength in structuring fiction, stylistic polish, a penetrating sense of social interchange and interpersonal tensions, and power in communicating (and subverting) the patterns of myth and romance.

This sextet of women published extensively between 1847 (when Leprohon's first story appeared) and 1927 (when Saunders' last novel came out). Their work taken as a whole suggests a time-tied shift in family and educational patterns, religious and economic concerns, responses to the environment, and concepts of an ideal society. Their work also clarifies a specialized aspect of literary history: the changing story of publishing conditions and reader responses.

These women came from varied backgrounds; they represent a range of lifestyles and achieved different forms of success. One was a university graduate; one left convent school at sixteen. Three were married; three remained single. Two were from Quebec, two from Ontario, two from the Maritimes. Their writings reflect those differences: one wrote domestic romances, one historical novels; another wrote gothic extravaganzas, still another tales of animal pets. Their diversity warns us against stereotyping. As Elaine Showalter says in *A Literature of Their Own*, "The knowledge that their individual achievement would be subsumed under a relatively unfavorable group stereotype acted as a constant irritant to feminine novelists."[1] Yet all six of the women under consideration here shared at least one quality: an enduring urge to write. They became deft at plotting, keeping the essential suspense, stirring the urgent question "What next?" They developed stories that were funny, moving, chilling, thought-provoking. Each sharpened her craft until she had built up a devoted, widespread audience.

Many of the characters their readers responded to are built on strikingly original or independent insights into both social and literary conventions. Fleming's Jemima Ann, for instance, in *Lost for a Woman*, is much more than a stock figure from below stairs: looking through the "six inches of green crystal" of a basement window, she responds to "all she ever sees of the outer world on its winding way. Hundreds of ankles, male and female, thick and thin, clean and dirty, according to the state of the atmosphere."[2] Leprohon's Blanche de Villerai is an epic heroine, defending her seigneury first against a British army and then against a confident suitor who expects to take over its management.[3] And Wood's Marriotte is an incendiary portrait of female grace, dancing in a flood of sunshine, swaying "in graceful arabesques so that she seemed surrounded by flashes of different lights – like a spark dancing in a flame."[4]

The diversity of their stories and strengths attests to the broad and varied tastes of the contemporary audience for popular fiction. Readers were roused by the courtroom scene in Saunders' *The Girl from Vermont*, where furious women, attending the trial of a child-abuser, are derided for their sentimentalism by the judge;[5] but they also loved Saunders' comic fantasy in *Beautiful Joe's Paradise*, where the narrator laughs till the chuckles die down to "a gasp of a squeak" – "I had used my laughing apparatus so hard, that it was all out of gear, and I felt sore!"[6] They relished the gothic frisson stirred by a story in Harrison's *Crowded Out*, when a parrot's mocking cry rings out over a scene of fire and destruction,[7] and they enjoyed the comic morbidity of a character in Wood's *Judith Moore*: "'She does look gashly!' said Mrs Morris. 'Whatever would I do if she was to be took! And this minute she looks fit for laying out.'"[8] They were provoked to meditation by another character's puzzlement: "How strange if all these restraints that we call moral laws were evolved from the moral deformity of some far back progenitor – some man in whom nature warped the free, true impulses, so that ever after he and his descendants were hived in cages of laws – well, it is hard to tell, and, at any rate, it would be madness to open the cages."[9]

Making readers laugh or cry or think, sharing a momentary flush of regal power, lending poignance to drab reality: these are the ways a good popular writer creates a loyal, grateful audience. Like all such writers, our six Canadians blended wit and wisdom, sense and sensibility. They were also sufficiently aware of their own métier to build in comments on the kind of literature they were producing. Fleming, for example, like a post-modernist interjecting a clever metafiction or self-reference, catches Jemima Ann just before real romance comes into her life:

"It would be awful pleasant to be like they are in stories," muses Jemima Ann, still blinking upward at the great squares of blurred light, "and have azure eyes, and golden tresses, and wear white Swiss and sweeping silks all the year round, and have lovely guardsmen and dukes and things, to gaze at a person passionately and raise a person's hand to their lips." Jemima Ann lifts one of her own, a red right hand, at this point, and surveys it. It is not particularly clean; it has no nails to speak of; it is nearly as large as that of any of the foundry "hands"; and she sighs … There are hands and hands; the impossibility of any mortal man, in his senses, ever wanting to lift *this* hand to his lips, comes well home to her in this hour.[10]

Such a passage also demonstrates another quality shared by our sextet of authors. They all present their stories in clear and effective style, unpretentious and without distracting mannerisms.

Yet, although in their own time each of these six women produced a body of work sufficiently varied and innovative to establish a wide audience and sufficiently well crafted to attract respectful critical reviews, for each this fame was surprisingly short-lived. Their fate is part of a general story about women writers now being uncovered by literary and social historians. The present study is designed to bring these successful, productive Canadian women from the shadows of literary half-life. We propose to re-examine their lives, to tally their literary achievements, and to explore some of the causes of the disregard of their work by critics in succeeding generations.

As their fame diminished, the books of these six authors went out of print. Consequently, copies of many of their stories are no longer easily available. In the chapters that follow, hard-to-find stories are summarized. Paraphrases are of course a poor substitute for the stories themselves, but they do suggest the range of interests and of imaginative creativity within each author's repertoire. Furthermore, although fiction is not autobiography, every story does reveal the author's experience, reading tastes, obsessions, and values. All novelists express symbolically their own ideals, longings, and frustrations. Women writers in the nineteenth century, as Sandra Gilbert and Susan Gubar have demonstrated in *The Madwoman in the Attic*,[11] were under particular pressure to devise indirections of expression. In Canada the pressure on women to present a façade of docility and propriety was perhaps less pronounced than in the old country; yet all six of the women under scrutiny here expressed many of their feelings and ideas obliquely. Recurring motifs and allusions in their novels clarify hidden pressures and feelings. The names they choose for their fictional characters, the plot events they devise, the elements in setting that they select for emphasis, all highlight particularly significant (and suppressed) parts of their real life experiences.

It is not easy to uncover all the details of these lives. Unlike their American compeers, who (as Mary Kelley notes in *Private Woman, Public Stage*[12]) came from upper- or middle-class backgrounds and were attached to politicians, military officers, or professionals – whose family papers were preserved in public archives – these Canadian women came from considerably less distinguished families. Joanna Wood was the daughter of a farmer who emigrated from Scotland; May Agnes Early (Fleming) and Rosanna Mullins (Leprohon) were the children of Irish working-class immigrants; Susan Frances Riley (Harrison)'s father was an Irish-born innkeeper. Margaret Robertson and Marshall Saunders grew up in small-town non-conformist families: Robertson's father was a Congregational minister, Saunders' a Baptist pastor. Without politically or economically significant male figures in the background, these women cannot be easily recovered through family biographical material, despite their having made names for themselves through their writing.

There are few sources in which we can trace their self-assessment, their management of personal stress, their efforts to balance family responsibilities and creative work – few journals or diaries, except in the case of Marshall Saunders, and very few letters. What records there are testify to courage, ambition, and ability.

We must turn to archival materials on regional history, family constellations, school curricula, travel conditions, and publishing opportunities to learn more about the experiences and the people that helped or hindered our six writers, and the circumstances and desires that impelled them to write and shaped their achievements. In some instances family members encouraged the young women: in Wood's case, an older brother, in Saunders', a sister. Early school-days also fostered the literary urge. As a girl in convent school in Saint John, New Brunswick, Fleming learned to compose and recite poetry and stories: she charmed the other little girls with impromptu fairy-tales. In a private school in Montreal, Harrison entertained a more formal audience with a prize-day poem. Saunders made literary acquaintances while attending boarding-school in Scotland. All six writers had at least high-school education, and at least one, Robertson, attended university – the prestigious Mount Holyoke in Massachusetts. Harrison moved in the McGill University orbit as a student in Dr Clark Murray's courses in philosophy. Records from Leprohon's Montreal convent school reveal that, even in the 1840s, women's education went beyond the traditional "finishing school" subjects to include philosophy, biology, and mathematics, for example; music and painting were by then optional extras. The result is a clarity in form, an elegance in diction.

Deep religious feeling played a powerful part in the lives of these six women. The didacticism that characterizes some though not all of their work is a lingering trace of moralistic upbringing. For Robertson in particular writing was a form of righteousness. For all, the sense of moral obligation and the commitment to truth and duty, sometimes at odds with reviewers' expectations, increased the tension of a period both pragmatic and puritan.

Reading was also a strong influence. None of these women was trained in the classics; all found inspiration and stimulus in contemporary works, British, American, and Canadian. Leprohon's first story, set in a British upper class she had never known, is clearly modelled on stories she had read in the *Literary Garland*; Fleming's was modelled on the romances she had read in the *New York Mercury*. But these women read much more than E.D.E.N. Southworth, Elizabeth Braddon, and other writers of popular sentimental romances. There are echoes of Scott and Dickens and Thackeray in many of their works; Jane Austen is an obvious influence on Leprohon, Swinburne and Hardy on Wood, and gothic novelists such as Ann Radcliffe and Edgar Allan Poe on Fleming. None of these women seems to have felt the "anxiety of influence" characterizing so many male authors. They learned from their literary contemporaries; reading widely, they admit and display the influence of others. Their attitudes to contemporary compatriots are particularly important. Wood's connection with William Kirby, her praise of Isabella Valancy Crawford, and Saunders' reaction to L.M. Montgomery help to define the cultural context of the times.

Indeed, their sense of the needs of their own country constituted another force impelling them to write. They express their patriotism variously. In *Shenac* (1866) Robertson quietly celebrates the gradual patriation of Scots immigrants in Glengarry, Ontario. Saunders assigns to a child in one of her early stories the rousing cry, "I am proud that I am a Canadian boy. When I grow up ... I will work for my country."[13] Wood expresses her national pride more directly in a letter written from Detroit during the First World War. A parade of Canadians passed her:

I was by the kerb and I raised my voice in what might be termed a yell. Canada – Canada – Canada For Ever – my dear, every man jack of them "faced" my way & the man in command saluted – Oh I was so elated – it was fun & I can assure you I was proud as a peacock – I suppose it was not strictly speaking ladylike – but oh my dear when I saw the maple leaf on their caps all the throng melted & I saw Niagara Common with the blue lake on one side & the green ridge of the mountain on the other.[14]

Canada in the later part of the nineteenth century was busy melding British, French, and American ideas and conventions into a new amalgam. Our authors reflect the emergence of peculiarly Canadian attitudes towards the three source cultures. All six of our authors came from British-born families. All six relished and imitated English, Irish, and Scottish literature. Yet all six show the loosening of unquestioned adherence to British ways, in particular to a snobbish class system. All of our authors read American books, submitted manuscripts to American publishers, and in all cases except Leprohon and Harrison spent time in the United States. Again, however, these authors defined their loyalties and interests in ways distinctly different from those of Americans. Major concerns in the United States, such as slavery and massive immigration, were not central in Canadian life or fiction. Robertson and Harrison, celebrating the ethnic mix in Canada in the post-Confederation period, reflect a common delight in peaceful adjustment of differences. French Canadian politicians such as George-Etienne Cartier and Wilfrid Laurier kept Quebec and the French presence in the public eye;

four of the six writers realized that French Canadian and Acadian manners and folklore made good copy.

Not chauvinistic in their attitudes to American and British life, not particularly concerned with bicultural politics, these women nevertheless shared with their male compatriots of the post-Confederation period a strong love of Canadian ways, Canadian scenery, Canadian mores and ethos. Their national pride explains the ease and composure of their work.

The careers of the six suggest that women in Canada generally led a life not as claustrophobic or class-conscious as in the old country, not as sentimental and spiritualized as in the United States. All of them travelled; several were educated abroad. Their fiction reflects cosmopolitan experience. At the same time, international travel helped them to realize a strong sense of national identity, which they in turn articulated through their fiction.

They came into the literary market at an auspicious time. Canadian fiction in the late nineteenth century was articulating the problems, personal and societal, faced in an emerging and increasingly complex society. After Confederation, editors, essayists, and anthologists avidly explored the nature of the new nation. Carole Gerson, in *A Purer Taste*, summarizes the general literary thrust of the period: "Each English-speaking community undertaking the process of cultural individuation drew on the common heritage from Britain, grappled with the torrent of publications from the United States, and strove towards the creation of a national literature that distinctively and appropriately referred to Canada."[15]

In a period when American editors and audiences relished local colour and regional realism, skilful work on Quebec, Maritime, or Ontario village life could reach across borders to find extranational publication. The proliferation of story papers in the United States in the latter half of the century played a part in the financial and popular success of many Canadian writers, including Fleming and Wood. The intense national pride of Canadians in the post-Confederation period, expressed in loving delineation of particular regions, proved highly acceptable to contemporary audiences abroad.

A different kind of publication opened up to Margaret Robertson and Marshall Saunders. The rise of the evangelical presses, as traced by Margaret Cutt in *Ministering Angels*,[16] meant that the Religious Tract Society in England and the Baptist Publication Society in the United States stood ready to welcome the work of competent Canadian writers.

In the earliest phase of anglophone literature in Canada, several women had arrived in the colonies trailing considerable literary reputations with them. Frances Brooke in the 1760s, Anna Jameson in the 1830s, Susanna Moodie and Catharine Parr Traill in the 1850s all commanded considerable respect for work already published in England – a phenomenon totally unlike the situation of any of the early women writers in the United States. In the later nineteenth century Canadian women such as the six novelists studied in this book enjoyed a kind of afterglow of acceptance that reflected the status of Brooke, Jameson, Moodie, and Traill, and could consequently find publishing outlets opened by these precursors. Moodie's publishing in the *Literary Garland* and founding and editing of *Victoria Magazine* created a model as well as a medium for later aspirants. Leprohon, for instance, began publishing in the *Literary Garland* under Moodie's aegis. "Seranus" Harrison became the editor of the *Week* in Toronto in 1886 – a later example of acceptance by a prestigious literary journal of a woman writer's leadership. While an ethos of modesty and quiet decorum propounded to nineteenth-century women shaped social and family life, an unusual publishing situation opened for many Canadian women the possibility of finding a full-time career in literary production.

Critical reviews, letters from readers, and, more practically, sales fed into each author's life and reshaped her self-image. The immense popularity of these writers' works changed their subsequent careers. Details of the real life and the literary works woven together and enriched by awareness of audience response thus reflect place and time: the changing minutiae of national and regional events. The successful careers of these six women form part of Canada's literary history.

Yet these six authors shared a common fate. When we look at the lists of nineteenth-century authors given respectful treatment in subsequent anthologies and critical surveys – those produced by Archibald MacMechan, O.J. Stevenson, Lionel Stevenson, Arthur Phelps, and Desmond Pacey, for instance – we do not find any serious attention paid to these productive and respected writers. In any national literature, the canon – the unofficial list of books accorded long-lasting reverence – consists of works that critics in subsequent generations feel able to comment on. None of the writers considered in this book gets more than passing attention – most do not receive even that – in subsequent studies of Canadian writers. And we note inaccuracies in biography and bibliography when attempts are made to include them, however marginally, in literary histories and literary companions. In R.E. Watters' useful *Checklist of Canadian Literature*, for example, Margaret Murray Robertson appears without life dates,

Joanna E. Wood with inaccurate ones, and Susan Frances Harrison as "Susie."

Various reasons can be suggested for this disregard. The reaction against romance and sentiment that followed the First World War contributed to the decline in interest in the work of the six. Then, because Canadian literature was not on school curricula, once their books ceased to be reprinted for a popular audience the authors disappeared from the general view. To the extent that twentieth-century literary research has examined the late Victorian period, it has tended to focus on a few well-known figures. Thus we have, in varying degrees, biographies, letters, critical studies, and reprints of the works of Bliss Carman, Sara Jeannette Duncan, William Kirby, Archibald Lampman, Gilbert Parker, Charles G.D. Roberts, Duncan Campbell Scott, and so on. But these "canonized" figures who have come down to us from the period are, as the writers of the *Literary History of Canada* have so convincingly documented, merely "the tip of the iceberg." Many serious writers who had strong critical reputations and/or popular followings are virtually lost to us.

Many of these writers were women. And as feminist critics before us have noted, some fiction writers have been ignored or dismissed by the critical academy not because they were naïve, awkward, or coarse, though popular, but because the academy itself in the early twentieth century – teachers, editors, and reviewers – was an all-male group, unable to see or appreciate the language, concerns, and structures of women's writing.

Women writers of the late nineteenth century were in no position to counter patriarchal disregard. Our six authors demonstrate the difficulty of forming a network of support. Rosanna Leprohon, living in Montreal and raising a huge family, had no way of making personal connections with her first patron, Susanna Moodie. Margaret Murray Robertson, who moved to Montreal from Sherbrooke, lived in a Protestant society walled off from Leprohon's Catholic one. May Agnes Fleming, born in Saint John, New Brunswick, would have been still farther removed geographically from a congenial sisterhood even if a dreadful domestic life with an alcoholic husband had left her free to develop a literary network. Susan Frances Riley Harrison, more happily married, and closer to vibrant literary circles during her successive residences in Montreal, Ottawa, and Toronto, always dreamed of a still wider and more congenial circle, and sited her dream in New York and London. For Marshall Saunders and Joanna Wood, such dreams became briefly an actuality. Then Wood, pulled by filial duty back to the Niagara district, dropped into domestic oblivion; Saunders, after a brief success in contributing to the mainstream of regional novels, drifted back into the subgenre of children's animal stories. Essentially, these writers were unknown to each other and unable to exploit each other's experiences.

The disappearance of comparably admired and popular women writers from later critical purview is a phenomenon observable also in Europe, the United States, Great Britain, and in Commonwealth countries such as Australia. Recent criticism in all these countries has offered theories about how and why popular women writers dropped from the canon of writing acceptable to later critics. Simone de Beauvoir's *Second Sex* opened the way to what is now called "gynocriticism": reconstructing and reassessing the way gender differences have affected literary as well as social status. Jane Tompkins, in *Sensational Designs: The Cultural Work of American Fiction, 1790–1860*,[17] has explored the social implications of the early popularity of women writers in America, and also of the later academic dismissal of them as sentimental, trifling, or trivial compared to the all-male mid-nineteenth-century American constellation – Hawthorne, Melville, Emerson, Thoreau, Whitman – with a late addition of Emily Dickinson as the lone female now in this canon. In Great Britain, obviously, a different situation held. No one interested in British fiction could dismiss Jane Austen, the Brontës, Mrs Gaskell, or George Eliot from a canon of durable classics. Yet British critics from Virginia Woolf to Mary Jacobus have drawn attention to the fact that writers like the Brontës and George Eliot were marginalized in subtler ways. They had to encode subversive ideas within the formulas of romance. In *Women Writing and Writing about Women*[18] Jacobus suggests that in Victorian Britain a woman's entry into literary discourse depended on silencing feminist elements and emphasizing feminine ones. Consequently, while these women gained respect, their true messages were bypassed or ignored, a point generalized by Gilbert and Gubar in *The Madwoman in the Attic*. Turning to more recent publications by women writers in Australia, Drusilla Modjeska explores the continuing exclusion of "merely popular" women writers there in *Exiles at Home: Australian Women Writers 1925–1945*.[19]

The question of "mainstream" authorship, and the academic exclusion of popular and successful women writers from the established lists of books to be studied in college classes and analysed in learned journals, has indeed been opened wide by such recent critics; there is a need for a comparable exploration of the fate of women writers in Canada. Two recent collections of essays have opened the way. *Re(Dis)covering our Foremothers*[20] raises general questions to which we offer particular answers in this book. *Gynocritics*[21] suggests the need for a new critical stance.

Like Jemima Ann looking through her six inches of green crystal, we see life from a new angle when we study women writers' language and literary structures. Recovering the facts about the lives of even six Canadian women, the audience they wrote for, and the values that audience found in them, we also fill significant gaps in our knowledge of this country in past days. This sextet of women, working in isolation in their homes, helped to shape Canada's national tradition. As well, by publishing in Britain and the United States and by maintaining international connections, they carried the profile of the new nation abroad.

Rosanna Mullins Leprohon: At Home in Many Worlds

LORRAINE McMULLEN

ELIZABETH WATERSTON

Rosanna Mullins Leprohon was a Canadian phenomenon – genuinely bilingual and bicultural. She was an Irish Montrealer who married into a prominent French-speaking family. Herself the daughter of an English-speaking business family, she managed to recapture in fiction the days of the British conquest, presenting the story of the ancient struggle from a French-Canadian point of view. Between 1847 and 1877 she wrote stories in English for anglophone magazines, presenting as her protagonists modern francophones such as Armand Durand or historic Québécois such as Antoinette de Mirecourt; her stories were translated into French for simultaneous publication in Montreal *journaux*. In Canada there have been few writers who moved this effectively between the traditions and languages of the two founding cultures.

But this Quebec writer was a phenomenon also in a different and wider world – the world of popular women novelists of the nineteenth century, the regiment of scribbling women who puzzled the male academy of writers, editors, publishers, and critics by their prolixity, and sometimes annoyed them by their popularity. Rosanna Mullins began publishing when she was seventeen. Except for a brief hiatus during the early days of her marriage to Jean-Lukin Leprohon she produced consistently readable stories, relished by a wide audience, until two years before she died at fifty. (She was biologically prolific also: she gave birth to thirteen children.) She tried her hand, successfully, at sentimental courtship stories, mysteries, gothic tales, translations, and poetry, as well as producing three major novels of Quebec life.

Surprisingly, considering how readable they still are, her literary products are now virtually unknown in Canada.[1] Rosanna Leprohon's relative obscurity raises questions about the critical standards of academic scholars and editors, especially as they apply to the women writers who satisfied so large an audience in their own time and who can still offer such provocative alternative visions of life to readers in our era.

Rosanna Ellen Mullins was born in Montreal on 12 January 1829.[2] Her father was Francis Mullins, an immigrant from Cork, Ireland, who had come to Canada shortly after 1819. Her mother, Rosanna Connelly, was the daughter of Michael Connelly, a schoolmaster, and Sarah McCabe of Montreal. Francis Mullins had established himself as a grocer and ship's chandler by the time he married Rosanna Connelly on 23 February 1824. Their first child, Sarah, was born 28 January 1827; Rosanna was their second. Four more children, three girls and one boy, were born by 1836.

Francis Mullins' business expanded. By 1847 he described himself as an importer and marine storekeeper; he had acquired large holdings of waterfront property on Commissioner Street and Place Royale. His family lived in the upper stories of the building that housed his store. Mullins later expanded his real-estate interests and moved his family to Wellington Street into a house that he named Erina Cottage. He sat on the city council for three years, 1858–60, and was recognized as one of Montreal's most successful businessmen. Six years after his death on 27 April 1866, a street near his home was named after him.

Rosanna was educated at the Convent of the Congregation of Notre Dame, then situated at the corner of Notre-Dame and Saint-Jean-Baptiste streets. She was by turns a "quarter-boarder" and a full boarder in the years 1839, 1841, and 1843 to 1846.[3] ("Quart pension" can be interpreted as living at home but staying at school all day, and being entitled to lunch and possibly tea.) The list of students registered at the convent indicates that at least one-third had English surnames – or rather, English, Irish, or Scottish surnames: part of the roll runs "Chauvette, Chenier, Modenne, Pépin, Baily, Dufresne, Seabre, Mullins, Duschesnois, Routh, Stuart, Driscoll, Delanaudière, McDonald, Thompson."[4]

French and English, the girls shared religious devotions, submission to the nuns' discipline, and at least a nominal acceptance of the values of the Sisters – otherworldly yet practical, chaste yet devoted to the development in their students of graces and skills that would make them attractive in society and effective as wives and mothers. The history of the Congregation outlines the education acceptable for young women of Montreal's best families – and indeed for young women who were sent to the convent from all over the country and abroad. Besides English and French, students worked at geography, history, arithmetic, philosophy, chemistry, botany, and geology. Rosanna Mullins' registration indicates that she studied piano, harp, guitar, and drawing as well. For the latter an additional fee was paid.[5] Judging from this record, the education of young women in Montreal was more substantial and scholarly than is sometimes thought, going beyond the finishing-school subjects (music, painting, embroidery). There was, of course, no thought of a young woman's pursuing further studies, as her brothers might do, at McGill University (founded 1821).

Rosanna Mullins' literary talents were encouraged in the Convent. Among teachers who influenced her was the Reverend Mother Sainte-Madeleine, three times elected general superior of the Congregation, and a young Irish nun, Catherine Cagger, from Armagh and New York, who had entered the convent as Sister of the Nativity in 1827 and become renowned for her pedagogical theories.[6] Years later Rosanna composed poetic tributes to these two nuns. These courteous tributes, produced long after her convent days were over, underline the fact that convent values would remain a constant part of Rosanna Mullins' life.[7] Yet her earliest publications show her casting to the side, perhaps unconsciously, some of the convent orientation.

While still a student Rosanna Mullins had begun to publish poetry.[8] In 1846 her early work was accepted for the *Literary Garland* by the publisher John Lovell, another Montrealer, who lived near and was probably acquainted with the Mullins family. Her first published fiction also appeared in the *Literary Garland*. *The Stepmother* appeared as a serial running from February to June 1847; it was followed by four more full-length serialized novels, all appearing in rapid succession in the same magazine. These early stories have never been reprinted, although even the weaker ones among them reveal a great deal about the tastes and literary techniques of the pre-Confederation period. Interesting in themselves as a series with subtle shifts in certain recurring themes, they are also interesting because they show no signs of the author's later focus on events in Montreal and Quebec and on aspects of Canadian social life and history.

The story of *The Stepmother* is set not in Rosanna Mullins' Montreal but in upper-class British society. Most of the *Literary Garland*'s fiction, written by expatriates like the Strickland family, naturally gravitated to that familiar milieu. Rosanna Mullins followed the trend very creditably, considering her real inexperience: she set all her early novels in rich, tastefully decorated rooms, in English country homes and London mansions. *The Stepmother* also adheres to other conventions of the genre: it focuses on courtship, uses surprise plot twists, sets its major scenes in ballrooms and by deathbeds, and it depends on quick dialogue to carry the story-line. In all these respects the young author shows herself capable of pleasing her genteel, early Victorian audience; but she adds some very personal touches. The plot focuses on an intense duel between a proper convent-bred young lady and a power-hungry, vivacious rival. The theme of the alien intruding into a family circle and disrupting its serenity will recur in Rosanna's subsequent stories, with varying emphases. It is a cliché of the courtship plot, of course, with sure-fire appeal to readers of romances; but it can also be decoded as a parable of this young woman's split desires, torn between convent propriety and a dawning sense of power and worldly ambition.

The story is told from the point of view of a gentle girl named Amy Morton who is just entering the adult world, though still devoted to her schoolgirl pursuits of reading, embroidery, and music. We see her first alone, in a dramatic pose, leaning against her harp and gazing sadly at the portrait of her recently deceased mother. Into this scene comes the stepmother – a lively young woman who is the antithesis of Amy. Louisa believes that life for Amy as well as herself should consist of driving out, receiving visits, dressing fashionably, and attending balls, theatres, and concerts.

The young girl and her stepmother are thus at odds from the beginning. The author, morally on the side of quiet Amy, nevertheless uses dramatic devices to show that her shy, withdrawn attitude marks her as unattractive. "Who is that pale, lifeless creature, beside Mrs. Morton? What a contrast the two present!" cries the handsome favourite of the fashionable set, Sir George Markham.[9] There is a trace of Jane Austen's influence in a central plot twist here: Amy overhears Markham's sneering comments, just as Elizabeth Bennet overhears Darcy in *Pride and Prejudice*; Markham, like Darcy, cannot understand the girl's coldness when he asks her to dance and when he subsequently offers himself as a suitor. But Rosanna Mullins works out this plot situation in a way different from Austen's. She deepens the antagonism as well as the contrast between her two young women characters. And in the end she awards Sir George not to Amy but to Louisa.

Louisa first drives Amy's father to his death by her hunger for power. He gives her, for instance, a diamond tiara he cannot afford;

her response is frightening: "It was not the rich setting, the sparkling brilliancy of the costly gems that caused her dark eyes to glow with such proud exultation. No! But in them she read a tale far dearer to her haughty heart. They told her she had – conquered!"[10]

A darkly effective death scene ends Mr Morton's life – and frees Louisa for further conquests. Louisa is always the spark that causes events to happen. Young Rosanna Mullins sympathetically portrays the convent-trained Amy, submissive and well-behaved; but she creates in Louisa a much more interesting character. Louisa has a quick wit. She sees the convent habit of getting up early as "rising with the lark, that senseless bird!"[11] Her manipulative skills lead eventually to a socially advantageous marriage, while her blameless first husband suffers sad punishment – presumably for trying to harbour two such different females within his heart.

For so young a writer, the mere fact of publication in a prestigious journal is impressive. But this story is also impressive in itself. Brought up to behave as Amy behaves, Rosanna Mullins was still lively and witty enough to create a Louisa. The young Montrealer was aware of the dangers of selfishness and materialism and flightiness; she seems to have been aware of their attractions also. She handles with dramatic flair the contrasting settings of country life and city bustle; the affecting deathbed scene and the elegant spectacular wedding; the melodramatic confrontations and the sophisticated ironies of social chat. Indeed, the bright lines of conversation among the social butterflies occasionally recall Jane Austen in deft handling and wit. As a first novel from a convent-trained seventeen-year-old, *The Stepmother* is a remarkable achievement.

Six months after the last instalment of *The Stepmother* was published, Rosanna Mullins' second novel began to appear in serial form. *Ida Beresford; or, The Child of Fashion* ran in the *Literary Garland* from January to September 1848. The disruption of a tranquil home by the intrusion of an alien is again the theme. But the treatment of the alien in this second novel shows a stronger sense of dynamic characterization. Ida Beresford, unlike always-gentle Amy and always-hedonistic Louisa, develops and changes. Furthermore, the shift in emphasis, from a focus of attention on the girl whose life is invaded to a sympathetic awareness of the emotions of the girl who does the invading, suggests an unconscious shift in the young author's sense of values.

Ida, a spoiled sixteen-year-old, accustomed to "boundless wealth," who has been left a penniless orphan by the death of her bankrupt father, is adopted by her relative, a middle-class country doctor. Dr and Mrs Vernon have two children: Lucy, almost fifteen, and Claude, a year or two older. The Vernon family is a generous and happy one – until disrupted by Ida's arrival. The author handles very well the mild banter of the Vernons' dinner conversation, cut across by the sharper arrogance of the newcomer's scorn for simple family pleasures. Claude Vernon resents Lucy's submission to the morose and irritable Ida. The stressful atmosphere created by the bickering of the young people, illustrated in a series of silent, repressed dinner scenes, is well caught. Dr Vernon kindly exclaims:

"Claude, what are you thinking of? I declare, you have not even offered Miss Beresford a biscuit, though they are just beside you. Fie! fie! my son," he smilingly continued, "to let an old man like myself surpass you in gallantry."

But no answering smile brightened his son's countenance, who gravely presented the plate to Ida, without even raising his eyes to her face; and then resumed his former position. Dr Vernon was astounded at the unaccountable taciturnity of his light-hearted son … It was a relief to all parties, when the servant returned to say "the doctor had just been sent for into the country." He hastily rose, and after a cheerful "goodbye," departed, whilst the remainder of the meal passed in a total silence, which no one, now, made the slightest attempt to break. At length they rose, and returned to the sitting room. [12]

This difficult situation is relieved when Ida's godmother, wealthy, aristocratic Lady Stanhope, appears. Like Cinderella's godmother, Lady Stanhope wants to give Ida a chance to meet her prince. The fairy-tale subtext seems to cast Ida, even in her disagreeable phase, as heroine. But another fairy-tale analogue underlines the ambivalence of the author's attitude towards her protagonist: in an effective scene before her mirror, the girl glances idly at her reflection: "Gradually, her look of pain, of abasement passed away as she gazed on the image of surpassing beauty it reflected … Long did the young girl survey her bright image, with a cold, listless air, but gradually the brightening eyes, the deepening colour, told her that her sadness had yielded to the consciousness of her own magic beauty … and whilst a radiant smile lit up her beautiful countenance, she exclaimed aloud, 'Yes, I am indeed beautiful!'"[13]

This is a remarkable passage. It reminds us of the fairy-tale queen who must constantly ask her mirror for reassurance: "Mirror, mirror, on the wall, who is the fairest of them all?" The incident also demonstrates a subtle awareness of female psychology, of self-shaping in response to an image. We can think of a modern parallel: as Marian MacAlpin in Atwood's *Edible Woman* looks at drops falling on the table which tell her she must be crying,[14] so Ida looks at the expression of her own face in the mirror and learns from it that her emotions are changing.

Ida is witty and beautiful. But unlike the witty and beautiful stepmother in the earlier story, she shows occasional gentleness and responsibility, which suggests she is not beyond redemption. She defends the Vernons when Lady Stanhope sneers at them as of "inferior class ... not of our set." The reader is prepared for a shift in her attitudes and values.

The Vernons agree that Ida should spend six months in London society, six months in country quietness. Persephone-like, she will enjoy half a year in the bright social world she loves but will be condemned to dreariness for the other half.

The author wittily reports the repartee of young London bachelors as the beautiful newcomer makes her debut at a duchess's ball, remaining poised, aloof, unimpressed by any of them. The device of an eavesdropping scene is used again; Ida overhears the handsomest of her admirers admit, "She is well enough and pretty enough, if she had but fortune; but were she ten times handsomer, wanting that qualification, she will not do for me. I but seek her society to while away an idle hour."[15] Ida avenges herself; she encourages him until he actually proposes marriage, then throws his words back in his face: "I have but whiled away an idle hour with your society."[16] Next, she entraps the Marquis of Pemberton, most eligible young man in society, of boundless wealth, and scion of one of the oldest families in England. Like the conquering, power-hungry stepmother – or the wicked queen of fairy-tale – she vows, to her own image in the mirror, "He will be mine!"[17] The plot-line, the device of overhearing, and the very name of Pemberton all suggest that the young novelist still had one eye on Jane Austen as she wrote.

Country life is a relief after this social whirl: "Was it that [the Vernons] had grown more witty, more affectionate? No! the change, however slight it may have been, was in Ida herself. The contact with a world, heartless as it was refined, had insensibly taught her better to appreciate the real affection now lavished on her. Unconsciously her manners had lost much of that insolent hauteur, her countenance the repulsive coldness which had so grieved and annoyed her kind friends on their first acquaintance."[18] The didactic touch marks a deviation from Jane Austen's detachment into the heavier mode of early Victorian domestic romance. The possibility of clarifying points of conduct, decorum, and morality was felt to justify "light reading." But Rosanna Mullins moves from the didactic mode into the dramatic one. Ida's gradual and hidden melioration leads to a suspenseful romantic development.

On her return to the country, Ida admits to herself her love for Claude. He treats her with cold indifference and interprets everything she says in the worst possible light. Neatly, the author untangles this impasse. The deathbed of Lady Stanhope, vividly described, offers a final, terrible lesson to the young girl (and to the reader) of the vanity of wealth, the fickleness of those it attracts, and the frailty of power. Ida returns to the Vernons and a last-minute reconciliation with Claude ensues. Proud Ida marries Claude, the poor son of a country doctor, "one of nature's aristocrats," while the gentle and humble Lucy marries above her station and becomes Marchioness of Pemberton.

We can postulate that the author, now eighteen, going into society as a member of a wealthy, respected family, was becoming aware of the unhappiness snobbery and selfishness can cause, of the hypocrisy inherent in many social situations, of the superficiality of many of the pleasures of the worldly. Yet in this story her object is to provide a happy social outcome because of her protagonist's capacity to change. *Ida Beresford* can be viewed as a girl's initiation story: the heroine passes her tests, endures suffering and humiliation, alters her view of the world, and is rewarded with happiness at the end.

It is easy for us to understand the pleasure the story gave its readers. Part way through its serialized publication it was praised by Susanna Moodie, who wrote of the young author in the *Victoria Magazine*, "Let her keep truth and nature ever in view, and scorn not the slightest teaching of the 'Divine Mother,' and she may become the pride and ornament of a great and rising country."[19] Canadian publishers were prepared to accept more from this young author, and she herself seemed happily compelled to keep on writing. There was no particular financial necessity for her to write – and certainly no great hope for financial rewards from Canadian publications. Perhaps the didactic impulse maintained that urge to write, marking a trace of the moralistic training of the convent. But more likely the sheer fun of creating, of imagining social scenes and suspenseful situations kept her pen flowing, even when her own entry into Montreal Irish society was taking Rosanna Mullins into a busy non-literary world.

A month before Rosanna Mullins' next novel began to appear in the *Literary Garland*, the magazine published an interesting attempt in another genre – the short story. "Alice Sydenham's First Ball" appeared in January 1849.[10] This story shows development in the use of two technical devices, already introduced in the earlier novels, that were to continue to appear in later ones: the use of a mirror-image and the device of an overheard conversation. Both devices work here to good effect as a way of compensating for the absence of psychological development in the short-story form.

In this story the protagonist and her mother are penniless, although they have rich connections. Alice's mother warns her not to accept an invitation to a ball since her lack of suitable clothes and jewellery will embarrass her. The mother's warning proves justified, as Alice overhears unkind remarks about her appearance. An older gentleman comes to her rescue. A surprise dénouement reveals that he is her wealthy uncle, long estranged but now ready for a reconciliation with his brother's widow and child. There is no preparation for this revelation, but it works well enough as a plot-turn typical of the short-story form.

Touches of social realism in the ballroom scene of "Alice Sydenham's First Ball" foreshadow a very similar scene in Louisa May Alcott's *Little Women* (1868). In both cases the writer illuminates the pettiness and competitiveness of a young girl's world; but where Meg and Jo withdraw from the fray, Alice Sydenham happily accepts the possibility of entering the lists again. She is grateful for her uncle's financial backing – of the kind that Alcott's Mr Lawrence offers and the March girls reject. The young Canadian author shows no tendency to reject the world and the flesh. As for the devil, there is no particular sense of evil in the thoughtless and shallow snobberies of the socialites of Alice's world.

In a new novel, already prepared for the press, Mullins would wrestle with much darker problems: with the social demons of sophistication, of careless wit, malice, and lack of charity. *Florence Fitz-Hardinge; or, Wit and Wisdom* began serialization in the *Literary Garland* of February 1849 and ran monthly for a year. It is longer than any of Mullins' previously published stories. Nearing her twentieth birthday, she creates an eighteen-year-old protagonist – consistent with her practice thus far of creating imagined characters about two years younger than herself. But she poses for young Florence a darker personal problem, and metes out a more tragic end than in her earlier work.

Florence is too satirical; as her aunt tells her, there is "more mirth than charity, more wit than wisdom" in her remarks.[21] The story will demonstrate the effects of her too-high spirits on herself and others. It clearly has a didactic purpose, but that does not detract from the entertainment young Florence's lively wit provides for the reader.

Beautiful as well as witty, Florence is well liked for both qualities. But she loses her suitor, the wealthy Earl of St Alban's, because of her malicious wit. The austere earl rejects Florence when her malicious gossip hurts her own young cousin Nina, a French-speaking girl who has come into Florence's household from her home in Switzerland.

The novel might well have ended here, but unfortunately it does not. It follows Florence into a later phase of life, and the tone now is so different that we seem to be reading a different novel. The writer provides an older, less romantic lover for Florence, a man who marries her despite the discomfort her wit causes him and others and despite her inability, much as she now seems to try, to curb her tongue. The last of a series of tragedies for which Florence is responsible is her husband's loss of an arm in a duel resulting from her mockery of one of his friends. The catastrophe causes her collapse; she barely survives, and remains in fragile emotional and physical health. The gentle cousin Nina, her victim, is in the end united with the Earl of St Alban's.

Florence has the lively wit and the artistic gifts of the heroines who preceded her. Her creative energy is unfortunately combined with her satiric skills, to no good end. The novel has entertaining, well-drawn scenes, sparkling with Florence's élan. The sharp turn to a new dark tone, however, is hard to accept. Florence has been compared to Jane Austen's Emma by a modern critic,[22] but of course her story has a radically different dénouement. Jane Austen, safely ensconced in a settled circle of gentility, perhaps had less reason to assign a harsh end to her thoughtless, sprightly heroine. Rosanna Mullins, younger than Austen but more actively involved in the challenges of social life, knew what a danger it could be to a marriageable young girl to acquire a reputation for too much liveliness, wit, and creative ability. Florence Fitz-Hardinge is the novel of a young author, now in society, aware of having her own share of wit – and aware that her cleverness may be dangerous.

The character of Nina, who comes into an unfamiliar society without having an easy control of its language, is another study of the alien. In contrast to the cool Louisa and Ida, however, Nina reveals the terrifying aspect of that situation from the point of view of the newcomer. The change in tone may reflect a new aspect of the young author's life in 1849. Rosanna Mullins was now becoming acquainted with the French-speaking Leprohon family, and may well have been concerned with their approval and acceptance of her. Quiet Nina's happy marriage is a comforting alternative to the sad ending Florence endures.

The weakest of Rosanna Mullins' novels appeared the next year in the Literary Garland (January–December 1850). Eva Huntingdon is too long, the changes in characters inexplicable; many of the characters are stereotypes, and it is conventional and predictable in plot. In fact this novel is more like a schoolgirl effort than the stories Rosanna wrote as a schoolgirl. One cannot help wondering whether it was indeed written earlier and whether, with a reputation now established, Rosanna Mullins pulled it out of the drawer to be accepted on the basis of earlier successes.

The novel begins with an improbable scene that is funny for the wrong reasons. Lord and Lady Huntingdon discuss the homecoming of their only daughter, Eva, now sixteen. As a sickly baby Eva had been given to the care of a widowed aunt, whose recent death now requires that the parents accept Eva once more. The father, who has not seen her since her babyhood, does not even remember her name. "Have you any idea of what she is like – of her age?" asks the father.[23]

From this bad start the novel winds through an improbable sequence of courtships by a group of stock characters: a rake, a dilettante, an older family friend. Eva also has an irresponsible brother, but again in an incredible sequence of events she reforms him and becomes his protector. This is not a well-written story, and it lacks the sparkle that makes a novel like *Florence*, though flawed, entertaining reading. Perhaps in writing *Florence* the author had talked herself into toning down her own wit.

Eva was followed by a much stronger but much more puzzling story. For the first time the author placed a male protagonist at the centre of her story, and a sorry example of manhood he is. *Clarence Fitz-Clarence; Passages from the Life of an Egoist* (1851) is less than half the length of *Florence* or *Eva Huntingdon*, but the shorter length proved better suited to Rosanna Mullins' skills.

Clarence Fitz-Clarence was to be the last in her first series of novels. The *Literary Garland* ceased publication that year. This magazine, so important in Canadian literary history, founded by Lovell and filled to a large extent with the work of British expatriates, had given the young Canadian writer a good start. The *Garland* had also published samples of her poetry since 1846, and she had been encouraged to send other poems to the *True Witness* and the *Montreal Pilot*. The demise of the *Literary Garland* was a real setback to Mullins, as indeed it must have been to the British expatriates like Susanna Moodie and her sister Catharine Parr Traill, who had also depended on it as an outlet for their artistry.

For other reasons as well, however, Mullins' writing career was to be virtually suspended for eight years. This was also the year of her marriage: *Clarence Fitz-Clarence* was concluded in the May issue of the *Literary Garland*; Rosanna was married in June. It is fascinating to conjecture what lay behind her production at this point of a portrait of an egotistical male, utterly devoid of any redeeming quality.

Clarence is a veritable Dorian Gray, painted forty years before Oscar Wilde's portrait, an Egoist conceived thirty years before George Meredith imagined the oddities of Sir Willoughby Patterne. And this tightly structured, cleverly written novel bears comparison with those better-known later works.

In this self-centred man Mullins concentrates all the faults of her *Stepmother* but without the stepmother's saving remorse. The novel begins with Clarence's consideration of his own superiority: "Clarence Fitz-Clarence was as proud of his studied elegance, his acquired lisp and drawl, as he was of his faultless face and figure, and when he chose to recollect that he was of high and honored extraction, his connections wealthy and titled, his own private fortune large and unencumbered, he wondered at his own condescension in holding any species of social intercourse with the inferior beings around him."[24]

The "passages" from his life are dramatic episodes that show how his unalloyed self-absorption takes him on a voyage of corruption, self-deceit, and final dissolution. The central thread of the plot ties his fate to that of a woman he carelessly uses and disregards. It begins with that favourite ploy, an overheard conversation. The inexperienced Blanche, discussing Clarence without realizing that he is listening, insists she could never be attracted to such an obvious fop. Clarence revenges himself by apparently changing his ways, convincing Blanche that he is a very different person, winning her heart, and then rejecting her.

In the next "passage," six years later, Clarence meets in Italy the beautiful countess Bianca, a widow renowned for her intellect as well as her beauty, but seemingly inaccessible to all admirers. She encourages Clarence, who finds himself for the first time in love. When he is completely won, she reveals to him that she is Blanche. Now it is Clarence's turn to be devastated, though unrepentant about his own earlier treachery. For five years he wastes his health and his fortune. In a very well-handled deathbed scene Blanche returns to ask forgiveness for her part in his fall. Clarence, unchanged, sneers with sardonic wit, "Like a true woman you cannot enjoy your triumph, when 'tis attained!" He continues, "Well, to satisfy you, I will amend, but listen, why! Not from the childish, absurd motives you would fain inculcate, but from the great motive which has guided me through life, and which, indeed, guides the whole world; the motive which forms the main spring of public, as of private life, *the love of self*. I would amend, to avoid the suffering and wretchedness I have already entailed on myself by my own folly, I would amend for my own sake alone."[25]

The story is structured effectively. The five disconnected "passages" are carefully fused by the linking device of a painting of an outward-bound ship, which reminds Blanche of her earliest love, helps Clarence to recognize her in the Italian Contessa Bianca, and finally permits the long-lost sailor to recognize her also. The competent use of an Italian setting is another mark of widening ambition in the young author. So too is the careful choice of epigraphs for each chapter, displaying her range of favourites: Shakespeare, Byron, Scott, and (an interesting addition to this august source-list) "L.E.L." – Letitia Landon. Landon's collected poems appeared in 1850; admiration of her work had become a kind of cult among contemporary women writers, especially with ambitious authors such as Elizabeth Barrett Browning.

Clarence Fitz-Clarence, then, represents a technical and stylistic advance. But what a bleak story from a woman about to be married! The male protagonist is a man with no redeeming qualities; surely Clarence is not meant to proffer a general view of men! A more suggestive interpretation would be that the author perceives such egotism and hunger for power as dangerous impulses, to be identified with masculinity, though women might sometimes be capable of nurturing them as well. A comparable fictional manifestation of power-hunger had appeared in Emily Brontë's 1847 creation of Heathcliff in *Wuthering Heights*. The recurrence of such a figure in fiction by women writers from the Brontës to the purveyors of Harlequin romances is more than a revelation of subliminal responses to male self-absorption. The force of such creations also presumably shows the existence within the writers of a comparable ego-drive. But for most women of the mid-nineteenth century such passionate self-absorption had to be repressed; both Emily and Charlotte Brontë damage and humiliate their powerful male beings. For a Roman Catholic girl like Rosanna Mullins, in a hierarchical colonial society, the need for repression and punishment of the creature who represented voracious pride was even stronger than in her English contemporaries. Furthermore, according to the orthodox beliefs of her time, her faith, and her class, there was a particular need to be rid of this dangerous and evil trait before entering marriage and taking on the accepted submissive role of Roman Catholic, French Canadian wife. So Rosanna Mullins created the strange dark figure of a male egotist, and then meted out to him a dreadful punishment for his pride.

One way Mullins showed her submission was in giving up writing – or at least publishing – for the first eight years of her marriage. She and Jean-Lukin Leprohon married 17 June 1851 in Notre-Dame Church, with her uncle, the Reverend John Connelly, officiating. Her husband's great-grandfather, Jean-Philippe Leprohon, had emigrated to Canada in 1758 as a sergeant in the French army, and after the Conquest in 1760 had settled in Montreal. Jean-Lukin's father, Edouard-Martial Leprohon, was a lieutenant-colonel in the War of 1812. His wife, Marie de Niverville, was of Swiss ancestry: the de Niverville family also had a long connection with seigneurial life in early Quebec. Jean-Lukin was born 7 April 1822 and baptized Jean-Baptiste Lucain. He was educated at the Collège de Nicolet, where his uncle, the Reverend J.O. Leprohon, was director. Jean-Lukin graduated from McGill University in medicine in 1843, spent two years in Europe, then began practising medicine at St Charles on the Richelieu River, east of Montreal. In 1847, at the age of twenty-five, he founded a medical journal, *La Lancette canadienne*, which he edited.[26]

Rosanna Mullins married a man of excellent family who shared her interests in writing and publishing; she brought to the marriage family wealth and a common religious faith. The twenty-nine-year-old doctor and twenty-two-year-old bride settled for four years into the small town of St Charles, about fifteen miles from the eastern tip of Montreal Island, on the wide Richelieu River, which flows northward from Lake Champlain, joining the St Lawrence at Sorel.

Their first child, Lucien, born in 1852, died in less than a year. A daughter, Gabrielle, was born in 1853, and a son, Rodolphe, in 1855. With these two young children the Leprohons moved to Montreal in 1855, to 6 St Antoine Street, in the heart of the old city. Soon they moved to a large mansion at the corner of Lagauchetière and Ste Radyone Street (now Beaver Hall Hill). Two more children were born in quick succession: Claude (in 1856) and Geraldine (in 1857).

Not only the children but also her functions as the wife of a very busy and socially conscious physician kept Rosanna Leprohon busy. Dr Leprohon was appointed justice of the peace the year of their marriage, and surgeon of the Tenth Battalion of Militia on their return to Montreal in 1855. He was one of the founders of the Women's Hospital of Montreal; he served on the city council for St Antoine ward in 1858.

To get back into writing at this time would not have been easy for Rosanna Leprohon. As a woman in a patriarchal society, with heavy family and social obligations – despite the help she must have had in the house – she would be expected to devote her energies completely to her duties. Yet in spite of all these responsibilities, the compulsion to write was obviously still strong, strong enough to impel Rosanna Leprohon to find time to produce a long short story and a full-scale novel in the space of two years. When Leprohon once more turned her hand to fiction in 1858, she was the mother of four small children under seven. Her first reappearance as a writer was with a story more sentimental and more didactic than the early courtship novels, a story more doctrinaire in its concern with the Roman Catholic religion she shared with her French Canadian husband. And the new story was set not in the aristocratic ballrooms and salons of an imagined England or Italy, but in middle-class America.

Eveleen O'Donnell appeared weekly in the *Boston Pilot* from 29 January to 26 February 1859. The *Pilot* was a widely circulated Roman Catholic weekly, and thus an appropriate journal for a devout young wife and mother to contribute to. According to historians of American journalism, the *Pilot* was the best of its kind in North America; as such it would be widely read in Montreal. If there was a way back into writing, it would be by the kind of inspirational fiction to be found in the *Pilot*.

There were many differences between Rosanna Mullins, daughter of Irish immigrants, and the old established French Canadian family into which she had married. She must at times have felt very much an outsider. It is not surprising that she returned in *Eveleen O'Donnell* with new intensity to her favourite theme – the coming of an alien into a family setting.

In place of the early plot cliché of a threatening stepmother, the new story is concerned with a more practical and more socially troubling problem. With the permission of her priest, Eveleen is about to take a position as governess in a Protestant home. She is given the usual admonition not to participate in any other form of worship, and never to deny the faith.

As in her earliest stories, Leprohon presents her heroine as an orphan in mourning for a recently deceased mother – at a moment marking passage into adult relationships. In *The Stepmother* the heroine was introduced leaning on her harp, symbol of her pleasure in art; in the new tale Eveleen O'Donnell is kneeling in church, metaphorically leaning on her religion, her church.

The scene of Eveleen's first interview with the Sydney family, her new employers, is well done. Mrs Sydney as interviewer of a prospective governess is drawn with a nice comic touch: "Left an orphan ... indigent circumstances, and all that sort of thing ... But now, as to your qualifications –."[27] Mrs Sydney, the fourteen-year-old Gabrielle, who will be Eveleen's pupil, the older daughter, who will display antagonism to the young governess, and the family friend Isabel Ashton, a giddy social butterfly, are all carefully distinguished by appearance and behaviour. All share and openly voice strong prejudices on learning of Eveleen's religion. She is accepted despite these attitudes – and also despite the fact that she has "no Italian." (Young Gabrielle pertly exclaims that "Some cross old bachelor or other has said that one language is quite enough for a woman to express her folly in.") Eveleen is also taken on partly because Mrs Sydney is as evangelical as Eveleen herself, and sees the possibility of winning her to the Sydneys' Protestant faith.

The most attractive member of the family is Eveleen's charge, Gabrielle, described on first appearance as a "golden-haired fairy-like being." She has more vitality than the earlier fourteen-year-olds, such as gentle Lucy of *Ida Beresford*, but seems socially younger. It appears that the twenty-nine-year-old mother of four sees a young girl with different eyes from those of the eighteen- or nineteen-year-old author. Something of Gabrielle's delightful yet ephemeral charm is conveyed in the metaphors – not found in the earlier stories – with which she is described: a "humming-bird," "a sunset cloud," "a rainbow." Gabrielle was the name of Leprohon's oldest child, who would have been five or six when the story was written, and it is possible to see something of her delight in her child in Mrs Sydney's fond and loving ways. The doctrinaire nature of the story does not prevent the portrayal of a convincingly warm (though Protestant) mother.

The story develops as expected. The family's antipathy to Catholicism provides Eveleen with opportunities to rebut their accusations of idolatry and superstition. Gabrielle, who takes no part in her family's criticisms, is eventually converted to Catholicism, to the horror of the Sydney family. Then Gabrielle's older brother Ernest, a shadowy figure at the outset of the story, drops his customary cool and courteous manner and proposes marriage. Eveleen rejects him, since the ceremony he proposes would be a Protestant one, but his offer forces her to recognize her own feelings of love for him, and she leaves the Sydney home to evade this distressing situation.

The story next follows Eveleen into a second position, as governess to two young girls being raised as Catholics in spite of the opposition of their Protestant father and the mockery of two brothers trained in his faith. Eveleen does what she can to ease the tensions and lessen the bickering and quarrels among both children and adults. This episode in the story is a demonstration of the disastrous consequences of a mixed marriage such as Ernest had proposed. In some ways the plotting creaks with the weight of didactic intention, yet the family scene in a mixed marriage is presented in effective detail. The story undoubtedly reflects the situation in many Montreal homes of the time. It shows in particular a woman's recognition of the male weighting of religious values. The Protestant husband and father in

Eveleen O'Donnell is prepared to allow his wife to practise her religion. It does not matter to him what religion his daughters profess, but with his boys it is a different matter. They must go into the world and make suitable professional and social connections, in a milieu not always receptive to Roman Catholics, so with his sons he maintains a mocking attitude, directed against their mother and sisters. Eveleen brings a change for the better into this unhappy household by helping the little girls to practise Catholic as well as Christian virtues, by taming the boys' wildness through gentle example, and finally by helping her employer to appreciate the fine aspects of his wife's religion. Realistically, the author does not concoct any scene of conversion in this part of her story.

Like so many mid-Victorian stories of this sentimental/pious kind, *Eveleen O'Donnell* proffers two affecting deathbed scenes. Isabel Ashton, wordly cousin of the Sydneys, in a melodramatic scene refuses to acknowledge that she is dying of galloping consumption and insists on talking of parties and admirers to the end. The second deathbed scene stands in contrast to Isabel's: it is the more genuinely touching death of young Gabrielle. Eveleen learns that through her young charge's influence Ernest too has become a Catholic. Gabrielle dies knowing they will be united in marriage. Hers is a joyous and holy death.

The author now returns to her old forte in a love scene handled with sentiment and grace. The young writer's concern with questions of courtship breaks through the pious matron's focus on questions of faith. Then the story of Eveleen returns to the conventions of its genre: Mrs Sydney, the once-hostile mother, is also eventually converted. By example rather than preaching, Eveleen has won her. *Eveleen O'Donnell* is in some ways close to *An Old-Fashioned Girl*, written a few years later by Louisa May Alcott, in its presentation of a moral lesson through the persuasion and example of an intelligent, independent, but courteous and gentle girl. To compare Alcott's story with Leprohon's and with the mass of comparable work in major magazines of the 1860s is to see a remarkable change in the kind of material enjoyed by domestic readers. The courtship scenes are definitely subordinated to the scenes of pious argument. The "ministering angel" has replaced the proud beauty as a fictional model.

But in Leprohon's story the specific idea of mission and conversion, burning strongly in Eveleen, shows also the local influence of convent training, reinforced in the late 1850s by the Catholic revival instigated by Cardinal Newman and very strongly felt throughout the British dominions. In Quebec sectarian religious sentiments were particularly inflamed at this time, intensified by linguistic, cultural, and political differences between the members of the two founding groups. Leprohon's shift to a doctrinaire theme, supplementing her earlier focus on the position of an alien, marks her absorption into one of the pervasive obsessions of her husband's cultural group. The intensity and accuracy of Leprohon's portrayal of religious arguments produce a story that, though set in New York, bears strong traces of a very local Montreal atmosphere. Maintenance of the Roman Catholic faith was perceived as an essential part of Quebec "survivance."

In her next work – in many ways her strongest novel – Leprohon turned to French Canada's second great obsession: cultural survival in the face of British domination. *The Manor House of de Villerai* is set very clearly and very effectively in the Montreal region, but in the situation of a century earlier, at the time of the Conquest of Quebec. It is the first novel Leprohon set in Canada and the first of a trilogy of novels concerned with French Canadian life.

The Manor House of de Villerai began publication in the first issue of the *Family Herald*, 16 November 1859, and ran until 8 February 1860. The editor of the *Family Herald*, commenting on the intentions of the new journal, announced his hope of contributing "to the creation of a healthy Canadian literature." His editorial declared his pleasure in obtaining Mrs Leprohon's "Manoir," which he had secured "for the Family Herald through the intercession of a mutual friend."[28] The tone of the announcement suggests the respect Leprohon enjoyed in local literary circles. This respect was buttressed by her continuing output of poems as well as by memory of her earlier appearances in the prestigious *Literary Garland* and the *Pilot*.

She had become a part of the English-speaking literary world of Montreal, a group that included John Lovell, publisher and printer of the *Literary Garland*, his brother-in-law John Gibson, initially editor of the *Garland* and after 1842 co-publisher (Gibson died in 1850), and John Reade, literary editor of the *Montreal Gazette*. (Reade's interest would be lifelong: he eventually wrote an introduction to the *Poetical Works of Mrs Leprohon*, published after her death by John Lovell.) Thomas D'Arcy McGee, who came to Montreal in 1857 and was elected to the House of Assembly in 1858 as an independent representing the Irish and Roman Catholics of his Montreal constituency, was a neighbour.

Leprohon was also now well acquainted with the old French-speaking families of Montreal, and well regarded by them. In 1859 *Ida Beresford* was translated into French and serialized in *L'Ordre*, a Montreal French-language magazine, an indication of interest in her work stemming partly from family connections. That early, witty story of a proud girl learning to accept a simple country life was translated by Joseph-Edouard Lefebvre de Bellefeuille, a nephew of Rosanna's husband. Dr Leprohon's sister Caroline had married Joseph Lefebvre de Bellefeuille, seigneur of Mille Iles and Cournoyer; their son Joseph-Edouard had been educated at the Jesuit St Mary's College, Montreal, so was bilingual and able to bring Leprohon's sentimental tale to her French-speaking friends. It may have been through this branch of the family that she learned about life on a seigneury. She was also by this time friendly with the Dumont family of Saint-Eustache; an ancestor of this family had married Geneviève de Villerai.[29]

Leprohon thus had access to the two cultural worlds of Lower Canada. She bridged the gap between the "two solitudes" when she began writing novels presented from the perspective of francophone characters. She wrote with accuracy of detail, working primarily for an English-speaking audience, but was quickly accepted and popularized in translation among French Canadian readers as well. There was something daring in the decision of an anglophone woman to tell the story of the Conquest of Quebec from the point of view of the defeated French.

The choice of period for *The Manor House of de Villerai* may be connected with a bit of personal history. In 1859 a third son was born to the Leprohons; he was named Edouard after Jean-Lukin's grandfather, a military hero of 1812 and child of the ancestor who fought in Montcalm's army, which offered so fine an example of valour on the Plains of Abraham in September 1759. That historic past became the inspiration of the 1859 novel.

Leprohon focuses on the complex of Quebec attitudes during the war: pride in the French heritage but bitter resentment of the condescending officers from Paris; a feudal sense of the dignity and responsibility of the seigneurial system, but interest and pleasure in the new, sophisticated pleasures of city activities; deep love of the countryside and of the rituals of church and community. Though she depended on historians for details of the campaigns before and after Wolfe's assault on the Plains of Abraham, she chose as settings for the major parts of the novel the two regions of Quebec that she herself knew well, the Richelieu River region, where she spent the first years of her married life, and the area of downtown Montreal where she now lived.

The author introduces local colour in her meticulous descriptions of snowshoeing parties, Christmas festivities, and later in her picture of a Montreal home, with its drugget carpet, dark chintz, oil paintings of religious subjects, alabaster groups of the Holy Family, ivory crucifix, and many books. But the life in an old-time seigneury is her more central concern.[30] There is little doubt that her success in this recreation played its part in stimulating Philippe Aubert de Gaspé to produce, in 1863, his own version of old-time seigneurial life in *Les Anciens Canadiens* (1863). Her use of local colour also predates the major period of regional stories in the United States.

In the opening scene of *The Manor House of de Villerai*, snow falling on a dark December day in 1756 covers the barren fields near the Richelieu River with a carpet of dazzling whiteness. The setting is presented as if in a movie: the narrative begins with a panoramic view of the landscape, fades into a description of the outside of the manor house, then pans across the hall and finally focuses on the two occupants, elderly Madame Dumont and her niece, the young seigneuresse Blanche de Villerai.

In choosing a female protagonist for her historial novel, Leprohon locks herself into some traditional romance conventions – but this is romance with a difference. At the outset of the story Blanche and her aunt await the arrival of Gustave de Montarville, to whom Blanche was engaged by her parents in childhood and whom she has not seen since. Blanche is being urged to accept the idea of marriage based not on romantic love but on family arrangement. Mme Dumont presents a traditional view of the situation: "If you do not like him, you have no alternative but to learn to like him. He was the husband chosen for you by your good, kind father, when you were, I may say, in your cradle – he was the husband chosen for you by your dear, good mother, who, when confiding you to my care on her death-bed, solemnly enjoined me to see that that sacred engagement should be fulfilled. Of course, in such a matter, no well-brought up or discreet young lady dreams of having a will of her own. Her parents select. That is their duty – hers obedience."[31] But Blanche has a mind of her own. Gustave arrives, handsome and charming. But when he leaves after this first visit Blanche tells her aunt, "I will never marry him, dear Aunt, till I have learned to love him."

There is no anachronism in placing such a discussion in the period around 1750, the time when novelists such as Richardson, Fanny Burney, Mrs Brooke, and others were obsessively discussing precisely this sort of choice between practical and sentimental considerations in the movement of young people towards marriage. But in creating Blanche, Leprohon has added some new attitudes of her own age. Blanche's early hesitation, when she waits to know Gustave better, becomes a determination not to marry him in spite of the long-standing engagement. She says, with dignity,

I hope, Gustave, you do not share the vulgar error, that an unmarried woman must necessarily be unhappy. Think you that in the exercise of charity and benevolence, the intercourse of friendship and congenial society, the resources of intellect both in herself and the companions she may select, she cannot find sufficient to occupy her time and heart? Certainly: and one unalterable resolution of mine I will communicate to you, which is, that though I may eventually marry, if I chance to meet one of your sex whom I may learn to love and respect, I certainly will never marry simply to please them, and to escape the dreaded appellation of an old maid.[32]

As well as rejecting Gustave de Montarville, Blanche rejects an offer of marriage from the Viscount de Mornaye, heir of one of France's noblest families. Blanche never does marry. When Aubert de Gaspé uses a similar rejection of marriage by his heroine as the ending of *Les Anciens Canadiens*, he imputes the heroine's choice to romantic, patriotic motives. His heroine rejects the young Scot she loves because she feels marriage would be a betrayal of her race. Blanche de Villerai's decision is more down to earth: she simply prefers not to marry.

Another interesting development in Blanche's story is that her beauty is destroyed by smallpox. Blanche faces her mirror (like Ida), not to say, as Ida did, "I *am* beautiful!" but to note "the changes that a terrible disease has made in colour and feature, the seams it has left in a once fair face."[33] This loss of beauty does not affect either her own self-esteem or Gustave's admiration of her. The shift from an emphasis on the heroine's pride of beauty to an emphasis on charity, duty, and inner strength is partly the mark of a maturing author, no doubt, but partly too it reflects a contemporary shift in women's stories towards unbeautiful heroines. Readers' acceptance of such a heroine as Jane Eyre or Jo March is a mid-century reflection of popular feminist arguments and sentiments. Blanche, accepting homeliness and a lonely life, marks a change in role models, not in the historic period of the story but in the author's own time.

Leprohon also departs from standard fictional conventions in her portrayal of two young women who are not antagonists. Blanche is a young seigneuresse, Rose the daughter of peasants on Blanche's estate. But Blanche has befriended Rose and educated her, so that she now has the gentle manners of her socially superior friend. Despite the way their names differentiate them, Blanche and Rose are both beautiful, quiet, virtuous, intelligent.

The relationship of Blanche and Rose, besides reversing the author's earlier use of a rivalry between her female characters, thus shows a broadening in the author's social interests. The novel suggests some mingling of Canadian classes and a possibility of upward mobility never remotely suggested in the novels set in English society. Leprohon's earlier novels had made no reference to any class but the fictional genteel; in *The Manor House*, although the upper-class milieu remains central, Leprohon gives colourful glimpses of other strata: the Lauzon habitant home, for instance, where Rose's mean-tempered stepmother battles the village curé. The charitable Mme De Rochon of Montreal, her social-climbing niece, and the foppish Parisian officers all help to suggest the complex social situation in French Canada and enrich the courtship story.

But although love and courtship are placed in the foreground of the novel, the author never drops her second thread – the story of the war. Gustave, as a young French officer, is engaged in battles, which are reported with historical accuracy. F.-X. Garneau was Leprohon's principal source for reports of these battles. Her reliance on Garneau defines her position: she accepts the French Canadian view of the historic conflict. The losers emerge with pride and dignity intact because of the valour of their defence of their native land.

Unfortunately, Leprohon was unable to weave the two threads of her story together in a convincing way. Awkward shifts of style occur when she moves from the domestic scenes to the military ones. Thus on one page the narrative moves with easy conviction: "Quickly and ardently De Montarville kissed the little white hand he so reluctantly yielded up; and in another second, he was gone." On the same page the heavy historic mode then takes over: "After some further time lost in expectation of help from France, Gen. De Montcalm, the French Commander-in-chief, resolved on profiting by the departure of Lord Loudon, general of the American army, who had left New York with part of the English troops for Louisbourg, to renew his (Montcalm's) attack on Fort Henry."[34] The sentimental force of the narrative mode is broken and is not replaced by any vigorous handling of feats of arms. The source of this weakness is the choice of Blanche as the central persona and the failure to devise a way in which that lady could participate directly in the military campaigns. Leprohon therefore tackles the military scenes with the coldness of a dry-as-dust historian. In later historical romances using the same settings, such as *Les Anciens Canadiens* (1863), William Kirby's *The Golden Dog* (1877), and Gilbert Parker's *The Seats of the Mighty* (1896), the male hero can move easily from love scenes to scenes of conflict. To mention the later writers, however, is to recognize that in spite of its weaknesses, *The Manor House of de Villerai* directed Canadian historical fiction into a choice of Quebec as a setting where romance and battle could be blended for the delectation of readers.

In 1860, the year following its publication in the *Family Herald*, *The Manor House* was published in French in serial form in *L'Ordre*. The translator was again Leprohon's nephew by marriage, Edouard

Lefebvre de Bellefeuille. *Le Manoir de Villerai* was published in book form in French translation that same year. This publication, by de Plinguet of Montreal, marked the author's first appearance in other than magazine format. Not until 1985 did *The Manor House* finally appear in book form in English, when J.R. Sorfleet edited and published it as a special issue of the *Journal of Canadian Fiction*.[35]

Leprohon herself acted as translator for an important social function in 1860. Her English version of a cantata by Edouard Sempé was performed for His Royal Highness the Prince of Wales on the occasion of his visit to Montreal. Her social status is indicated by the invitation she received from city officials to prepare this translation. Her poetry also earned her the distinction of being included in E.H. Dewart's *Selections from Canadian Poets* (1864), the major pre-Confederation anthology, selected not by her Montreal friends but by a Methodist editor in Toronto. Her re-establishment as a writer of fiction was perhaps slowed down by the demise of the *Family Herald*, which abruptly ceased publication after a single successful year, because of the death in August 1860 of the editor, George Ure.

In the meantime, however, in 1862 another son, Joseph Arthur Lukin, was born, but died in infancy; and in 1863 Leprohon gave birth to Gertrude Ida – so her family now comprised six children under ten years old.

It was 1864, four years after *The Manor House*, that the second novel about French Canada appeared. Appropriately, it deals with the period immediately following that of *The Manor House*, the years following the fall of Quebec to the British. *Antoinette de Mirecourt; or, Secret Marrying and Secret Sorrowing* deals not with the sentiments of the Québécois alone but with the relationship between French and English in those post-war years. It is set primarily in Quebec City, with several episodes in the nearby seigneury of Antoinette's father.

This was a period of reconciliation and adjustment rather than of conflict; Leprohon here could exploit her old deft touch in handling romantic intrigue. The confrontation occurs not only between victors and vanquished but between adherents of two different religious faiths, the one now officially established, the other guaranteed survival and protection as part of the treaty that ended the Seven Years' War. Leprohon is able to summon the interest in sectarian differences that animated *Eveleen O'Donnell*: the "secret marrying" of the subtitle is one between Roman Catholic Antoinette and a Protestant British officer.

This is exactly the period described in the very first Canadian novel, Frances Brooke's *History of Emily Montague* (1769). Brooke largely confined her fictional romance to the intrigues between British officers and the English ladies of the Quebec garrison –

although one charming French widow appears in her story. But comparison of *Antoinette de Mirecourt* with *The History of Emily Montague* leads to a conviction that, especially in the sprightly opening chapters of *Antoinette*, the mid-nineteenth-century novelist has admirably caught the atmosphere reported by the contemporary observer. Leprohon adds darker tones to her story because of its cross-cultural, cross-sectarian problems; but her heroine shares the ebullience and charm of Brooke's Emily and Arabella.

Further, although Edouard de Bellefeuille, Leprohon's nephew, did not translate the French edition of this novel, he may have played a part in connection with it. In 1859 he had presented his thesis to the law school of St Mary's College; it was published the next year under the title *Sur les mariages clandestins* – the subject Leprohon here takes up.

Antoinette is a motherless young woman (as are so many of Leprohon's heroines) who visits her worldly married cousin, Lucille D'Aulnay, in Quebec City. As a couple the D'Aulnays resemble Jane Austen's Mr and Mrs Bennet. M. D'Aulnay remains in his study, allowing his wife to do as she pleases. What she pleases is to entertain the British officers stationed in Quebec and to encourage her young country cousin in romantic entanglements.

Some of the officers who appear recall the Parisian officers of *The Manor House*. There is a comparable condescension, and a comparable triumph when a supercilious fop, "as thoroughly infatuated with himself as ever lover was with mistress,"[36] is quickly put in his place by "the obscure little colonial girl" for his rude and condescending attitudes to Canada and Canadians, thus becoming the laughing-stock of the regiment.

The entertainment of British officers by French Canadian women as described in *Antoinette de Mirecourt* became in fact so much accepted that a new word was introduced into the English language. "Ma femme" became "muffin" – a term used to describe the young French-Canadian woman companion. The *Oxford English Dictionary* gives one example: "Every unmarried gentleman, who chooses to do so, selects a young lady to be his companion in the numerous amusements of the season … When [she] acquiesces she becomes his 'muffin.'" In the early years of British rule there were many men like M. D'Aulnay and Antoinette's father who preferred not to associate with the British; but there were those like Lucille D'Aulnay who, though passionately patriotic during the war, had no trouble welcoming the victors.

The end result of Mme D'Aulnay's ill-considered chaperonage is Antoinette's secret marriage to the most handsome and charming of the British officers. The marriage is performed by an Anglican clergyman. It is agreed that the marriage will not be consummated until approved by Antoinette's father and blessed by a Roman Catholic clergyman. This secret marriage involves religious and racial differences, as well as lack of parental approval.

Madame D'Aulnay is in a long line of misguided chaperone figures in Leprohon's works. She has the liveliness of manner and speech of Leprohon's worldly British women. Antoinette, too, has a lively manner until the full impact of her situation strikes her. Her handsome husband is soon revealed to be a gambling, flirtatious fortune-hunter. And no sooner are they married than Antoinette realizes her attraction to the somewhat dour Colonel Evelyn. The colonel, under a Byronic exterior, is actually kind and courageous, while Antoinette's husband under his charming exterior hides a sadistic and villainous nature.

All ends happily. Antoinette's husband is killed in a duel, freeing her to marry Colonel Evelyn, who, although British, is at least Catholic, and has won her father's esteem by defending a French Canadian innkeeper from a brash British merchant.

Leprohon shows that there are good and bad among both the French and the English. She also demonstrates the importance of knowing someone well before marriage and of sharing religions. She suggests that marriage between the races may have been difficult but could be very happy, as Antoinette's promises to be.

With this bright young heroine, in fact, Leprohon had gone back, past the severe self-sufficiency of a Blanche de Villerai, to a feminine character absorbed, like the heroines of her earliest fiction, in the business of finding a husband. Perhaps this more orthodox fictional characterization made *Antoinette De Mirecourt* more popular than *The Manor House of de Villerai*. The other source of its power, however, is the real tension, real fear, and real hostility suggested in Antoinette's plight. This female protagonist is involved in scenes that are for her and for women readers as tense, as agonizing, and as potentially destructive as scenes of armed battle would be for a male hero. The assaults on Antoinette by her secret husband are frightening, insulting, and contemptible. And the shifts in her sentiments from the fascination exercised by the egotistical officer to the respect aroused by Colonel Evelyn are delicately traced – especially effective in suggesting how respect can develop into a convincing romantic attachment.

Like *The Manor House, Antoinette de Mirecourt* was translated into French and published in *L'Ordre*, as well as in book form, in 1865. The translator this time was Joseph-Auguste Genand, editor of *L'Ordre*. This novel and the preceding one were intended by Leprohon to be contributions to a specifically Canadian literature, as her preface to *Antoinette de Mirecourt* makes clear: "Although the literary treasures of 'the old world' are ever open to us, and our American neighbors should continue to inundate the country with reading-matter, intended to meet all wants and suit all tastes and sympathies, at prices which enable everyone to partake of this never-failing and ever-varying feast; yet Canadians should not be discouraged from endeavoring to form and foster a literature of their own."[37] In the same preface Leprohon modestly introduces her novel with the phrase "essentially Canadian" – words she had used in early pages of *The Manor House*: "If *Antoinette de Mirecourt* possesses no other merit, it will, at least, be found to have that of being essentially Canadian."

The author's view of Canadian life is not a picture of "roughing it in the bush." Even in the 1750s, 1760s, and 1770s, she implies, and even under conditions of siege and post-war reorganization, life in Canada could be gracious and spirited. Here, as in *The Manor House of de Villerai*, she presents cultivated conversations, luxurious furnishings, people with fine libraries, good domestic organization, and a variety of social pleasures. In spite of social and domestic tensions Antoinette enjoys society and relishes garrison pleasures. "Garrison life" is not a pejorative term for Leprohon. She presents the officers as men of social finesse, artistic tastes, and sportsmanlike behaviour. "Essentially Canadian" life for Leprohon blends city and country pleasures, and the country people, such as Antoinette's father and her rural suitor, are amiable and energetic.

Perhaps the gracious social atmosphere in the novel reflects Leprohon's own way of living. Her husband was increasingly important in Montreal circles. In 1864 he was appointed consultant to the Montreal Dispensary, adding further to his responsibilities. In 1866 he was appointed, with another doctor, to present an official report on the sanitary conditions in Montreal.

Rosanna Leprohon must have been very busy indeed. In 1865 another little girl had been born, and christened Marie Antoinette Selby – first of the children to be given a combination of French and English names. But this little namesake of the fictional Antoinette was ill fated; she died within the year. Two years later the Leprohons endured the same sadness again: another daughter, named Eleanore Florina, was born and died in 1867. In 1868 another baby girl was born and christened Marie Florence – a poignant combination of the names of the two little predecessors; Marie lived, to swell the family to seven children. The oldest child, Gabrielle, was fifteen.

Years later the wife of the oldest son, Rodolphe, would speak of his mother as "of a sweet and kindly disposition," and a granddaughter would affectionately recall the way Rosanna pushed her children towards social accomplishment: "I remember my late father, Col. Edouard Leprohon, telling me that grandmother, although the very soul of kindness and motherly love, used to stand over him, at his piano practice and whenever Dad would stop he'd get a gentle little rap on the knuckles with a ruler, hence in later years, father was quite well known as a pianist."[38]

In such a busy home environment and with such social commitments, it is small wonder that four years elapsed between *Antoinette de Mirecourt* (1864) and Leprohon's next novel, *Armand Durand; or, A Promise Fulfilled* (1868). This was the third and last of her trio of novels set in French Canada. It is wider in scope than the other two, and very much darker in tone. *Armand Durand* is a study of marital relations, traced through two generations of a family in rural Quebec. It was first published serially in the *Montreal Daily News*, beginning 1 October 1868, and in book form in English the same year by Lovell. The French translation followed within a year, from the Montreal publisher J.B. Rolland. According to the notice in the back of the Lovell edition, it was "written for and presented to the DAILY NEWS by Mrs Leprohon."[39]

The first half of this new novel is concerned with the two marriages of Paul Durand, the second half with the lives and marriages of his two sons. For the first time since *Clarence Fitz-Clarence* Rosanna Leprohon had chosen to focus attention on the experiences of male protagonists. Perhaps this marks her sense of a new audience, developed by the interest in her historical novels; perhaps it marks her determination to enter a fictional world more complex and troubled than the parlours of Blanche or Mme D'Aulnay, or of those earlier heroines Amy, Ida, Eva, Florence, and Alice. Certainly the *Montreal Daily News* catered to an audience more mixed, more robust, and less genteel than the readers of the old *Literary Garland*. At any rate, Leprohon, now nearing forty, dared to tackle marital unhappiness, drunkenness, and jealousy – as well as love, self-sacrifice, and gentleness – in her new novel. Like *Clarence Fitz-Clarence*, *Armand Durand* marks the end of a stage in Leprohon's career. Unlike *Clarence* it is a mature novel, valuable for its complex human relationships and also for its glimpses of Montreal life in Leprohon's own time and of rural Quebec life in somewhat earlier days.

The action of *Armand Durand* begins on a seigneurial property on the St Lawrence River. Paul Durand, who works a prosperous farm on the seigneury, decides, upon the death of his mother, to marry. Instead of one of the many attractive girls of the area, he chooses young Geneviève Audet, recently come from France as governess to children in the seigneur's house. As a penniless member of a superior family, she is miserable in her position. Paul pities, admires, and finally loves her. But she is not a farmer's wife; she can neither cook, sew, nor keep house. The community, and Paul's own family, resent her. Yet Paul is happy, despite the chaotic housekeeping and disastrous quarrelling: "feminine gentleness, more powerful than anger, logic, or pride, ... demolished in one instant the wall that passion and suspicion had raised between them."[40] Geneviève never does learn housekeeping. Her character is strongly reminiscent of Dora in Dickens' *David Copperfield*. Like Dora, she dies very young; unlike Dora, she leaves her young husband with an infant son, Armand.

Paul, a practical man, decides to remarry to provide a mother for his child. This time he selects a girl from the community: the plain, virtuous Eulalie Messier, generally accepted as an old maid. The author compares their wedding day to the intensely hot day in Marseilles described in Dickens' *Little Dorrit*. Local colour is touched in with a lengthy description of the eight-day wedding celebration, the custom of the time. Eulalie, an excellent housekeeper and a quiet hard-working peasant woman, offers a contrast to the fragile Geneviève. She too has a son; she too dies shortly after giving birth. Both Paul's marriages have been happy, but he continues to mourn the impractical, high-born Geneviève, the true love of his life.

The two sons grow up to be opposites: in physical and psychological characteristics each reflects his mother. Geneviève's son Armand is tall, slight, handsome, sensitive, gentle in manner, very intelligent. Eulalie's son, named Paul after his father, is of stronger build, more thoughtless, rougher in manner, excitable, but not interested in studies. When they attend a Montreal college Armand is so girlish in appearance he has to beat up another boy to prove his manhood. The contrast continues: Armand enters legal studies with a Montreal lawyer, but Paul gives up college to join his father in farming.

In an archetypal situation, recalling Cain and Abel, Jacob and Esau, Paul becomes jealous of his more talented brother and discredits him with the father. He prevents delivery of letters. As a result Armand, returning home to his father's deathbed, finds he has been disinherited. This plot is potentially melodramatic; but Leprohon handles it unsentimentally, with a cool delineation of the character differences between the two half-brothers. She adds eccentric, individualistic touches to an essentially archetypal story of sibling rivalry.

The focus of the novel now swings to Armand's adult life and to the two marriages that he in turn contracts. While an impoverished law student Armand marries a girl who is his social inferior, Delima, the seventeen-year-old niece of his landlady. She is beautiful, quiet, gentle, and submissive – until they marry. Then she becomes rude, nagging, bad-tempered, and extravagant. The story of Armand's marriage is an excellent portrayal of a miserable mismatch.

Meanwhile, at the old seigneury, another young woman, the seigneur's niece Gertrude, has grieved over Armand's fate and, unknown to him, has come to love him. Armand's marriage has cut him out of good society, but Gertrude, meeting him accidentally, observes Delima's behaviour and sees the unhappy man slipping into habits of drunkenness, urged on by careless city friends. Gertrude is able to persuade him to stop drinking; a move to a new locale – Quebec city – frees Delima from some bad influences and makes Armand's life more bearable. Delima becomes more amenable; then she, like Armand's own mother, dies in childbirth.

Again there is a second marriage. This one, to Gertrude, brings happiness. For a wedding gift Gertrude asks that Armand forgive his rough brother Paul; this "gift" frees Armand of all bitterness. As the story ends, Armand, a brilliant lawyer, is moving into politics, with his wife's support. His brother Paul is unmarried, rumoured to be drinking himself to death, and, although still using his ill-gotten inheritance, apparently unable to achieve happiness.

The stories of the father and the son, though similar in outline, are quite different in quality, in tone, in troubles, and in rewards. In this curious double story of two generations of marital histories, Leprohon shows us a young man repeating his father's pattern of two marriages. Both husbands find their happiness with the socially higher wife, the father moving from that happiness to a lifelong sense of loss, the son moving from a much sharper mésalliance up to an idyllic union. In both the view of courtship and marriage has a sardonic bite not found in *Antoinette de Mirecourt* or in any of Leprohon's earlier work, except for *Clarence Fitz-Clarence*. Unlike that naïve study of a totally depraved character, the new novel presents three seriously flawed male protagonists undergoing interesting and unpredictable transformations as circumstances, fortune, and time bring changes. The three Durand men develop within themselves, and in relation to each other, as well as through their relations with women. There is a particularly interesting effort to distinguish between the different kinds of drinking problems experienced by Armand and by Paul.

In comparison to the first two of Leprohon's "essentially Canadian novels," *Armand Durand* drops the historical distance and moves closer to the worlds she knew directly – the professional world of Montreal and Quebec City, and the seigneurial world of rural Quebec. The realism of this novel of manners is of a different order from the antiquarian tone of *The Manor House of de Villerai*. The city scenes, though they suggest the influence of Dickens in richness and oddity of detail, do not carry the symbolic weight of Dickens' labyrinths; and there is no Dickensian build-up to strange revelations of unsuspected identity, no sudden unmasking of evil or sudden emergence of the angelic. Instead, the plot unfolds with sociological conviction. Strongly plotted, convincing in characterization, this underestimated novel focuses on Leprohon's central continuing interest – the essential problem of finding an appropriate mate. But along with its focus on strong male characters, it adds another note new for her: the recognition of potential dark hostility within a family group.

Appearing in the year following Confederation, *Armand Durand* was to be the last work in which Leprohon focused on her francophone compatriots. We might say that Leprohon celebrated Confederation by imaginatively moving beyond the confines of Quebec or Lower Canada and choosing an Ontario setting for her next novel. *Ada Dunmore; or, A Memorable Christmas Eve: An Autobiography* appeared in a new Montreal weekly, the *Canadian Illustrated News*, which began publication in 1869 and advertised itself as "Canada's First National Magazine." Like Lovell of the *Montreal Daily News*, the editor solicited work from Leprohon, and like the editor of the *Family Herald*, he wanted a contribution from her in his first volume. These facts attest to her outstanding reputation as a writer, a reputation reinforced by the inclusion of an entry on her in Canada's first important cyclopedia, Henry Morgan's *Bibliotheca Canadensis*, published in Ottawa in 1867.

Ada Dunmore; or, A Memorable Christmas Eve was an appropriate title for a story that was inaugurated 25 December 1869; it would run weekly until 7 February 1870. The novel seems even more obviously designed for a Christmas issue because Ada's father is named Noel. But the tone of the story is surprisingly dark. It is like the opening movement of Charles Dickens' Christmas stories without the outburst of joy and celebration with which Dickens ends his tales. Those stories – *A Christmas Carol* (1843) and four further Christmas stories published in each of the next four years – maintained an immense popularity; Dickens' second visit to America in 1867 had intensified imitation and admiration of his work. But if *Armand Durand* reflects Leprohon's response to Dickens' rich vision of city life (perhaps the part of Dickens' work still most appreciated by modern readers), her new novel imitates what is to us his least attractive feature: his dependence on incredible plot twists – masked identities, sudden returns, cruel abandonments.

Ada Dunmore begins with a direct address: "Reader, are the reminiscences of your childhood gay and happy, are they connected with pleasant scenes and pleasant places, interwoven with loving smiles and tender voices? Well for you if they are so! Listen now to mine."[41] Obviously, neither the Christmas occasion nor the Confederation shift from a Quebec scene to Ontario was going to lighten the dark tone established in *Armand Durand*.

In the bleak opening scene, in a farmhouse on the Bay of Quinte in south-central Ontario, the seven-year-old Ada and her brother "celebrate" Christmas in poverty and isolation, and in fear of their morose widowed father. Nothing could be further from the sense of seigneurial interconnections, or the social complexity and sophistication of the Montreal scenes in the earlier novels. The children are being educated by their father: Ada acquires none of the convent graces of embroidery or music, but she is taught, like her brother, mathematics, science, Italian, French, and some Greek and Latin. Fear and loneliness forge a strong tie between brother and sister.

At seventeen George sets off for University College, Toronto. The point is made that Ada, equally prepared for university, cannot attend. The memorable Christmas Eve of the subtitle is Ada's seventeenth birthday. In the snow-filled darkness a terrible accident occurs. George kills a neighbour, then escapes from the scene, helped by Ada and their father. When, a short time later, a body is discovered some distance away, the neighbours assume that this is George, and take the discovery as proving his innocence. Ada and the father accept the assumption, although they in fact know the body to be that of a young vagabond to whom Ada had given some of George's clothes.

On this complicated plot device Leprohon constructs a slow, dark resolution for her story. Ada's life becomes linked with that of an old friend of her father's, and after many trials she marries this prosperous Toronto man. Despite the disparity in their ages, it is a love match. Their happiness is intense until disrupted by a tragic misunderstanding. Ada's husband, returning unexpectedly from a business trip, sees his wife in the arms of another man. In a rage he refuses to listen to explanations and leaves with no indication of where he is going. The man with Ada is in fact her brother, George, still a fugitive, seeking money to leave Canada. In *Armand Durand* Leprohon had used this same motif of a husband's unjustified jealousy in a minor way, when the senior Paul Durand mistrusted his Geneviève briefly; in *Ada Dunmore* the motif is central and tragic.

Although George's ultimate death releases the truth and the contrite husband returns to beg forgiveness, Ada has borne – and lost – a son before the return and reconciliation. Ada's deep despair at her husband's abandonment and at the loss of the child, and the absence of any spirituality on which she can draw for comfort, are well described. The moving scenes of the mother holding her dying child in her arms are ones Leprohon was only too well equipped to handle, four of her own babies having died in infancy. (Maud, not born until 1872, would bring the number to five children dead within the first year of life.) The young woman in the novel eventually arrives at spiritual awareness through suffering; the story ends as the couple renew life on a less self-centred albeit loving plane.

Ada Dunmore returns to a focus on female sensibility. But here Leprohon imagines a setting, an education, and a marriage completely different from her own. The excursion into a dark alternative life shows her continued readiness to tackle new materials. The shift is not as radical as when she moved from the light elegance of English drawing-rooms to the more complex realism of Quebec historical fiction, but it is another example of her flexibility and openness.

Yet another shift, and she produced "My Visit to Fairview Villa." This witty little story also appeared in the *Canadian Illustrated News* (14–28 May 1870).[42] The tale is again told in the first person, but the voice now is not that of the gloomy Ada but of a bright, sophisticated young man. "My Visit to Fairview Villa" is a charming courtship story set in Quebec, not in francophone society but in an elite English-speaking country milieu. The story appears to consist almost entirely of conversation, for when the protagonist is not engaged in reports of bantering talk, he is addressing the reader in the same chatty tone he uses to his Fairview Villa acquaintances.

Young Saville, the narrator-protagonist, has fallen in love with a beautiful, witty, and wealthy girl, Geraldine, who like him is a guest at the villa. He overhears her, at the outset of the story, mocking men and deriding marriage, and declaring that she would recognize any proposal made to her as the machination of a fortune-hunter. Amusing encounters at the tea-table, at a hunt, and on a picnic develop the young man's love, and also his dread of being ridiculed and rejected. Like Shakespeare's Beatrice and Benedict, the two young people carefully disguise their feelings. The narrative is skilful, as Saville reveals to the reader more than he understands himself.

As readers we enjoy this intriguing situation. We also relish the bright banter. We may, however, cavil at the device used for a denouement. The young man, sitting in the dark and happening to hold a perfumed handkerchief, is mistaken by Geraldine for a girlfriend whose perfume she recognizes. To her "friend" she confesses her love for Saville. Still, this unlikely scene is carried off by the author's light tone. Even the threat of a duel is treated lightly – a sharp change from the author's use of a duel for melodrama in earlier novels, including *Antoinette de Mirecourt*. In "Fairview Villa" the true duel is

the verbal one. This is a real comedy of manners, reminiscent of Jane
Austen, Anthony Trollope, or George Meredith rather than Dickens.

With the quick succession of *Armand Durand*, *Ada Dunsmore*, and
"Fairview Villa" between 1868 and 1870, Leprohon seems once again
to have been in full stride as a productive writer. It could not possibly
have been easy for her to find time to write in this period, however.
In 1871 Dr Leprohon was appointed vice-consul for Spain at Montreal
(an honorary position, but with some responsibilities for screening
immigrants). In the same year he took on the position of professor
of hygiene at Bishop's College in Lennoxville, Quebec, a teaching
post that must have involved considerable travelling to the townships
of Quebec that lie south of the St Lawrence. No doubt her husband's
appointments added to Leprohon's social responsibilities. A twelfth
child, the third living son in the family, Jean de Niverville Leprohon,
was born in 1870. A slowing-down of her activities would not be
surprising. In fact, however, she managed to contribute poems to
the *Journal of Education*, the *Saturday Reader*, the *Hearthstone*, and
various other publications, according to Henry Morgan's *Types of
Canadian Women*.[43]

Her next major story, "Clive Weston's Wedding Anniversary," was
published in the *Canadian Monthly* in August–September 1872.[44]
Again she was appearing in a new review, founded in 1872 by the
"Canada First" group of Ottawa and characterized by modern critics
as "popular-academic."[45]

This story of a modern marriage that comes close to breaking
down returns to Leprohon's earliest plot formula: an outsider joins a
family and threatens to disrupt its happiness. The setting is Montreal.
Clive Weston and his bride are affluent middle-class people. At their
wedding the bridesmaid begins her assault on the stability of the
marriage with sly, cynical comments. On an extended visit to the
young couple this disturbing young woman drives a wedge between
them by interfering with their routine, taking up much of the young
wife's time in entertainment that excludes the husband and finally
introducing her to an attractive young officer who soon makes
improper advances. The young wife rebuffs him, of course. But
communication with the husband has almost completely broken
down, and the friendship between the young women is also endan-
gered. Business troubles now add to the marital problems of the
morose young bridegroom. When he is finally forced to tell his wife
that he is bankrupt, her support of him in his trouble reunites them.
The "friend" leaves, misunderstandings are cleared up, a new business is started – all's well.

This story is set in a grey area of social morality. Neither of the young married people has done anything wrong, but Leprohon has shown how easily relationships can run into trouble. She suggests the need to work at a marriage to prevent its developing difficulties. The trouble-making friend is also an interesting study, not of evil but of rather petty malice and selfishness. Leprohon shows the danger such a person can pose, even to a warm relationship, especially in a busy, urban, socially and economically complex life. The social set is rather like that of "Fairview Villa," but the view of affluent, apparently successful socialites is here less affirmative. Though her examination of jealousy is here never allowed to develop the mordant tragic tone of *Ada Dunmore*, Leprohon is demonstrating again her ability to trace subtle and rather sad changes in marital relationships. The story was an appropriate one for the new *Canadian Monthly*, with its socio-economic seriousness; Leprohon could contribute to this new national journal a touch of Montreal urbanity along with a focus on a modern moral predicament.

A year and a half later Leprohon's next story appeared. She returned to the *Canadian Illustrated News* in January 1874 with the two-part "Who Stole the Diamonds?" Despite the title, this is not a mystery story. The protagonist and the reader watch the diamonds being stolen. The interest of the story is in its study of a young girl in complex relations with people in her circle. As in the early story "Alice Sydenham's First Ball," the heroine is named Alice, but this Alice is the only child of very wealthy parents. She tells her own story, like the narrator in "Fairview Villa," but the course of love here is muted and melancholy.

Wealthy Alice looks in a mirror as the story opens; what she sees is not beauty but homeliness. She feels fortunate in being engaged to handsome, debonair Harry Severton, who works for her father. It is the Christmas season, and all in the household except Alice are bound for a party. Later, alone in the house, Alice is awakened by sounds under the study window; she watches a figure enter, move to the safe, and remove some valuable jewels. It is Harry. Confronted with this story on the next day, Harry admits his guilt and agrees to leave the country. Years later Alice learns that not only did her father suspect Harry of treachery but that her pretty young cousin Carrie had also been alert to his falseness.

The obvious moral of "Who Stole the Diamonds?" seems to be that we should not judge by appearances. The more subtle lesson concerns the willingness of Alice to be deceived. Because she was pretty, Carrie had had to learn to recognize deceivers. The unattractive Alice had not had the same protective experience. Quite humanly, she has been happy to accept at face value the admiration and professions of love of a man as charming as Harry. The didactic touch was in keeping with the "household fare" offered in the *Illustrated News*, and the intriguing plot twist also adhered to the policy of lively entertainment in that magazine. In Leprohon's own development, the story also reveals a change from early days, when her fiction encouraged female readers to fantasize about a Cinderella shift of fortune. Now she is prepared to urge caution to young girls – no doubt an inevitable development in a woman whose oldest daughters, Gabrielle and Geraldine, were now twenty-one and seventeen, while their little sisters were also rapidly approaching the age for entering society.

The same year that "Who Stole the Diamonds?" was published, the Leprohons moved into a mansion at 237 Saint-Antoine Street, which was to remain their home. The family of eight children was now complete. In 1875, when her former teacher the Reverend Sister of the Nativity died, Leprohon published a poignant memorial poem. But her own health had begun to fail, primarily due to a heart condition. She published only one more story, a short one, which appeared in the *Illustrated News* 25 August to 17 September 1877.

Its title, "A School-Girl Friendship," is somewhat misleading. The story begins at the point when school is being left behind, and friendship is not the central theme of the tale. The story is told once again by the protagonist, who is an eighteen-year-old girl named Gertrude. (The Leprohons' daughter Gertrude was now fifteen; perhaps that schoolgirl daughter was in the mother's mind as she wrote this cautionary tale.) Gertrude's friend Charlotte, a penniless orphan, has been brought up by Gertrude's parents. The difference between the two girls is shown in the first scene, when Charlotte reveals that her success in class has been due to cheating, while Gertrude complains of doing poorly, despite studying – a difference in character very different from the histrionic antithesis between Amy and Louisa, or Lucy and Ida, those melodramatic heroines devised in Leprohon's own schoolgirl days!

In the new story Gertrude is re-establishing acquaintance with a young man whom her father hopes she will marry. The situation is similar to that of Blanche and Gustave in *The Manor House of de Villerai*. But here the beautiful, self-confident Charlotte sets out to win Rodney away from Gertrude. Gertrude, quiet and unpretentious, notes her fiancé's friendly overtures to Charlotte and becomes increasingly withdrawn, increasingly self-conscious, increasingly awkward. Fortunately, she matures sufficiently to speak up and to offer to free

Rodney from his engagement. She learns, happily, that he loves her and has been pleasant to Charlotte only for her sake. Once again, as in responding to the vivid Louisa or to Ida Beresford, the reader can feel some sympathy for the aggressive alien. Here again is a character like Thackeray's Becky Sharp, forced to live by her wits; such liveliness and high spirits are more interesting to read about than Gertrude's withdrawn self-consciousness. Gertrude's behaviour, nevertheless, is very realistically portrayed and psychologically appropriate.

In 1879 Rosanna Mullins Leprohon died. A volume of her poetry remained, to be collected and edited by John Reade, a neighbour and editor of the *Gazette*, who published it in 1881, with a critical introduction. That same year *Antoinette de Mirecourt* appeared for the second time in a new French translation. In 1884 another French edition of *The Manor House of de Villerai* appeared. Interest among French Canadian readers continued well into the next century – 1925 saw yet another new edition by the Beauchemin company. Yet only in 1973, with the New Canadian Library edition of *Antoinette de Mirecourt*, did many English Canadian readers turn their attention once more to Leprohon's works.

To read carefully through the sequence of these works is to recognize her discipline and determination as well as her creativity. She was concerned with exploring human nature and problems of relationships, not solely with entertaining her readers, although she does that too. The quick wit of her protagonists suggests her own wit and humour, developed from a very early age.

Her interest in the traditions of her country, her love of Canada, and her ambition to contribute to an "essentially Canadian" literature are all very much part of her work, and become more pronounced on her marriage into a family with strong roots in French Canada. Her Canadian patriotism is evident well before the Confederation period, which was the impetus for others to develop a "Canada First" spirit. Few other writers in the nineteenth century grasped as she did the intrinsic interest of biculturalism: she made herself at home in French Canadian materials and presented to anglophone compatriots a sensitive, clear-sighted narrative of stories uniquely Québécois. Only in James Macpherson Lemoine do we find a comparable ease of movement between the two founding cultures. Lemoine's forte is historical research and reporting; Leprohon brings the Quebec past to life in imaginative narratives and romances. Her inclusion of local colour as well as her careful research into historical detail, well before other local colourists, is another indication of her strong Canadianism. Interestingly, one of her greatest (and least known) successes in this genre is *Ada Dunmore*, the story in which she left her own Montreal scene and attempted to delineate life in an Ontario village and city.

But Rosanna Leprohon wrote not only to "capture Canada" in fiction but also to catch some of the interests of women – young women, or older women remembering their own preoccupations, worries, triumphs. For most women of her class and her century, the arena for dramatic action was the sitting-room, the parlour, the dance-floor, where girls met their fate by meeting and attracting suitable husbands. Most of her stories may be termed in a superficial way "courtship and marriage stories," but they are much more. They deal not only with the minor obstacles and misadventures that must be straightened out to reach the happy ending, but also with the inner problems of the protagonists, the maturation that occurs when young women face and attempt to cope with frustrations. Such problems may sometimes seem slight, home-bound, without consequential resolutions. But for young people the maturation process is experienced with intensity and puzzlement. Leprohon catches the sense of that absorption in her stories.

And in many of her stories she implies – by the foiling of the women characters, by their names, by their symbolic gestures – that romantic dreams of finding the "right" man are often illusory. Her strongest characters, those with whom most readers identify, either refuse to marry, or marry unhappily, or marry someone old or selfish. The weaker, less dynamic women characters are rewarded with the traditional romance heroes, those glamorous males who are most eager and best equipped to protect, nurture, and adore their womenfolk. In a sense Leprohon thus writes "failed romances," following many formulas up to a point but rejecting some of their essential illusions. Her women characters are close to the real world of anger, fear, sadness, and loss. Only on the surface are Leprohon's stories a facile reflection of women's desires. They suggest always, as a subtext, a realistic awareness of the truth about women's lives.

Rosanna Leprohon must have had a compelling desire to write, which drove her to make time in her overloaded life as mother, wife, member of a public-minded family, and bearer of thirteen children. Whether from early literary ambition or from a sheer bubbling-over of wit and the pleasure of invention, she hit an early stride in the light entertainments of the *Literary Garland*. She broke that stride completely during the hiatus from writing in the early days of her marriage. When she resumed writing, it was to produce a quite amazing variety of literature. From the sentimental pietism of *Eveleen O'Donnell* to the high martial idealism of *The Manor House of de Villerai*, the intrigue and coquetry of *Antoinette de Mirecourt*, and the dark modernity of *Armand Durand*, she moved always unpredictably into new settings, new periods, new themes. In the last period, when she returned from the serialized novel to the short-story form – perhaps for health reasons – she could still shift easily from one type of fiction to another.

The very virtuosity of her performance raises some important conclusions about the limitations of her life, as professional writer, as a Canadian, and as a woman. Like her character Ada Dunmore she had grown up without the possibility of a thorough intellectual education. The tastes inculcated at the convent led to early conformity to the sentimental formulaic patterns that suited readers of the *Literary Garland*. She was talented enough to slip in and out of various modes, without lingering to perfect her work in any one of them. Working in her middle years for an insecure, ephemeral range of publications, she lacked a serious editor, consistent enough in interest to push her beyond the easy successes and intent enough on excellence to demand it.

In her later years she lived in Montreal when that city was in a period of transition from its earlier focus on the provincial interests of Quebec to an ambitious stretching towards a place in continental Canadian culture. This transition in Montreal's intellectual and commercial life may have distracted Leprohon from the subject she had proved herself to be uniquely qualified to handle: the bicultural tensions of Quebec, as they were worked out in domestic scenes. She produced three first-rate Quebec novels in *The Manor House of de Villerai*, *Antoinette de Mirecourt*, and *Armand Durand*; then she slipped back into producing magazine entertainment. Finally, in spite of having a supportive husband whose wealth provided adequate household help, she probably never had time to concentrate on her art long enough to find her own best note. And so as a literary woman in the mid-nineteenth century, she was, for all her talent, industry, and charm, an alien.

May Agnes Fleming:
"I did nothing
but write"

LORRAINE McMULLEN

"I did nothing but write," said May Agnes Fleming to a New York
World correspondent,[1] explaining how she began a career that was
to make her one of North America's most popular and financially
successful fiction writers of the 1860s and 1870s. What she wrote
may seem at first glance to be the hectic stuff of routine gothic
romance. Considered more carefully, her work reveals a competence
in creating unusual women characters – obsessive, strong-willed,
sometimes ruthless. These women serve as a release for rebellious
impulses, both in the author and in her ostensibly tame domestic
audience. Near the end of her life May Agnes Fleming did something
else: she created a lively novel about a young woman who weathered
changes and vicissitudes as trying as the author's own, and under-
went transformations of name, role, and character to emerge as a
new kind of woman.

Published in New York at the age of seventeen, and a sought-after
writer of serial novels by her twenties, May Agnes Early Fleming
became Canada's first best-selling writer. In her balancing of career
and domestic life she speaks to today's woman. In the 1860s and 1870s
a highly paid contributor to New York and London story papers, with
novels appearing in book form in both the United States and Britain,
she was at the same time wife and mother, coping with the demands
of a growing family of four young children, all born within a six-year
period. Like the modern career woman she had to balance the
demands of her two lives, professional and domestic. And like many
of today's women she eventually found herself a single mother, coping
alone with the multitudinous demands of career and family. In her

life she faced pressures and barriers almost insuperable; in her writings she sublimated her resentment and created good escapist fiction.

May Agnes Early was born in the Portland area of Saint John, New Brunswick, on 14 November 1840.[2] She was the eldest of five children born to Bernard Early and Mary Doherty, who had come from Donegal, Ireland, to Saint John in their early twenties. Three of the Early children died in childhood: Catherine, born 4 October 1844; Joseph, born 22 December 1847, and Bernard, born 7 April 1850.[3] The only surviving sibling of May Agnes was James Patrick, fourteen years her junior.[4] May Agnes was thus brought up virtually as an only child, her one brother nearly a generation younger.

May Agnes grew up during the golden age of sail, when Saint John, Halifax, and Quebec were Canada's three major ports. Saint John became a boom town as merchant shipping expanded rapidly in the mid-1800s, with timber trade to Britain, coastal trade to the United States, and expanding trade to the West Indies and South America. During the April to November sailing season the port was crowded with sailing ships of all sizes, from brigs to schooners. The waterfront swarmed with seamen, merchants, carters, provisioners, labourers. The thousands of sailors from many lands moving in and out added colour and vitality to Saint John. Their boisterous, sometimes rowdy behaviour as they made the most of their evenings ashore enlivened port life. Winter, when most seamen had left for their homelands, was a quieter time; it was the shipbuilding season for Saint John and the Bay of Fundy area.

There was plenty of work for Bernard Early in the port city. As a ship's carpenter his skills were needed for repairs to docked ships in summer and shipbuilding in winter. A port city in the 1840s and 1850s would be a lively and cosmopolitan, if sometimes boisterous place for a girl growing up. It is easy to understand the wish of May Agnes's parents to have their daughter educated in a more tranquil setting. They arranged for her education at the Convent of the Sacred Heart. This local institution was respected for its academic standards and its formation of young women of virtue and refinement. An advertisement that appeared regularly in the Saint John Catholic paper, *The Morning Freeman*, underlines the formative aspect of the convent:

The institution embraces every means calculated to form young persons to habits of order, neatness, and polite deportment; but more especially to the practise of moral and Christian virtues.

The Course of Studies includes all the branches pertaining to a finished education. The health of the Young Ladies is the object of the most assiduous care.[5]

A Saint John paper reporting the annual exhibition of the Convent of the Sacred Heart gives a more specific account of May Agnes's educational milieu:

The annual exhibition at the Convent of the Sacred Heart took place on Wednesday. The bishop, several priests and a large number of relatives of the pupils, and of strangers, attracted by the fame of these Exhibits, were present. A large classroom, about 60 feet in length, was tastefully fitted up for the occasion. About half the room was occupied by the students, the Ladies of the Sacred Heart, and by the platform on which the recitations, etc. took place. The rest of the room was filled with visitors who must have numbered from 250 to 300.

On the arrival of the Bishop, six young ladies played the Entrée Victoria Quadrille on two pianos with excellent effect. Then one of the senior pupils read the Welcome, a very beautiful original composition and various recitations and dialogues in French and English: songs, duets, choruses, interspersed with instrumental music followed to the delight of the audience, who, although the Exhibition lasted several hours, gave no sign of weariness. To speak, read and write the English language correctly and elegantly are decidedly most important parts of a good education, and in these essentials, the ladies of the Sacred Heart are peculiarly successful teachers. The excellence of the original compositions spoken on this occasion, the purity of the language used, the accuracy and emphasis in pronunciation all proved this. It was positively amazing to hear little children recite, not as if hurriedly performing a painful task and muttering words they did not understand, but in an easy, graceful, natural manner with well modulated voices that would do credit to an orator.

After the Prizes were given for English, French (grammar and composition), Music, Writing, ARITHMETIC, Philosophy, Logic, etc., the Bishop briefly expressed the gratification afforded to the whole audience by what they had heard and witnessed. In one of the parlours were displayed specimens of the pupils' skill in needlework, embroidery, fancy work, wax work, drawing, penmanship, etc. The great advantages offered to parents by this establishment, unequalled by any in this Province, are beginning to be appreciated as they deserve.[6]

The emphasis on speaking, reading, and writing referred to in this report contributed no doubt to May Agnes's preparation for a writing career. The wide range of poetry quotations and references to literary works in her novels indicates her literary education.

The convent also provided her first audience. Like many only children, May Agnes was highly imaginative. She began her literary career as a very little girl telling fairy-tales to the other convent girls.

But the children, "to do them credit," she said later, "were never so completely carried away with my tales as I could have wished." "Perhaps," as she herself suggested, "it was this unappreciativeness of my audience that turned my thoughts to my pen."[7]

The Convent of the Sacred Heart provided an added, somewhat different source of education of which the Sisters were likely quite unaware, novels and papers that the girls smuggled into the school. As a schoolgirl May Agnes was a voracious reader. She read all the fiction she could get her hands on. By this time, story papers that published several short stories and several serials in each weekly edition were just coming into their own. Among the earliest of these papers, the New York *Mercury*, established in 1838, was also one of the most popular. May Agnes and her companions always contrived to secure copies, and May Agnes soon decided that she could do as well as its most popular contributors. At the age of fifteen she sent the *Mercury* a story inspired by her enthusiasm for the period of history she was studying at the time, titled "The Last of the Mountjoys; or, a Tale of the Days of Queen Elizabeth." Her assumption that she could do as well as the writers in the *Mercury* was justified. The paper accepted her first story and paid her three gold dollars for it.

Encouraged by her initial success, May Agnes sent stories to several other papers, including the local *Western Recorder and Carleton Advertiser and Home Journal*, and to two Catholic weeklies, the New York *Metropolitan Record* and the Boston *Pilot*, while continuing to write regularly for the *Mercury*. "'I should probably have remained longer at school, but for my success,'" she was to say later. "'Cousin May Carleton,' the name under which I used to write, soon thought herself too fine for a school."[8] From this beginning of her writing career in her teens, May Agnes remained a prolific writer. Committed to four or more papers, she might well say of these early years, "I did nothing but write."

May Agnes's success is all the more remarkable in that she was unlikely to have found much reading matter at home. Her mother could not even write her own name.[9] However, the Reverend Edward John Dunphy, pastor of St Malachy's Church, who had baptized her, encouraged May Agnes's intellectual development, and the stress on reading and writing in her convent school had its effect. Her religion remained an integral part of her life, and she remained always an active member of her church. She reportedly taught school for a short period at this time, but the demands created by the success of her stories cut short this career. Father Dunphy, who had established the Roman Catholic parish at Carleton in 1852, built the Roman Catholic school there. The school building was completed in 1856 and regular school classes began in January 1857. May Agnes, who had just turned seventeen, became the first teacher for the girls of the parish. She taught for two to three years before the success of her fiction led her to retire from teaching to work full time at her writing. In the words of Father Dunphy's biographer: "Miss Early continued her arduous duties till wearied of the monotonous routine of teaching she retired from the situation to engage in a no less arduous but much more lucrative calling."[10]

Her remarkable success so early in life can be ascribed partly to timing. The extension of education and expansion of literacy in the nineteenth century had led to a much wider reading public. More readers meant greater demand for reading material. As a result, the first great development in cheap paperback publishing began in the 1830s, and at the same time the story papers, as they were called, came into being. By mid-century circulation of the story papers had expanded to the hundreds of thousands, and writers for them were much in demand. Often novels serialized in these papers were quickly republished in cheap paperback.[11]

But a teenage convent girl's experience of life is limited. Where does such a girl find material for her fiction? Stories that May Agnes wrote at sixteen and seventeen demonstrate her sources of inspiration to be her reading of popular fiction in the story papers, her high-school education, and her religious upbringing. She had a quick mind, as the rapid improvement in her craft indicates. Her first story, "The Last of the Mountjoys,"[12] reveals as well her ability at the age of fifteen to transmute history into melodrama. An aristocratic young woman haughtily rejects the unpleasant Sir Hugo Mountjoy. Her response is nothing if not definite: "I would not be thy wife to save my head from the block, my estates from confiscation, or my soul from perdition! Sooner than mate with thee, I would dwell with the fiercest brutes of the forest, and make my home in the scorpion's nest" (27–8). The rejected suitor vows vengeance, which he quickly achieves by falsely accusing his rival, who is arrested at his wedding festivities and soon beheaded. His young widow achieves her revenge three years later, when she kills Mountjoy's infant son and then the villain himself at Elizabeth's court, calls down a curse on Elizabeth, and plunges the dagger into her own breast. The melodrama is excessive; nevertheless, the story is tightly constructed, with a series of scenes consisting almost entirely of dialogue and a minimum of description establishing the setting and the situation. The schoolgirl is already consciously crafting her story.

Another early story, "The Lady's Choice," appeared under the pseudonym Cousin Mary Carleton on page one of the *Western Recorder* on Saturday, 28 November 1857, less than two weeks after the author's seventeenth birthday. One can imagine the pride of May Agnes's mother, unable to write her own name, at seeing her daughter's story on the first page of the local Saturday paper. In this story the lady of the title, a beautiful, proud young aristocrat, rejects the man she loves because of his poverty, only to regret her decision when he returns five years later, an acclaimed author wedded to another. Thereupon the proud lady marries an elderly suitor and lives unhappily ever after. The language, stilted and formal, is almost childishly archaic, yet the brief story is carefully structured and economically told. Of most interest is the Pre-Raphaelite setting of the first scene, in which the fair-haired lady in a white robe sits in a room of crimson damask, carpet patterned in white lilies, golden sunlight pouring in. The setting and heroine are obviously derived from Tennyson's "Lady of Shalott" and Rossetti's "Blessed Damozel." The hero may well be acting out the young writer's own dream of future fame.

Another story in the same paper a year and a half later shows a clear advance in writing style and handling of plot. "Zion: An Old Man's Tale," also given prominence on the front page, appeared in two parts, on 23 and 30 April 1859. The narrator falls in love with Zion, a beautiful Jewish singer-actress, who reveals that she is secretly married to a young aristocrat. Later, after the narrator has learned that Zion's nobleman-husband has married a peeress, a baby girl, Zion's daughter, is left on his doorstep. He brings her up to follow her mother's profession. When she makes her stage debut, her father is in the audience and realizes from her strong resemblance to her mother who she must be. Otherwise childless, he adopts her. Hardly realistic, yet this is less a fairy-tale than the earlier story; it is the sort of sentimental story with complicated plot that would appeal to the story-paper reader, showing more kinship with the usual sentimental romance of the story papers than with Tennyson or Rossetti.

A third story, "Little Lily," also in the *Western Recorder* (21 May 1859), is obviously indebted to May Agnes's religious background. Lily, a blind, delicate little orphan, is befriended by an attractively hoydenish little girl, through whose carelessness Lily is left alone one stormy night at her mother's graveside. Found the next morning, Lily dies joyfully with the vision of her mother before her. Her remorseful friend enters the convent.

In this story there is more emotional intensity, and there is an attempt at realistic dialogue. It is twice as long as "Zion." The plot is more involved than that of earlier stories, and the introduction is more dramatic, one might say melodramatic: "'I am dying – dying – dying! There is no hope, I must die!' and the speaker, an emaciated woman whose skin shone like burnished copper with the fierce heat of fever, raised herself partly on her elbow and glared around wildly." Religious this story may be, but it also shows us that even at this age May Agnes has captured the popular mind; for this was the time of graveyard literature, with deathbed scenes, ghosts, and cemeteries prevalent in illustrations as well as stories.

"Nora; or, Love and Money," a story appearing in the New York *Sunday Mercury* the next month, is closer to the conventional sentimental romance.[13] The story takes the reader into the aristocratic world of the Anglo-Irish. Intending to marry a wealthy young woman solely for her money, a handsome young aide-de-camp to Dublin's Lord Lieutenant is injured in an accident. He regains consciousness in a simple Irish home, where he is nursed back to health by Nora, a lovely young Irish girl. They fall in love, but he leaves Nora to marry his wealthy fiancée. Hearing that Nova is seriously ill, he returns from his honeymoon to be with her when she dies. In lifelong remorse, he visits her grave daily.

The story of a rakish young man who repents too late and a young girl who dies of a broken heart is hardly original. Nevertheless, the story has appeal. Introductory dialogue arouses interest and quickly establishes the situation, and the story-line moves quickly. For a young, relatively inexperienced writer it is well crafted. Some years after the author's death this story was republished as the lead story, with the new title "Married for Money," in a collection of three Fleming stories.[14]

"Love's Young Dream" in the *Sunday Mercury* of 20 November 1859 is an embittered young man's story of being jilted. It differs slightly from preceding stories in being structured as a frame story. Also, the story is set in the United States, an obvious accommodation to the American audience. Another *Mercury* story some months later, "The Wages of Sin," is also first-person narrative, set in the fashionable American world of New York, Newport, and Washington. Well named, "The Wages of Sin" is the unhappy story of a young woman who, on her wedding day, meets her bridegroom's cousin, falls precipitately in love with him, and runs away with him while on her honeymoon. Later, deserted and destitute, she accidentally meets her husband, who forgives her before he dies. She looks forward to her own death to unite them. Of interest is a reference to Gradgrind of Dickens' *Hard Times*.

While these early stories are sentimental and romantic, set in England or in New York, where the readership was, many of them differ refreshingly from most sentimental writing in the flashes of humour that were to characterize May Agnes Early's novels. "The Philopene,"[15] for example, is consistently light in tone as the observer-narrator tells of a winter visit to Canada with a charming and flir-tatious friend. Local colour is added with the description of sleighing and skating as well as dancing and partying as the young flirt charms all the men. Then she overhears a handsome new arrival vow that he will not succumb to the bewitching man-killer of whom he has heard. The young woman accepts the challenge but finds the tables turned; she falls in love with the newcomer while he remains ostens-ibly heart-free. At the last minute, of course, he confesses that he too has fallen in love, and proposes to her for a happy ending. In action and tone this story is much like "My Visit to Fairview Villa," one of Rosanna Leprohon's later stories. With its light, ironic tone it shows a sophistication not evident in stories of two years earlier.

These stories show May Agnes Early developing her craft and attuning her plots and settings to her audience. In three years she progressed from the stilted and unreal "Lady's Choice" to the sophis-ticated comedy of "The Philopene." As well, her stories were becoming longer and more complex, and by twenty she was writing novels, most of which were published in cheap paperbacks following serialization.

Her indebtedness to the popular and sentimental novels of her school days is still apparent in these first serials, but now, with the longer length, Early added elements of the gothic novel as well. There is no clear demarcation between the two, inasmuch as both involve courtship and romance in which a series of obstacles must be over-come before the happy ending of marriage. The gothic, stemming from Horace Walpole's *Castle of Otranto* (1764), had been popularized by Ann Radcliffe and Edgar Allan Poe, both of whom were widely read at this time. It added fear and terror to the sentimental novel, creating mystery and suspense by such gothic conventions as hidden identities, inherited curses, family secrets, and melodramatic villains. To arrive at the marriage of the hero and heroine, the mystery had to be resolved and the villain defeated. Since each instalment would leave the reader waiting impatiently for the resolution of yet another crisis, the genre was admirably suited to serial publication.

Possibly the most popular of Early's early romances was *Sybil Campbell; or, The Queen of the Isle* (1861),[16] a novel with a remarkably intricate plot. It begins with the return of twenty-year-old Sir Guy Campbell and his seventeen-year-old sister Sybil to their ancestral home, a small island off the coast of North America. Complications develop immediately. For example, Guy falls in love with a woman married to a villainous husband, and Sybil's lover becomes infatuated with and secretly marries a young girl he meets on the island. Of course both spouses must be eliminated, and they are – both die so that love can triumph. But mysteries from the past also intrude and must be resolved before the happy ending can be achieved. Central to these mysteries is a ghostly white-robed figure glimpsed occasionally at night – in one instance running through the woods shouting, "Murdered! Murdered!" This figure is revealed to be the second wife of Sybil's father, whom her insanely jealous husband had walled up with her suspected lover, an incident possibly suggested by Edgar Allan Poe's well-known "Cask of Amontillado" (1846), in which a man recounts walling up his enemy alive in an alcove of his wine cellar. In Early's novel the companion has died, while the woman was rescued but has gone mad. This unfortunate woman is called Bertha, an indication of her source – the mad Bertha Rochester of *Jane Eyre*.

Other gothic elements in *Sybil Campbell* include a plethora of harrowing incidents involving murder, attempted murder, several deaths, a secret marriage, startling revelations, a dream foreshadowing future events, and a fortune teller who does the same. Like her best-known predecessor, Ann Radcliffe, the young May Agnes Early explains seemingly supernatural events as resulting from natural causes. She indicates her literary interests by using appropriate quotations, largely from Shakespeare and Byron, to introduce her chapters. Characters are stereotyped, as might be expected; to control a complex, multi-threaded plot such as this was sufficient challenge for a young woman of nineteen or twenty without her attempting to develop characters as well. Most refreshingly, and as unusual in gothic as in sentimental novels, there is some humour.

Sybil Campbell was frequently republished. It appeared as *Sybil Campbell; or, The Queen of the Isle* in 1861 and 1863, as *An Awful Mystery* (1875), and as *Queen of the Isle* (1886). That many of Early's novels were published under different titles by different publishers, along with the ephemeral nature of some of the publications she wrote for, makes it next to impossible to determine the number of novels this popular author wrote.

In *The Twin Sisters; or, The Wronged Wife's Hate* (1864) emotional intensity reaches new heights, and the woman villain makes her debut. Again, gothic elements are present, including a murder, a secret marriage, two kidnappings, and two suicides. The main impetus to the plot is the vengefulness of a deserted wife whose husband has kidnapped their infant twin daughters, then planned a socially and financially suitable marriage, ignoring his earlier, secret marriage. The heroines are dark and the evil women blonde and angelic in appearance, an inversion of the stereotype and one that would recur in many of Early's stories. Another deviation from stereotype is the introduction of a poor cousin – in the vein of the well-born governess – who is not gentle and submissive but jealous and resentful. This figure too would become a stock character in Early's romances. Here she also uses landscape effectively to reflect the mood and action; the "gray spectral sunlight," for example, could be compared to the evocative poetry written by Wilfrid Campbell twenty years later. Once again the sensational, one might say melodramatic plot is well handled. This novel, too, appeared under several titles, including *The Rival Brothers* and *A Wronged Wife*.

Another novel of about the same time, *Eulalie; or, A Wife's Tragedy* (c 1864), published not under her usual pseudonym but under the author's own name, Miss M.A. Early, provides for the first time an erotic element, a sensuality that is threatening and a passion that is disastrous. By telling the story largely from the perspective of the young hero, Arthur, Early is able to show the emotional swings in his response to a young woman whom he both loves and fears, the darkly beautiful Eulalie. His first vision of this young woman is both erotic and threatening. She is seated on a red-cushioned window-seat surrounded by red drapery, wearing a scarlet shawl and a circlet of emeralds. "Somehow he had thought of the fatal greenish glitter of a serpent's head." Later in his thoughts he sees her as a "black-eyed houri" of "darkly-gorgeous beauty,"[17] and that night he dreams of her along with, and in contrast to, the young woman he had planned to marry, "blue-eyed Isabel, robed in white and illumined by the sunlight as he had seen her last." The dream becomes terrifying when, "out of the black shadow of the trees a tall serpent reared itself upright with a hiss, and the sunshine was suddenly darkened. The serpent had an emerald flashing in its head, and looked at him with the great black eyes of the Creole heiress" (46). The two women are opposed as archetypal virgin and temptress or fatal woman. The woman-serpent recalls Keats's Lamia. Time after time in the next few days the fascinated Arthur thinks of Eulalie in terms of her bewitching power: "the dark-eyed siren," "the dark little witch." But when she agrees to marry him, gone are witch, serpent, houri, siren. "Eulalie is an angel; and he is in paradise" (166). When he proposes to her, this reversed symbolism is equally explicit:

"To-night, the world was all Eden, and she the happiest Eve that ever danced in the sunshine" (116). An astonishing transformation.

Unlike most gothic novels, the woman's troubles, instead of being resolved by marriage, begin after the wedding. The troubles are not altogether surprising to the reader after the portentous imagery used earlier to describe the bride. While Eulalie has been instantly transformed from serpentine to angelic, other figures quickly appear as representatives of evil threatening the happiness of the young couple in their Eden. First, the darkly handsome Gaston Benoir appears, threatening to divulge a secret from Eulalie's past that is so dreadful she dare not tell her husband. Described as having "the look of a demon," Benoir remarks of Eulalie, "She hates me, as I suppose an angel would hate Lucifer" (257). He extorts money and jewellery from the unhappy Eulalie, who finally runs away before he can reveal her secret to Arthur.

The plot is further complicated by the introduction of the darkly beautiful and passionate Rebecca, who has followed Benoir to insist he keep his promise to marry her. She too is aligned with the powers of darkness. Benoir wonders, "Has Satan sent her here to balk me? I wish he had her, body and bones; for she is as near akin to him as anything in woman's shape can well be ... Rebecca Isaacs, I wish the old demon had you!" (260) Rebecca's vengeful murder of Benoir is too late for Eulalie; rather, having run away, Eulalie is the prime suspect. Rebecca contrasts with Eulalie; she fulfils the promise that Eulalie's erotic appearance erroneously suggested but that hid the conventional helpless and sentimental woman. In the words of Benoir: "If that unfortunate little beauty, Eulalie, had a tithe of her [Rebecca's] spirit, I would have a hard fight for the victory" (328).

Sir Walter Scott's *Ivanhoe* is the probable genesis of Rebecca. In that novel the dark-haired Jewish Rebecca was a foil for the blonde Anglo-Saxon Rowena. Early's Rebecca fits into the tradition (discussed at length by Leslie Fiedler in *Love and Death in the American Novel*)[18] of dark and dangerous women – usually Jewish, Oriental, or Mediterranean – who bring with them the threat of sexuality and/or death. Eulalie, a Creole uniting both dark and light, is an equivocal figure. At first she appears threatening to the hero; then, when the light side of her nature wins out, she becomes the virtuous white maiden. But later, after their marriage, the darker side of her nature leads to disaster. The secret that her dark complexion is not derived from French or Spanish heritage but, in fact, from a black mother, a runaway slave, is the hold Benoir has over her. Eulalie runs away from her Eden to her tragic end. One can never return to Eden. Eulalie-Eve is found dead, leaving Arthur free to marry his fair-haired first love, who in the meantime has married but has conveniently been widowed.

Arthur is an inept hero, his name ironic. No knight in shining armour, he displays neither courage, initiative, independence, nor intelligence. When Eulalie runs away, for example, he is so distraught that he falls ill and for several months is unable to search for her. When Rebecca's letter arrives confessing to Benoir's murder, Arthur's mother, not Arthur, decides what to do, which should be obvious – notify the police. "Drive to St. Mary's immediately," she orders her son, "and do as I tell you!" (414).

Despite its heavy-handed imagery and symbolism, the novel has many interesting facets: the charming, ruthless villain with more personality than the hero, the villainess with the intense passion of the spurned woman, with initiative and determination as well. As for Eulalie's role, it seems that the sensuous woman does not bring lasting happiness to marriage. The novel ends with the hero's marriage to the cool and proper young woman he should have married in the first place.

The novel's subtext is subversive. Despite her obvious feminine virtues, despite proving herself, as does the traditional gothic heroine, "worthy of salvation through the love of the hero, who becomes her deliverer from the terrors that beset her,"[19] the heroine is not rescued by the hero. Nor is the gothic villain defeated by true love, as he should be, but by true hate; he is defeated not by a male hero but by a female avenger. Nor does solution of the mystery bring a happy ending for the heroine. The happy ending is reserved for the failed hero and is achieved through the brief frame story – the conventional woman met in the early pages of the novel, who has had no part in the action, is brought back for a happy marriage in the last pages. This frame story has no real connection with the rest of the novel. It could easily have been tacked on to the completed novel as an afterthought to give readers the happy ending they would expect, and probably it was. It is interesting to speculate whether the editor or the writer herself deemed it necessary to add this ending.

A year after the publication of *Eulalie*, unusual in its passion and eroticism and its handsome but weak hero, May Agnes Early married, stepping into a situation that was to be almost a working-out in real life of the plot of her novel. On 24 August 1865, at the Cathedral of the Immaculate Conception in Saint John, she married John William Fleming,[20] a handsome boilermaker a year her junior, who swept her off her feet in a whirlwind three-week courtship.[21] Thus began a marriage based on passion, to a man who was to prove himself very weak indeed. The Flemings remained in Saint John, living in a small house in Brittain Street near the harbour, next door to Bernard and Mary Early. The young bride, superior to her husband in education, intelligence, and material success, did not give up her career but continued writing for several papers and republishing her novels in book form, at the same time taking on the additional responsibilities of domesticity and, within two years, the care of her first child, Frederick, born in 1867.

Three years after her marriage Mrs Fleming's success led to an offer to write exclusively for the Philadelphia *Saturday Night*, a paper that had been established only in 1865 and was looking for successful writers to build up its readership. By 1868, the time of Fleming's first appearance in the paper, its circulation had reached at least one hundred thousand, and it maintained one of the largest circulations of any American weekly. It had the usual story-paper format, consisting of eight pages, usually running three serials and several short stories. At this time payment to writers varied widely from paper to paper and from writer to writer. Some paid one-half to two cents per word, others seven dollars per page. Ten dollars per page was paid by higher-class magazines.[22] Fleming's agreement with *Saturday Night* was to write three stories annually at $666.66 each, or $2,000 annually,[23] an excellent contract for that time, which made it well worth her while to give up her other magazine writing. It took away some of the pressure of deadlines – she was later to blame her poor health on the earlier years of hard work trying to fulfil her commitments to three or four papers. John Fleming later claimed that although he was, on their marriage, "only a hard working, hard fisted mechanic," it was "with my advice, and partly through my exertions" that his wife "made connection with the story papers."[24] While John's involvement in the negotiations is debatable, it is certainly possible that he pushed her to try to get more money for her stories if she could. There was never any chance that Fleming, unlike her contemporary Rosanna Leprohon, could give up her writing in the early years of housekeeping and childbearing.

Fleming's entire family shared in her good fortune. Her father, listed in the 1863–64 Saint John city directory as ship's carpenter, is listed in the 1869–70 directory as grocer. It seems most likely that his daughter, with her now secure source of a comfortable income, assisted him in setting up his business, one more suitable to him at the age of sixty than carpentry. It also seems most likely that she was responsible for her husband's going into business for himself. John's advertisement for his own business as boilermaker also appeared in the 1869–70 city directory.

Considering Fleming's central place in her family, it is interesting to note the listing of her household in the 1871 Saint John census. By this time she had been under contract to *Saturday Night* for three years. According to the census report, the family consisted of two children, Frederick, aged three, and Maud, aged two, one servant, Ellen Murphy, aged sixteen, John, a boilermaker, and May Agnes, who – despite her popular and commercial success, despite earning an income far beyond that which a Saint John boilermaker could ever dream of, and despite her traditional duties as wife and mother – is credited with neither career nor employment.

Saturday Night, however, made much of its new contributor. More than two months before her first serial began, the paper announced: "We shall soon give to our readers a romance by a new contributor to these columns, although she is well known and deservedly popular in the field of American Romance,"[25] and on 19 September the paper noted of her novel, *The Baronet's Bride*, which was to begin in two weeks:

It has been written especially for SATURDAY NIGHT by our new contributor, MRS. MARY AGNES FLEMING, who, under the *nom de plume* of "May Carlton" [sic] has been one of the most successful novelists of the day.

In "The Baronet's Bride" Mrs. Fleming has given us a romance which, for continued thrilling interest, cannot be surpassed; and we are happy to announce that she has been engaged to write exclusively for this paper.[26]

Fleming's career with *Saturday Night* was launched on 3 October 1868, when the first instalment of *The Baronet's Bride; or, A Woman's Vengeance* was featured on page one, with a large illustration of a scene from the novel. The story continued for thirteen weeks and, according to the number of editions that were published in book form, proved to be another of Fleming's successful novels. On the insistence of *Saturday Night* Fleming henceforth dispensed with her pseudonym.

The novel's subtitle, "A Woman's Vengeance," is appropriate. The plot hinges on a search for vengeance through three generations of women. A Spanish gypsy, loved and deserted by an English baronet, gives birth to a daughter. First the gypsy, then her daughter, and finally her granddaughter plot vengeance against the betrayer's family. The novel deals primarily with the plot of the granddaughter, Sybilla, against the baronet's son Everard and his bride, Harriet. Everard is unaware of his father's history and of the plot against him. The novel is complicated by a dreadful secret in Harriet's family as well, so there are two plot threads; the expected conventions of the gothic genre are all here as well – secrets, hidden identities, attempted murder, mysterious meetings, letters conveying urgent messages.

This novel is less formal in narrative method than Fleming's earlier fiction. Occasionally, the narrator makes asides to the reader, reminders that this is, after all, a novel. After Harriet has been stabbed and thrown over a cliff, her body to be washed away by the waves, and Everard, having been framed for her murder, awaits execution, the next chapter begins: "And while Sir Everard Kingsland lay in his felon's cell, doomed to die, where was she for whose murder he was to give his life? Really murdered? Is there any one above the artless and unsuspecting age of six, who reads this story, does not know better?"[27] At another time the narrator chattily remarks, "What is it that Byron says about solitude, and moonlight, and youth? A dangerous combination, truly" (56).

An innovation for Fleming is the introduction of a Scotland Yard detective to solve the supposed murder. He is employed by Everard, and ironically he quickly picks up clues, planted by the villainous Sybilla, that incriminate Everard, leading to his arrest and conviction. Fleming, who continued to be a voracious reader, was aware of the evolution of the mystery and detective story. She disliked Wilkie Collins, whom she considered overrated.[28] *The Woman in White* had appeared in 1860 and been an immediate sensation, but *The Moonstone* was published only in 1868, the same year as *The Baronet's Bride*. As an ardent admirer of Dickens,[29] Fleming would have known *Bleak House*, first serialized in *Household Words* in 1852–53, which is credited with the first police-detective hero. The outstanding success of Mary Elizabeth Braddon's *Lady Audley's Secret* (1861) and of Mrs Henry Wood's *East Lynne*, serialized in Colborn's *New Monthly Magazine* in 1860–61, were probable influences. Both of these novels concerning sensational crime in aristocratic circles had complicated plots leading eventually to the revelation of the mystery. Such mystery plots led to the development of the detective novel,[30] and with *The Baronet's Bride* Fleming took her first step in that direction.

In the gothic, as later in the detective novel, character is subordinate to plot. Because the conclusion must be carefully planned, the novelist cannot allow characters to take on their own lives to the extent that the story changes as it is being written. Nevertheless, Fleming was beginning to develop her women characters more fully. Harriet, introduced as a tomboyish seventeen-year-old, gives promise of developing into an engaging heroine. She first meets Everard at a hunt, where she proves herself a first-class rider; more daring than the men, she leads the hunt. Like Diana Vernon, the heroine of Sir Walter Scott's *Rob Roy*, who shocks Frank Osbaldistone with her riding and shooting and her freedom from convention, Harriet's behaviour shocks and amazes Everard. But once engaged to him she spends a year at a convent in France, where she makes the transition from lively, independent tomboy to loving, submissive bride, much as Eulalie in *A Wife's Tragedy* changes from femme fatale to submissive wife. Harriet is then a foil for Sybilla, whose hatred for Everard's family is her sole motivation in life. Sybilla, another of Fleming's strong villainous women, beautiful, passionate, and clever, insinuates herself into Everard's home and there lays her plans for Harriet's murder and Everard's death on the gallows – the fate her family has decreed for him. She very nearly succeeds. Only coincidence – part of a carefully integrated plot involving Harriet's family secret – results in Harriet's rescue and the failure of Sybilla's plan.

In much women's fiction, contrasting women characters reflect the author's conflicting attitudes to her society and women's role in it. Since the authors are creative and observant, they cannot help but perceive the disparity between the power and freedom of their male colleagues and the lack of power of their own sex, and the limited range of experience open to them. Consciously or unconsciously, they reflect their own dilemma, their ambivalent response to their society and the role it seeks to impose upon women, by personifying in two women characters the conventional and unconventional aspects of their own personalities.[31] This is what we see happening in Fleming's creation of Harriet and Sybilla. Sybilla, like Rebecca in *A Wife's Tragedy*, exemplifies the "monstrous woman" of whom Sandra M. Gilbert and Susan Gubar speak in *Madwoman in the Attic*: "By projecting their rebellious impulses not into their heroines but into mad or monstrous women (who are suitably punished in the course of the novel or poem), female authors dramatize their own self-division, their desire both to accept the strictures of patriarchal society and to reject them ... the madwoman in literature by women is not merely, as she might be in male literature, an antagonist or foil to the heroine. Rather, she is usually in some sense the *author's* double, an image of her own anxiety and rage." In the nineteenth century, say Gilbert and Gubar, "even the most apparently conservative and decorous women writers obsessively create fiercely independent characters who seek to destroy all the patriarchal structures which both their authors and their authors' submissive heroines seem to accept as inevitable."[32] Sydney Conyer echoes this observation in a study of the gothic novel, most of whose nineteenth-century women authors, "even when they do not overtly criticize patriarchal institutions or conventions ... almost obsessively create characters who enact their own, covert authorial anger ... over and over again they project what seems to be the energy of their own despair into passionate, even melodramatic characters who act out the subversive impulse every woman inevitably feels when she contemplates the 'deep-rooted' evils of patriarchy."[33]

Fleming had every reason for anger when she considered her place in patriarchal society. She was a successful professional woman who had shown herself to have talent, ambition, drive, and initiative, a popular and commercially successful and sought-after writer, yet her social status remained strictly domestic, that of a boilermaker's wife. Her successful career came while bearing and bringing up children. She had good reason to be rebellious at the status society ascribed to her and at society's expectations of her.

With *The Baronet's Bride*, her first suspenseful serial in *Saturday Night*, Fleming captivated the paper's eager readers of gothic romances. Within five weeks her next story, *The Heiress of Glen Gower; or, The Hidden Crime*, began (23 January 1869), continuing weekly to 17 April. *Estella's Husband* began the following week and continued to 24 July; *Sybilla's Marriage* appeared from 11 September to 30 October; *Lady Evelyn* from 1 January 1870 to 16 April; and *Who Wins?* beginning the same week *Lady Evelyn* ended, to 23 July – six novels in less than two years. The dates of these novels suggest that Fleming continued to write under some pressure. After *Who Wins?* the pace slowed: *Magdalen's Vow* did not begin until 18 February 1871, seven months after the conclusion of *Who Wins?* It ran until 3 June. Almost five months later, on 28 October, Fleming's last novel for *Saturday Night, Which Will She Marry?* began, concluding 3 February 1872.

Copyright problems were to prove troublesome to Fleming, who complained of the pirating of her novels by Canadian publishers.[34] But this time an instance of piracy of a *Saturday Night* story proved to be advantageous. When the *London Journal* published *The Heiress of Glengower*, it did so under the title *The Sister's Crime*.[35] Several New York story papers began reprinting it, not realizing that it was also published in an American paper and thus was protected by copyright. *Saturday Night* took out an injunction prohibiting continued publication.[36] The discontinuance of a suspenseful serial midway caused quite a stir, which resulted in a bidding war for the services of the popular May Agnes Fleming and in her transfer to the *New York Weekly*, where she was to be paid three times her *Saturday Night* fee, six thousand dollars a year for three stories.[37]

With her second serial for the *Weekly, A Wonderful Woman*, Fleming also began publishing regularly in the *London Journal*. A note appears under the title of the first episode (6 July 1872): "N.B. – This story is copyright. Proceedings will be taken in case of infringement." The same note states that Fleming is author of *The Sister's Crime* and also of *The Mystery of Mordaunt Hall*, which had appeared anonymously 16 July to 1 November 1870. This novel proves to be *Who Wins?* which ran in *Saturday Night* 16 April to 23 July. In pirating this story *Saturday Night* had carefully changed the names of the characters and of the English estate on which much of the action takes place. The *London Journal* was paying Fleming twelve pounds weekly for serialization of her novels[38] – approximately sixty dollars in American currency, amounting to eighteen hundred for a thirteen-week serial – and G.W. Carleton began publishing all her novels directly after their run in the *Weekly* and paying her 15 per cent royalty. Her annual income was well in excess of the ten thousand dollars estimated by literary historians.[39] Later the *New York Weekly* reportedly paid her fifteen thousand dollars for two novels.[40]

The *New York Weekly*, which had so aggressively gone after the popular writer, claimed to have the largest circulation of any paper at this time. It was owned by Francis S. Street and Francis S. Smith. Both men had worked for Amos J. Williamson on the *Sunday Dispatch*, Street as the bookkeeper, Smith as a reporter, later as editor. At Williamson's suggestion they had bought from him in 1858 the *New York Weekly Dispatch*, which they re-christened the *New York Weekly*. Smith as editor and Street as business manager set out to expand circulation by recruiting famous writers, to whom they paid enormous fees.[41] Obviously, their plan worked. By 1874 they could claim a circulation of 350,000, the largest of any weekly in the world.[42] Smith himself also wrote serials for the paper and published his poetry in it.

When Fleming was writing for the *Weekly*, it was one of two leading story papers. Its rival, the *New York Ledger*, edited by Robert Bonner, also recruited famous writers, including William Cullen Bryant, Henry Wadsworth Longfellow, and, of the popular women writers, Harriet Beecher Stowe, Sara Parton, and E.D.E.N. Southworth.[43] The *Weekly* countered with Horatio Alger, Jr, Mary Jane Holmes, and May Agnes Fleming.

Fleming was fortunate in her book publisher as well. George W. Carleton had gone into publishing in 1857 and soon acquired a list of successful authors, including Josh Billings (Henry Wheeler Shaw), Artemus Ward (Charles F. Browne), and many of the popular sentimental novelists, including Mary Jane Holmes and E.D.E.N. Southworth. He was known to be generous to his authors. James Derby, a contemporary publisher, mentions May Agnes Fleming as among the most popular American novelists published by Carleton.[44] On his retirement in 1886 his associate G.W. Dillingham took over his list.

Later reprints of a number of Fleming's novels appear under the Dillingham imprint.

Early in 1873 Fleming's first story for the *New York Weekly* appeared: *A Leap in the Dark; or, Wedded Yet No Wife*, which was titled in book form *Guy Earlscourt's Wife* (1873). This was followed by *A Wonderful Woman*, *A Terrible Secret*, *Norine's Revenge*, *A Mad Marriage*, *One Night's Mystery*, *Kate Danton; or, Captain Danton's Daughters* (in the *London Journal* titled *In Golden Bondage*), then *Silent and True; or, A Little Queen*, which began in October 1876 – eight novels in less than four years.

Within a year of joining the ranks of *Weekly* writers, Fleming moved with her family to Brooklyn to be near her publishers. By this time the Flemings had four small children: Frederick was seven and Maude five; and there were now two more, Agnes, three, and Charles, one. The family set about looking for a house, and on 1 April 1875 May Agnes Fleming – not her husband – bought a house on DeKalb Street for which she paid $4,200 in cash.[45]

Fleming was at the peak of her career, but personal and health problems began to complicate her life. Her father died on 13 August 1875, and some time after that her elderly mother came to live with her. Not many months after her father's death, John and May Agnes's marital difficulties surfaced when she made a carefully worded will to exclude her husband not only from a share in her estate but also from guardianship of their children. Fleming's will, dated 1 February 1876, left all her assets, with the exception of a few small bequests, and all future royalties to her four children. She included in her will instructions for her children's education in Roman Catholic schools, specifically requesting that the girls be educated at the Sisters of Charity school, Mount Saint Vincent, on the Hudson River, the boys at the Jesuit Fordham College. To forestall her husband, she instructed that should he assume control of the children or remove them from the guardians she had named, the trustees should pay no part of her estate to their education or support.

She made a sensible choice of executors for her will and trustees and guardians for her children, selecting Patrick Meade, a fellow parishioner at the Church of Saint John the Baptist, who presumably would see to the children's upbringing and education as she wished, and Francis S. Smith, publisher and editor of the *Weekly*. Smith, himself a writer as well as a publisher, was well placed to supervise the children's financial affairs, including future payments and royalties. The trustees were to handle the estate until the children reached their majority, when each was to receive an equal share of the estate. There was a further proviso to her will, resulting no doubt from her own unhappy experience, that should a daughter marry before she was twenty-one, she was to receive her share of the estate, but that share was to be "immediately invested for her benefit by the trustees in such a manner as to be for her sole use, not under the control or subject to the debts of her husband."[46]

According to contemporary sources John Fleming was an intemperate man who made life extremely difficult for his family.[47] A report that she had "a husband who made her life wretched, and from whom she was always hiding," and that "she worked hard for the money that he claimed as his right,"[48] helps to explain the careful wording of her will to protect her children. It also helps to explain her hectic pace of writing, spurred on to support herself and her four children and to prepare for their future. John Fleming was to maintain later that their domestic troubles began soon after they moved to Brooklyn, when "she grew wealthy and famous and I remained what I was when I married her – a hard working, hard fisted mechanic," and to complain that "she, as good a woman as ever breathed, was easily led in a certain direction. She was taught to believe she was better than I – perhaps she was; that the children would not receive an orthodox training in my charge, although remember I am a Roman Catholic, and so we quarrelled and I went west."[49] He also blamed the Church of Saint John the Baptist, of which Patrick Meade was a trustee, as having something to do with her will. It seems more likely that her publishers, successful businessmen, were her advisers, as both were involved in drawing up the will, Street as a witness and Smith as an executor and guardian.

On 4 December 1878 Fleming sold her house and moved to a larger one nearby, at 98 Lewis Street.[50] A journalist gives us a brief description of the house and its owner at this time:

Arriving at a neat little white-painted two-storey house in one of those outlying eastern avenues of Brooklyn ... he was shown into a small but trim parlor, which was evidently not the workshop of the story writer, inasmuch as it was spick and span, with snowy tidies on the bright-colored satin furniture, and not a suggestion of a book, or of the tools for making one. Wax flowers were set about here and there under shining glass globes, and a few pictures were on the white walls, indistinct in the dim light that found its way in through tightly-closed window shutters. It was like "the best parlour" of the New England housewife, and the lady who presently stood in the room was not unlike the lady one would have expected to see there. She was tall – her height perhaps a little increased by the long morning wrapper in which she was dressed – and of a gentle cast of features. Her face was pale, showing to better advantage the richness of auburn tresses, which she wore brushed well back from her forehead. In voice and manner

Mrs. Fleming confirms the opinion that her appearance forms. Her eyes are pale blue, and modestly seek the ground when she speaks, looking frankly into your face when she listens.[51]

The spotless house and serene hostess are all the more impressive considering that the interview took place only one week after the purchase of her new house. Already everything was perfectly in place. The reporter noted the absence of any sign of her writing – or even reading. Later Fleming's work habits were described by another visitor: "Her own home, on the outskirts of Brooklyn, was as plain as a home could be. There was not the first sign of luxury about that little frame house on Lewis Avenue. There was no library; in fact, nothing indicated the house of a woman who made her money writing books. Her bedroom was her study and she generally, after the manner of schoolgirls, wrote on her lap, an old atlas serving as desk.[52] It seems that despite her success, Fleming's domestic identity took precedence at least publicly over her professional one, which was carefully hidden away. One who visited her would see "the New England housewife."

During these difficult times, by now estranged from her intemperate husband, Fleming's health was declining. She had developed Bright's disease. Her literary output lessened as she no longer had the stamina to write at her earlier pace. She was reduced to writing only one novel a year. *Shaddeck Light!* began in the *Weekly* in October 1877. It was titled *The Forced Marriage* in the *London Journal*, where it appeared weekly from 3 November 1877 to 13 April 1878. *Carried by Storm* began in the *Weekly* in October 1878, and *Lost for a Woman* in October 1879. The dates of these serials are in keeping with Fleming's work habits as she described them in 1878:

I cannot write with any advantage except in the spring. I seem to have to get thawed out. I usually begin my stories about the last of April and finish them in the middle of June. I lock myself in a room at 9 o'clock in the morning – the merest sound disturbs me – and I write, steadily if I can, if not, perseveringly, until 12 o'clock. Then I stop and do now allow myself to think of the story until 9 o'clock the next morning. It is sometimes very difficult to do this, but I believe it is necessary to my health. Do you know I find that the most effective means for putting my work quite out of my mind is a ride up and down Broadway in the stage. The hurrying masses of people distract my thoughts completely.[53]

She goes on to explain that she completed the first draft of a book in a month and a half. Usually she took this first draft to the countryside, where she copied it over. A novel she estimated to cover seven hundred to one thousand pages of foolscap, which she revised quickly, rewriting from the first draft at up to thirty pages a morning. She had the novel rewritten, ready for the printer, by mid-July. The story would then be ready to start in the *Weekly* in October. It would run for up to thirty weeks, usually, in the *Weekly* and the *London Journal* simultaneously, and would then be published by Carleton.

Fleming's novels after she moved to the *Weekly* show that her craft was changing and developing. She restrained the gothic and melodramatic elements while retaining both mystery and romance. She shifted for the most part to American settings – New York City and small-town New England, with which she was by then familiar – from the English settings she had favoured earlier. From time to time she added episodes set in Canada, in what to Americans would appear to be Canada's most exotic setting, Quebec.

A Little Queen (later published as *Silent and True; or, A Little Queen*), which began serialization in October 1876, exemplifies Fleming's change of style. The introduction is skilful, quickly establishing setting, creating atmosphere, and introducing the central characters. Disinheritance is a key ploy in the novel, an interesting parallel given Fleming's real-life disinheriting of her husband in her will the same year. While there is mystery, including a secret wedding and a mysterious robbery, the plot is less complex than usual, thus allowing for more character development.

The central characters are contrasting sisters. The elder, blonde and coolly beautiful, is linked as a femme fatale with Cleopatra and Helen of Troy. She has only one area of unselfishness, her devotion to her younger sister, the "little queen" of the title. The younger girl, neither blonde nor beautiful, is attractive in manner and, in further contrast to her sister, sensitive and unselfish. New for Fleming is the introduction of another kind of woman, a modern, independent, unmarried woman of thirty-seven (Fleming's age when the novel appeared, but far from her domestic situation – one can picture her fantasizing such a life free from family responsibilities). This woman plays an important role in the novel as the confidante of a younger man and later of the younger of the two sisters. She rejects the younger man's proposal, being not so independent-minded as to consider such a marriage appropriate, which frees him to marry her young friend later. The central characters are realistic and better developed than in Fleming's earlier fiction.

The following October *Shaddeck Light!* began its serialization. When published in book form as *The Heir of Charlton: A Story of Shaddeck Light*, it proved one of Fleming's most successful novels. As in *Silent and True*, the central characters are sisters, but this time they are half-sisters. Again, the elder sister is blonde, beautiful, calculating, and strong-willed, while the younger is lively, gentle, and naïve, but not beautiful. Two such contrasting characters may, like the submissive heroine and passionate villainess of earlier stories, express the author's ambivalence to her position in society and to expectations of her as a woman, but the opposing elements are here less extreme.

The novel begins well, the first chapters narrated from the varying perspectives of the different characters, who are then all brought together. Thereafter, the plot becomes too involved and strains credibility. Nevertheless, the characters are, as in *The Little Queen*, plausible and individualized. Of special interest too is a private detective, hired by one of the protagonists, who solves a crime in which all the central characters are enmeshed. He is presented as a man of a lower class who speaks in a dialect that sets him apart from the protagonists.

Lost for a Woman, which began in October 1879, is Fleming's best novel. Its protagonist faces psychologically complex problems and demonstrates the initiative, liveliness, and courage heretofore evident in some of Fleming's villainous women but only occasionally and fleetingly in her protagonists, in whom it disappears with marriage. The novel is more socially inclusive, moving beyond the sentimental novel's, and Fleming's, usual preoccupation with the wealthy and aristocratic to give some insight into the lives of working-class and middle-class women as well. It includes a perceptive portrait of a woman trapped in an unhappy marriage, and it comments ironically on the sentimental novel.

Jemima Ann, with whom the novel opens, is far from the expected heroine of any novel – a twenty-four-year-old kitchen maid who seven years earlier had come from the country to work in her aunt's boarding-house for working men. She is addicted to romantic novels that take her, at least briefly, out of her dreary workaday world, a world realistically described in the early pages of the novel: "Mrs. Hopkins' basement kitchen is lit by four greenish panes of mud-bespattered glass, six inches higher than the pavement. Through these six inches of green crystal Jemima Ann sees all she ever sees of the outdoor world on its winding way. Hundreds of ankles, male and female, thick and thin, clean and dirty, according to the state of the atmosphere, pass these four squares of dull light every day."[54] As the narrator comments, "all the romance of life that ever came near her, to brighten the dull drab of every day, was contained in the 'awful' nice stories devoured in every spare moment, left her in the busy caravansera of her aunt Samantha Hopkins" (9).

"It would be awful pleasant to be like they are in stories," muses Jemima Ann, still blinking upward at the gray squares of blurred light, "and have azure eyes, and golden tresses, and wear white Swiss and sweeping silks all the year round, and have lovely guardsmen and dukes and things, to gaze at a person passionately, and lift a person's hand to their lips." Jemima Ann lifts one of her own, a red right hand, at this point, and surveys it. It is not particularly clean; it has no nails to speak of; it is nearly as large, and altogether as hard, as that of any of the foundry "hands"; and she sighs ... There are hands and hands; the impossibility of any mortal man, in his senses, ever wanting to lift *this* hand to his lips, comes well home to her in this hour. The favorite "gulf" of her novels lies between her and such airy, fairy beings as the Duchess Isoline. And yet Jemima Ann fairly revels in the British aristocracy. Nothing less than a baronet can content her. No heroine under the rank of "my lady" can greatly interest her. Pictures of ordinary everyday life, of ordinary people, pall upon the highly-seasoned palate of Jemima Ann. Her own life is so utterly unlovely, so grinding in its sordid ugliness, that she will have no reflection of it in her favorite literature. Dickens fails to interest her. His men and women talk and act, and are but as shadowy reflections of those she meets every day.

"Nothing Dickens ever wrote," says Jemima Ann, with conviction, "is to be named in the same day with the 'Doom of the Duchess,' or 'The Belle of Belgravia.'" (10–11)

Fleming is obviously commenting on the sentimental novel as escape literature for women such as Jemima Ann whose social situation provided little relief from their dreary round of duties and no possibility of permanent escape.

In the midst of Jemima Ann's thoughts on literature the doorbell rings, and in answering it "there opens for poor, hard-worked Jemima Ann the one romance of her existence, never quite to close again till that life's end" (16). Jemima Ann walks into a sentimental novel, for, with the opening door, the glamorous circus star Mimi Trillon and her tiny daughter Snowball enter Jemima Ann's life. Jemima Ann is enthralled by the circus performer and adores the pretty, precocious fair-haired child. Mimi, as it turns out, was the wife of George Valentine, son of the town's wealthy summer resident. In a reversal of the usual gender roles, the innocent son had eloped at eighteen with the worldly-wise Mimi and been disowned by his family. He has since reportedly died. Mimi visits her mother-in-law to acquaint her with the existence of a granddaughter, then dies in a fall from the tightrope. Wishing to see the child cared for but unwilling to become personally involved with this unexpected granddaughter,

Mrs Valentine arranges that the child be brought up in a small Quebec settlement on the St Lawrence River.

This little girl is the novel's protagonist. We watch her character and personality develop through the various roles she is required to play over the first twenty years of her life. Each change in her role is signified by a change in her name. First, as the daughter of a circus performer, appearing herself as a tiny child in a circus act and leading the irregular life of the travelling performers, with a mother of questionable morals, she is Snowball. Then, in a Scottish–French Canadian family in Quebec, she is christened Dolores by the nuns who educate her – an ironic name, inasmuch as she is happy and carefree in this milieu, but it hints at the unhappiness to come. As Dolores Macdonald she grows up beautiful, talented, lively, and self-willed. At sixteen she joins her grandmother and becomes Miss Dolores Valentine, heiress to a fortune.

For the next three years she travels through Europe learning the manners and sophistication of the cosmopolitan world. Putting aside the tomboy ways of Dolores Macdonald, Dolores Valentine becomes the loving and dutiful granddaughter and heiress. She accedes to her grandmother's wish that she marry her British cousin Vane, who has inherited a baronetcy and an impoverished estate. Since he had expected to inherit Mrs Valentine's fortune had the granddaughter Snowball-Dolores not appeared on the scene, their marriage seems a suitable solution for everyone.

As Vane's wife she takes on another role, that of Dolores, Lady Valentine. At this point Fleming gives us a realistic portrait of an unhappy wife. Since her grandmother dies shortly after the wedding, Dolores is alone when she realizes what a dreadful mistake her marriage was. Vane loves her fortune, not her. Ensconced on his estate are his spinster sister, in charge of the household with no intention of relinquishing her position, and Vane's "cousin," Camilla Routh, the woman Vane has loved for years and who has waited for him to return with the Valentine fortune and marry her. Now he returns with a bride as well as the Valentine fortune. As might be expected, Camilla is bitter and resentful. Vane and the two women form a cohesive, unfriendly group isolating the young bride. The constant psychological pressure on Dolores intensifies: there is no question of the husband's power over his wife; she must obey him in all areas of her life.

Dolores has one friend and support from the past, Jemima Ann, now her personal maid. Jemima Ann has walked into one of her novels of British aristocracy, but life with the aristocracy is not entirely what her novels had led her to expect. The first scene on Vane's estate is designed to foreshadow Dolores' resolution of her predicament. She returns from a solitary ride on a large black horse, which she leaps fearlessly over the gate. Within the submissive wife lives the passionate and courageous girl, this incident suggests. When her husband pushes too far, she will have the courage to leap over the barrier of her marriage to freedom.

The oppressiveness of Dolores' married life and her sense of entrapment are well drawn, as is the desperation that leads her to run away. Our awareness of Fleming's unhappy marriage, which ended finally in separation, adds significance to comments in the novel about marriage and to the later description of Dolores's sense of release when she gains her freedom from her husband.

Fleming introduces part four of the novel, which deals with Dolores's married life, with the epigraph: "Marriage is a desperate thing. The frogs in Aesop were extremely wise; they had a great mind to some water, but they would not leap into a well, because they could not get out again" (328). Dolores – like the author – is very conscious of a husband's power over his wife. When she has run away, she knows that Vane will do everything he can, including hiring detectives, to find her. She is determined never to return: "'I will die first!' she cries, and she means it. Death holds no terror so great as the terror of returning to that horrible life. 'I will never go back!' she exclaims; 'he may do what he likes. The law that takes the part of the husband always against the wife, may do its utmost. I will bear all things, but I will never go back'" (419). Of the irrevocability of marriage, the narrator says: "She is a slave who has escaped, but a slave her whole life long none the less, and liable to capture any day. She is Vane Valentine's wife – no power on earth can alter that. Life or death – what do they matter?" (421) Dolores's words as she recalls her unhappy marriage could be May Agnes Fleming's:

If one could forget! If I could but shut out the last horrible year, with all its hateful remembrances, its bitter humiliations, its heart-burnings, its shame, its insults. But I will carry it with me always, a plague-spot in my life, down to its very end. And though I have snapped my chain, I shall carry my half clanking with me to my grave. What latent possibilities of evil lie undreamed of within us. I am afraid of myself when I think what a few months more of that life might have made me. I don't wonder women go wrong so often through sheer desperation. I have felt the capability within myself. Thank God! all these evil thoughts of hatred and vengeance have been left behind. I am conscious of nothing now but an unutterable longing to be out of England. Go where I may, endure what I will, I can never suffer again as I have suffered here. (420)

Dolores' next role is that of a young career woman living in New York with Jemima Ann, now her friend and equal. Jemima Ann continues to see life in terms of fiction, saying, as they sail to America, "We are free, and off at last, and all the world is before us to seek our fortunes, like the princesses in a fairy tale!" (421–2). When they are settled in New York, the narrator continues Jemima Ann's metaphor: "And no queen recently come into her kingdom was ever prouder of that dominion than is Jemima Ann of this furnished 'floor through' in the third storey of a third-rate New York house, in a very third-rate street. For it is their own, their very own, and they are together, and happy, and free, and she helps to keep it – is not only sole housekeeper and manager, but also part bread-winner" (427). After years as a scullery maid in a dreary boarding-house, this is surely a fairy-tale life for Jemima Ann.

As for Dolores, "There is no longer a Dolores, Lady Valentine – only a Mrs. Trillon, who teaches for a salary, and walks the New York streets in shabby dresses" (436). Another role, another name. Life is comfortably domestic, with Snowball, as Dolores calls herself once again, returning home from a long day's work to a cosy fire and a pleasant supper, to reading and sewing. Such a life, free from the pressures and responsibilities of husband and family, may have been for Fleming as delightful a fantasy as were the lives of the wealthy and aristocratic for the usual readers of sentimental novels. "'How cozy it is here,' Dolores says [returning from the mansion of a wealthy client] with a delicious sense of rest well earned, and of the long evening to come, with two or three new magazines to speed its flight. 'What a dear little home we have, and what a queen of housekeepers in my Jemima Ann. It is very splendid up there in the Pettingill palace, but I really do not think I would care to exchange. I like our duodecimo edition of housekeeping best'" (433–4). A charming use of a metaphor from Fleming's publishing world to indicate where real happiness lies – despite what the sentimental novels may say. Free of role-playing in a life spent fulfilling the expectations of others, Snowball is using the skills she learned in her convent school and with her grandmother to teach others, and is living a free and independent life.

For the conclusion of the novel, Fleming returns us to the real world of the sentimental novel, or should we say the world of the real sentimental novel. Snowball's husband conveniently dies in an accident, leaving her free to marry her Canadian childhood sweetheart, who has been popping up in her life from time to time. The novel ends with the revelation of secrets, the unmasking of disguises, the resolution of all complications; this time the obligatory happy marriage fittingly takes place outside aristocratic or wealthy circles.

A marvellous achievement. Although it possesses the conventional characteristics of the sentimental novel, with its secrets, disguises, villain, and beautiful heroine, at the same time *Lost for a Woman* takes every opportunity to poke fun at the genre, and in many ways it overturns the expectations of the reader. Its attractive, believable heroine is more individualized than is usual in a sentimental novel. She finds happiness ultimately in neither wealth nor title but in a simpler way of life. She possesses the initiative, courage, and drive seen earlier only in Fleming's villainous women, here balanced by the virtues expected of the heroine. She is rescued not by a hero but by her own initiative. The novel is also unusual in the episodes it chooses to develop, giving us insight through Vane and Snowball into the desperate mind of a woman trapped in an unhappy relationship, through Jemima Ann into life below stairs, and through the episode in New York into the real possibility of autonomy for a woman. Fleming had emerged from her marriage to create a new kind of independent life for herself and a new kind of heroine in her novel.

Fleming had no opportunity to develop further this new direction in her writing, or in her life. *Lost for a Woman* was running in the *Weekly* when she died on 24 March 1880. Although she had suffered from Bright's disease for some years, her death was unexpected; she had planned to leave for a trip to England in April, to visit for the first time some of the settings of her stories. For the first time, too, she was breaking into her writing routine, allowing herself a holiday during her usual working period.

Fleming's death merited considerable attention in the New York papers. Because she died during Holy Week, the usual funeral requiem mass was precluded. She was buried at nearby Calvary Cemetery after a brief service at her parish church of St John the Baptist. Papers disagree as to whether her husband was present. One paper reported that he was not present, that her four children and her mother were the chief mourners,[55] another that her husband arrived for the funeral.[56] Most report that her funeral was attended by a crowd of friends from her parish, whose poor she "so liberally and unostentatiously assisted for so many years,"[57] and by members of the papers for which she wrote. At her funeral the priest confirmed her charity to the poor of the community. Her pallbearers included Patrick Meade, the parishioner she had appointed executor of her will and trustee and guardian of her children, her publisher W. George Carleton, and *New York Weekly* editor Francis S. Street.

The *New York Telegram* hailed Fleming as "the American Miss Braddon," claiming that she "occupied on this side of the Atlantic a position akin to that won by Miss Braddon in England."[58] She has also been termed "Mrs. Southworth's most successful imitator."[59] These were the two most popular writers on either side of the Atlantic. There is no doubt of Fleming's popularity. Her novels were reprinted for years following her death. Ealier novels were republished. Her short stories were collected, some from very early years, and published in volumes. That titles were often changed has led critics to think it likely that stories by others were published under Fleming's name because of her popularity. This now seems unlikely. There are many instances where her novels were published in paperback in two parts. The first part was given the novel's title, the second part a different title. For example, *A Mad Marriage*, which was serialized in the *New York Weekly* and the *London Journal* 1874–75, and published by Carleton in 1875, appears reprinted in Street and Smith's paperback New Eagle series as two novels, the first titled *A Mad Marriage*, the second *Woman without Mercy; or, A Heart of Stone*. Her fame justified the late publication of her early stories and novels. But readers of these half-novels who thought they were reading complete books would find them somewhat lacking in clear character and plot development and would not be in a position to judge the calibre of writing. Fortunately her family seems to have been able to maintain control of the copyright. As late as 1915 reprints appear copyrighted by Maude A. Fleming, May Agnes's elder daughter.

The talent that Fleming evinced from her early years, the ingenuity of her plot structures, the evolution of her style all suggest that she had the potential to develop much more as a creative writer. In speaking of her method of working Fleming once said that she had to have the plot completely clear in her mind before she began to write, that she never allowed the story to change its development significantly once she had started to write. This method is understandable for a writer handling the complex plots of most of Fleming's novels. But she also spoke of a creative element that intruded in her writing: "Occasionally, she explained, new characters will obtrude themselves, and often so persistently that she is obliged to introduce them, but she takes good care that they shall not interfere with the tale that she has arranged and is telling."[60]

We cannot help wondering what this woman would have been capable of had she not felt compelled to work so hard to satisfy popular taste, not only to support her four children but also to prepare for their future, knowing as she did that her life was to be short and that their father was irresponsible. The welfare of her children came before further development of her talent.[61] And we wonder what she might have been able to do had she lived another thirty years. Her last novel suggests a deeper development of character, greater realism, and a developing social consciousness. In itself it is a fine novel. It also indicates what we lost with Fleming's death at thirty-nine.

Margaret Murray Robertson: Domestic Power

LORRAINE McMULLEN

"She wrote at first with no thought of publishing, but because she loved it," reports a friend of Margaret Murray Robertson. Then, when over the age of forty she did decide to publish, with her first novel she "stepped at once into fame."[1] With this success Robertson quit her teaching position and devoted herself to writing. Within twenty-five years she published more than a dozen works of fiction.

Almost forgotten today, this late-blooming author was well known in the late nineteenth century, popular primarily for her lively yet moral stories for young people. Published in Britain and the United States, most of her books went through many editions. Her stories of Scottish or Scottish Canadian families are well crafted, entertaining, always didactic. The strong religious theme in her novels was a major reason for their popularity. The fact that preaching – even in fictional form – had slipped into women's hands shows a major shift in religion itself. Calvinist rigidity, with its emphasis on a patriarchal God of wrath, was modulating into a milder preaching of love. Margaret Robertson's fiction presents in lively, realistic form the result of this transition.

Margaret came easily by that religious bias. Her father, James Robertson, was a minister in one of Scotland's first Congregational churches. The new denomination had been formed by adherents of a late eighteenth-century evangelical movement who withdrew from the Church of Scotland when they encountered opposition to their propagation of support for Sunday schools, libraries, and private reading of Scripture.[2] In 1801 a small group of these dissidents in Stewartfield built a small chapel, seating three hundred, and the following year they called James Robertson to be their pastor.[3] James, born 1 June 1776, had studied theology in Glasgow and completed his studies in 1800.[4] He was twenty-five years of age when ordained pastor of the Stewartfield church. Here he remained for thirty years; here he married, and here Margaret Murray Robertson was born and began her schooling.

Stewartfield, originally called Crichie, is a small village in Old Deer Parish, Aberdeenshire, founded in the late eighteenth century. Situated in rolling countryside, it is today a tranquil, picturesque village of neat stone cottages, with a small central green and at one end of the village an old mill. The cottages have been carefully restored, and newer houses have been designed to blend in with the old. A general air of prosperity is likely due to the North Sea oil boom, as the village is within easy commuting distance of both Peterhead, only eleven and a half miles northeast, and Aberdeen, about nine miles to the southeast.

On 2 June 1807 James Robertson married Elizabeth Murray.[5] Elizabeth's was a staunchly religious family that had been established for several generations on the Aberdeenshire sheep farm of "Lofthills." Elizabeth's two brothers, John and Andrew, both became clergymen. John, an Evangelical minister, remained in Aberdeen. Andrew settled in South Africa. His son, also named Andrew, became internationally respected as an eminent religious thinker and writer.[6]

Marrying James Robertson, Elizabeth Murray performed a female version of her brothers' choice of a career in the Christian ministry. As a minister's wife she would provide her children with a model of piety, propriety, and industry. As for the Reverend James, his impact on his Stewartfield parish was remarkable. Sixty years after he left people asserted, "The name of James Robertson is still frequent in the countryside."[7] Elizabeth and James's children all were born in Stewartfield; Margaret Murray was baptized there on 23 April 1823.[8]

After Elizabeth's death in 1832, James emigrated to Derby, Vermont. There he ministered to the parish for four years, before being called in May 1836 to a newly established Congregational church in Sherbrooke, Quebec.[9] Although Margaret was only nine years of age when the family moved to Derby, and thirteen when they moved to Sherbrooke, the Stewartfield area of Scotland and the Vermont area of the United States feature in her writings, along with the Eastern Townships of Quebec, where she lived until she was nearly fifty, and Montreal, where she lived in later years.

All the Robertson children, girls as well as boys, were well educated and successful. Joseph Gibb Robertson, three years older than Margaret, became a businessman. Involved in many commercial enterprises in Sherbrooke, he was also politically active. For eighteen years he was mayor of Sherbrooke. In 1867 he was elected a Conservative member of the provincial legislature, and in 1869 appointed to the cabinet as treasurer of the province, a position he held for eleven years. Three other brothers – Andrew, George, and William – became successful Montreal lawyers.[10]

Margaret and her sister Mary were also given unusual educational opportunities. Both attended Mount Holyoke College, then termed Mount Holyoke Female Seminary, in Massachusetts, founded in 1837 and reputedly the most prestigious women's educational institution in the United States at that time. Mary graduated in 1847.[11] Many years later her son reported that she had been such an excellent student she completed the second and third year in one,[12] graduating at the age of nineteen.

According to Mount Holyoke records, Margaret was a second-year student in 1847–48 but did not return for her final year.[13] This was not surprising as Mount Holyoke accepted students for one, two, or three years of study. The seminary's principles of education are clearly stated in "Female Education," an essay by its first principal, the much respected Mary Lyon. Underlining the religious principles on which Mount Holyoke had been founded, its strict admission requirements, and its high intellectual standards, Lyon emphasized that the seminary sought to develop independence in young women and to prepare them not only for household responsibilities but for teaching and other useful social activities. Composition and reading were required each year, as was calisthenics; Lyon insisted upon the importance of physical activity to maintain physical health.[14] The course of study also included algebra, geometry, botany, geology, chemistry, Latin, and philosophy. Samuel Philip Newman's *A Practical System of Rhetoric* was the composition textbook.[15] With its high standards and its emphasis on writing, the seminary undoubtedly shaped Robertson's prose style and reinforced her native industry and intellectual seriousness.

Both Mary and Margaret taught at the Sherbrooke Ladies' Academy. Mary became principal. She had been teaching for several years when, on the death of Mary Lyon, a delegation from the board of directors of Mount Holyoke came to Sherbrooke to invite her to take on the position of principal of that college. Her son reports that Mary "was eager to go, but not quite sure of herself."[16] Her father, however, advised against her going, and the following year, 1851, she married Daniel Gordon, an Aberdeen-educated Presbyterian minister whom she had met two years earlier, and went with him to his parish among Scottish settlers at Lingwick in the Lake Megantic area. This clever, gifted sister of Margaret Robertson became the mother of a boy who would become one of Canada's most popular novelists. As "Ralph Connor" Charles Gordon pleased a world of readers with his blend of piety and adventure. He wrote lovingly in his biography of his mother's influence; an even stronger testimonial is the fictional portrait in *The Man from Glengarry*.

Margaret taught at Sherbrooke Ladies' Academy until approximately 1865, and she loved teaching. She was successful, popular, and respected in her profession. Opposed to class distinctions, she wished the poor student to have the same opportunity for education as the wealthy. To friends who urged her to open a private school, she would reply, "If I have any talents, then they shall be devoted to the girls of Sherbrooke." She was described as neither emotional nor demonstrative in her attitude to her students, but much concerned with their development. Reportedly, "It became a common saying that it was impossible to puzzle any pupil of Margaret Robertson's." She advised against trying to cram children with knowledge, and is remembered as saying, "Look at — . He has been stuffed and crammed, and crammed and stuffed, till he is nothing but a skin crammed, full of facts, and no individuality at all." In response her students were said to have revered rather than loved her. When asked whether Robertson was fond of children, one student replied, "Perhaps not in the way of mother love. She looked more to the intellect, and was always on the lookout for new development of that."[17]

After fifteen years Margaret Robertson's professional interests led to her first successful venture into writing. She entered "An Essay on Common School Education," subtitled "Wisdom is the principal thing," and won the Galt Prize essay competition. This competition was open to teachers in the St Francis district. Essays were submitted anonymously, and announcement of the award, offered by the Hon. A.T. Galt, MPP, appeared in the *Sherbrooke Gazette and Eastern Township Advertiser* for 17 December 1864. The winning essay was printed in two parts in the same paper, 14 and 21 January 1865. It was then published separately as a short monograph.[18]

Robertson's essay provides us with an expression of her views on education. While stating that developing mental powers and imparting knowledge are the aims of education, she nevertheless insists that moral training is more important than either of these objectives. She recommends Bible reading and, acknowledging that sectarian religion cannot be taught, advises that moral truth and religion in a general sense should be.

As well as being a clear statement of Robertson's staunch religious principles, the essay perhaps also represents a growing restlessness, a feeling that schools were not the only channel for reaching young people, and a desire to move to a field where religious values *could* be taught – the field of moralistic fiction. In shifting into fiction Robertson followed a trend encouraged by the establishment of evangelical publishers such as the Religious Tract Society. These publishers were ready to buy the work of women writers who voiced in their stories the new softer dogmas of love and domestic charity. The very fact that women had assumed this role of lay preaching marks the easing of church patriarchy – particularly notable in Presbyterianism, so long a bastion of Mosaic patriarchy.

On 7 September 1861 the Reverend James Robertson died in his son Joseph's home at the age of eighty-five. Margaret's father had continued his ministry until his death.[19] It seems likely that Margaret, with her father, lived with Joseph, who by this time was a leading member of the community. He was elected mayor of Sherbrooke in 1854 and, with two or three exceptions, annually thereafter until 1872.[20] He was unmarried, and no doubt appreciated having his sister with him.

Margaret's teaching career likely ended in 1865. The *Sherbrooke Gazette* reported on 16 September of that year: "The Fall Term of the female department of the Sherbrooke Academy opens on Monday, next, under the tuition of Miss F.L. Merry, a graduate of McGill Normal School. Miss Merry comes highly recommended, and we have reason to believe will sustain the reputation which the institution has acquired under its late teacher."

The "late teacher," now aged forty-two, had begun working in earnest on her writing. It is interesting to speculate on the development of Robertson's writing career. Her first novel, *Christie Redfern's Troubles*, appeared in 1866, the year after we assume she retired from teaching. But she loved to write, at first, we recall, "with no thought of publishing." And late in 1864 two anonymous stories appeared in the *Sherbrooke Gazette*, which was edited by Joseph S. Walton, a good friend of the family, of Robertson's brother Joseph in particular, and a member of James Robertson's Congregational church. This was a novel departure for the paper, which usually published authors' names with their fictional pieces. We must consider, then, the possibility that Margaret Robertson wrote these pieces as a means of exploring public response to her work.

Both of these short pieces centre upon small children. The first, "Little Ben,"[21] tells of an elderly man's attempt to befriend a small shoeshine boy in New York. The child is receptive to his overtures, but his drunken, impoverished parents prevent the gentleman's kindliness from having any significant effect. The child dies of injuries inflicted by his abusive father, but, visited on his deathbed by his benefactor, he is able to greet him as "friend" before he dies. That the old man's kindness has at least been recognized and valued by the child lessens the sense of despair that otherwise pervades the story. The second story, "Miriam,"[22] appearing in the same issue of the *Gazette* as the announcement that Robertson had won the Galt prize, also focuses on a poor child. Miriam is adopted by a kindly couple and grows up with their children. The father's angry words on inadvertently learning that Miriam and his eldest son, for whom he has ambitious plans that do not include marriage to a penniless orphan, are in love and intend to marry, cause Miriam to run away, though the father quickly regrets his harshness. A serious epidemic the following year brings Miriam back to nurse her lover, and she dies with him, to be united to him in death if not in life. Both stories are moralistic and sentimental, two characteristics of Robertson's fiction but also of much other fiction of the time. There are no special qualities that link them with her novels or can be advanced as conclusive evidence of her authorship.

Within the next few years Margaret moved to Montreal. Her three brothers – Andrew, George, and William – were there, working as busy lawyers. Since the death of their father, only Joseph was now living in Sherbrooke. Joseph was elected a Conservative member to the Quebec legislature in 1867, and he now spent much of his time in Quebec. Two years later, when he began a twenty-five-year appointment as provincial treasurer, this would be even more necessary. Finally, with his marriage to Mary Jane Woodward, daughter of his business associate Albert Gallatin Woodward, in 1870, there would clearly be no need for Margaret in her brother's household. In 1871 we find the name of Margaret Robertson in the Montreal census, with the following notation: "Born in Scotland, Presbyterian Congregational in religion, unmarried, no occupation, age 44."[23] "No occupation" is not surprising. May Agnes Fleming, a very successful Maritime writer, was similarly listed as without occupation in the 1871 Saint John, New Brunswick, census. Margaret Robertson is reported in the census as living with Sara Robertson, a widow seventy-six years of age, Presbyterian Congregationalist, also born in Scotland, more than likely a relative.

In the meantime Robertson's writing career had begun. Her first full-length story was published anonymously and its author apparently not known for many years.[24] First appearing in 1866 as *Christie; or the Way Home*, the novel is better known as *Christie Redfern's Troubles*,[25] a title Robertson never approved.[25] This is the story of the maturing of a young girl, ten-year-old Christie, a member of a large

Scottish family settled for three years on a backwoods farm in the eastern Ontario county of Glengarry. Christie's mother has died, her Aunt Elsie has come to care for the younger children, and Christie's three older sisters have shouldered some of the responsibilities – Effie, the oldest, is the local schoolteacher, and the next two work on the farm. Christie is having difficulty adjusting to the loss of her mother and her home in Scotland. She finds Aunt Elsie severe where her mother was gentle, and the farm bleak and dreary in contrast to her remembered Scottish home by the sea. When family troubles increase with the death of their father and loss of their farm, Effie struggles to keep the family together, and Christie too must now shoulder some responsibility. Ill-equipped to make a living, she becomes a nursemaid, supporting families through difficult periods of illness or other trials by caring for the children.

The change in Christie's personality and her positive influence on others, as her sisters gently move her towards more responsibility, is well drawn. We see her mature from a peevish, dissatisfied child to a loving, responsible young woman. That she is of delicate health has been evident from the beginning, and the novel ends sentimentally with Christie's happy and pious death while she is still a young woman. The novel was written at a time when the death of a young woman, especially from tuberculosis, was not uncommon. The much-loved youngest of the Robertson sisters, Jennie, had died in 1850 at the age of nineteen.[26] Margaret and Mary were deeply affected by their youngest sister's death; the death of a beloved young sister occurs frequently in Robertson's novels.

Critics of sentimentalism observe with condescension the kind of deathbed scene described by Robertson here and elsewhere. But the religious belief underlying Robertson's writings asserts such a death as the final victory. Christie's name is appropriate to the author's purpose, for Christie becomes, in her self-sacrificing devotion to others, and ultimately by her pious death, Christ-like. Deathbed scenes such as Christie's were popular in nineteenth-century novels not because readers enjoyed the tear-jerking sentimentality but because the culture within which Robertson and her readers lived accepted such a death as the ultimate vindication, the final glory of a Christian life.

Clearly this is an admonitory novel. It was published by the Religious Sunday School Union in the United States and by the Religious Tract Society in England. Robertson wrote it "chiefly to do what one woman could to supply Sunday School libraries with something better than the twaddle with which they had long been over-stocked."[27] An overtly didactic novel, "twaddle" it is not. Emphasizing religion, daily prayer, the joy of true Christianity, it is nevertheless written in a lively, entertaining style. Robertson, the admired and dedicated teacher, had taken her vocation into a new and different phase in which she could hope to influence an enormously wider number of young people. Despite its moralistic message Robertson was providing for readers of Sunday-school stories a work refreshingly different from their usual fare, with attractive characters and interesting plot development.

The response was immediate. An acquaintance wrote: "The way it [Christie Redfern's Troubles] came into notice in England is very interesting. A lady friend of hers was visiting England at the time and was present when a box of Sunday-school books from an American publisher was opened by the secretary of the British and Foreign Tract Society. 'Poor stuff,' he had been wont to pronounce most of such volumes printed on this side of the water. On the top of the package lay 'Christie or the Way Home,' in two volumes. He groaned. As if trash in one volume was not bad enough. But the friend recognized it and urged him to read it. He did, and became so fascinated that he forgot even his dinner-hour, and pored over it while he missed train after train that should have taken him home. Then other members of the society read it, and so charmed were they that they at their next meeting voted twenty-five pounds to be handed by the publishers to the unknown author, as a mark of their appreciation of the work."[28] An example, perhaps apocryphal, of Christie Redfern's popularity with children is the report of a letter in the British children's periodical Aunt Judy's Magazine offering a copy of the novel in exchange for a kitten.[29]

Setting and character for this story are taken from real life. Margaret's sister Mary and her husband, the Reverend Daniel Gordon, had moved in 1853 to Glengarry, where Gordon was the Presbyterian minister at Indian Lands, an area on the western edge of Glengarry, so named because originally leased from the St Regis Mohawk tribe. The Gordon family lived in the St Elmo area. The liveliness and accuracy of detail in the novel thus stem from Robertson's knowledge of the community; furthermore, the character of Christie was reportedly the portrait of a real-life Christie, a young woman of that name who was for years with the family of Margaret's sister and had been considered "a blessing to all around her."[30]

This story of the novel's origin is credible, inasmuch as Robertson's subsequent fiction is set in locales with which she was very familiar and many of the experiences she describes are those she had experienced or observed in her own family. Robertson had lost her mother at nine; in the novel, Christie at ten has recently lost her mother.

Robertson frequently writes of a Scottish family that has moved to North America, as had the Robertsons. This novel establishes other patterns that will recur in Robertson's later fiction. Her stories are usually structured about a large, closely knit, strongly religious family – all characteristic of the Robertson family. Often, as with the Robertson family, the father is a clergyman, and often too one of the girls marries a clergyman, as did Mary Robertson. The fictional family, always Scottish, lives in an area of Scotland or New England or Canada familiar to the author: Glengarry would become a frequent setting.

Robertson writes in more detail about the Maxville and St Elmo area of Glengarry in her next novel, possibly her most popular, *Shenac's Work at Home*.[31] That this novel appeared so soon after *Christie Redfern*, perhaps even the same year, gives credence to the speculation that Robertson began writing before her resignation from teaching in 1865 and that she left teaching only when convinced that she had found an equally valid, useful vocation.

Essentially *Shenac* is, like *Christie Redfern's Troubles*, the story of the maturing of a young girl, this time earnest Shenac (Gaelic for Janet). But Robertson expands her canvas to write a family chronicle of two generations, beginning with two brothers who emigrate with their parents from Scotland, settle on Glengarry homesteads, and bring up their large families – eight children each – on the land. Of the two brothers, the younger, Angus Dhu, prospers; the other, Shenac's father, Angus Bhan, does not. As a result Angus Bhan agrees to sell half his farm to his brother, and his two elder sons leave seeking employment to help support the family. The eldest, Allister, leaves for the California gold fields; the next year the second, Lewis, goes off to a lumber camp for the winter.

Troubles multiply. Angus Bhan dies, leaving heavy debts. Lewis drowns. The house burns down the day before Angus Bhan's burial. As the bereaved widow is clearly unable to cope, Shenac, not quite sixteen, must take charge, with the support of her delicate, crippled twin brother Hamish. Neighbours help the family move in to the old log cabin their pioneering grandfather had built. One of Shenac's first decisions is to reject indignantly her uncle's over-eager offer to buy the farm. He, of course, rationalizes that the family will be unable to cope and that his offer arises as much from a desire to help as from a will to expand his own property.

The story provides a colourful picture of early Glengarry life, describing farming and leisure activities in the changing seasons and the strong sense of community spirit, including bees organized to help neighbours, and the important role of religion in the everyday lives of the Scottish pioneers. The novel describes the split within the Church of Scotland, which had spread to Canada and divided the parish of Robertson's own brother-in-law, Daniel Gordon. He had been a theology student at Aberdeen in 1843 when the Disruption in the Scottish church led some congregations to break away and form the separate Free Church of Scotland.[32] The same upheaval reached Glengarry in 1864, when Gordon and his followers built a new church, known as the Gordon Free Church.[33]

Religion is important in the maturing of Shenac. Headstrong, accustomed to having her own way, the young girl is at first severe and impatient with the younger children, all of whom must contribute to keep the farm going. The weakness of her religious practice is shown to be central to her failure to treat her young siblings with tact, gentleness, and understanding. Exhausted from the physical work on the farm, Shenac stops attending most church services because she falls asleep when she does so. She also loses the habit of morning and evening Scripture reading. When Shenac attends a missionary revival meeting at the behest of a younger brother, she is converted, returns to the regular practice of her religion, and becomes more loving in her attitude to others. Historian Royce MacGillivray, in his essay "Novelists and the Glengarry Pioneer,"[34] notes that it is the religious revival of 1864–65, which actually occurred in Glengarry, that Robertson describes.

All ends happily. After four years Allister returns successful from the gold fields to repay family debts, buy back the property sold to his uncle, rebuild the home, and relieve Shenac of family responsibility. Allister's marriage to his young cousin, Shenac's best friend, cements family relations, which were understandably under some strain because of the uncle's acquisitiveness. Shenac agrees to marry the young clergyman who first came to the area as a teacher, and, in preparation for her role as clergyman's wife, goes off to school for two years.

The novel's narrative strategies are worth noting. From time to time the narrator addresses the reader directly in a conversational tone that takes the reader into her confidence. The easy informality of such remarks as "I suppose I ought to describe Shenac more particularly, as my story is to be more about her than any of the other MacIvors" (16) or "I am not going to tell all about what was done this spring and summer; it would take too long" (104) lend the story the aura of an oral tale, which would be especially attractive to those the narrator refers to as "my young readers." But this sentimental, religious novel is attractive to a wider audience because of its liveliness of style, its vivid portrayal of Glengarry life, and its depiction of the maturing of a strong, determined young woman under great difficulties.

The twins' reversal of traditional roles is significant. Hamish's delicate health allows the author to give the dominant role to Shenac, while her gentle brother takes on a supporting role, helping her to curb her quick temper, strong will, and tendency to extremes, and to develop patience and tact in dealing with the younger children. When Hamish dies, as piously as Christie in the earlier novel, it is clear that his work in this world has been accomplished. Shenac's twin, her alter ego, by his example, support, and encouragement has been the source of her maturing in patient, loving understanding of others. Shenac's acceptance of the impending death of her much-loved twin is final proof of her moral maturity. Throughout the novel Hamish has demonstrated the spiritual and moral qualities that Shenac lacks. When Shenac, under his guidance, develops these qualities, Hamish is no longer needed. Although he dies, he lives on spiritually in his twin.

Of added interest are the parallels between this novel and the much better-known Glengarry novels of Robertson's nephew Charles W. Gordon, who wrote under the pseudonym of Ralph Connor. Born at St Elmo in 1860, Gordon was six years of age when *Shenac* was published and ten when he left Glengarry with his family for his father's new parish at Zorro, Ontario. While no letters have yet been found indicating the extent of Robertson's contact with her sister Mary in Glengarry, her use of the area as setting for the first two novels suggests strong ties. We can assume that Charles Gordon knew his aunt well. He refers in his autobiography to talking with her of his mother's experiences at Mount Holyoke College.[35]

Roger MacGillivray and Ewan Ross in their *History of Glengarry* have noted the accuracy of the geographical and religious background Robertson and Ralph Connor both provide.[36] The Presbyterian church Robertson describes in *Shenac* as "the great gray, barn-like house of worship which had been among the first built in the settlement"[37] Connor describes thus: "No steeple or tower gave any hint of its sacred character. Its weatherbeaten clap-board exterior, spotted with black knots, as if stricken with some disfiguring disease, had nothing but its row of uncurtained windows to distinguish it from an ordinary barn."[38] MacGillivray and Ross also note the following two parallels between Connor's *Man from Glengarry* and Robertson's *Shenac*. Robertson observed that, "though there were those among the aged or the discontented [among the first settlers] who never ceased to pine for the heather hills of the old land, the young grew up strong and content, troubled by no fear that, for many and many a year to come, the place would become too strait for them or their children."[39] Connor wrote: "By their fathers the forest was dreaded and hated, but the sons, with rifles in hand, trod its pathless stetches without fear, and with their broad-axes they took toll of their ancient foe."[40] Of the opening of the new church Robertson wrote:

A few of those to whom even the dust of Zion is dear, seeking to consecrate the house, and with it themselves, more entirely to God's service, met for prayer for a few nights before the public dedication; and from that time for more than a year not a night passed in which the voice of prayer and praise did not arise within its walls. All through the busy harvest-time, through the dark autumn evenings, when the unmade roads of the country were deep and dangerous, and through the frosts and snows of a bitter winter, the people gathered to the house of prayer.[41]

Connor wrote:

For eighteen months, night after night, every night in the week except Saturday, the people gathered in such numbers as to fill the new church to the door. Throughout all the busy harvest season, in spite of the autumn rains that filled the swamps and made the roads almost impassable, in the face of the driving snows of the winter, through the melting ice of the spring, and again through the following summer and autumn, the great revival held on.[42]

Besides the specific echoes, Ralph Connor's work shows the influence of his aunt's work in a more subtle way. Her popularity proved the existence of a market, and of readers ready to hear about pioneer life and to respond to a blend of poetry and romance.

Following the success of *Shenac*, published in London and New York and running through at least five editions, Robertson continued with the family chronicle. *The Bairns; or, Janet's Love and Service* (1870) is more ambitious than *Shenac*, just as *Shenac* was more ambitious than *Christie Redfern's Troubles*. *The Bairns* is a chronicle of a Scottish family and their housekeeper, Janet Nasmith, who move from Scotland to New England to Canada following the death of the family's mother. The father is a clergyman; the seven children range in age from two to fourteen years.

The novel centres first on Janet, a young widow who leaves her own small son and her mother in Scotland to move to a new land with the family she serves and which, she is convinced, needs her more than her own does. The novel gives an account of the Elliott family's adaptation to a vastly different culture and climate in New

England, and shows the family discussing with Americans some of the differences in outlook and culture, including an involved exploration of the relative merits of British and American forms of government. The discussion of British versus American life is very interesting in light of Alexander Galt's continuing importance in Sherbrooke. His father, John Galt, had written two novels about the two versions of pioneering, in Canada and in the United States. Robertson's interest may reflect this specific Galt interest. It may also, of course, be a simple response to life in the Eastern Township region, south of the St Lawrence River and nearer to Vermont and upstate New York than to many parts of Canada.

The family prospers; the children grow up, and Graeme, the eldest daughter, with Janet's support replaces her mother. On the death of their father the family moves to Montreal, joining the eldest son, Arthur, who had remained in Scotland to continue his education and now, having completed law school in Canada, is well established. We are reminded of Robertson's brothers, successful Montreal lawyers. There is a description of Montreal, including a McGill University convocation.

Janet's acceptance of a marriage proposal from a staunch American widower, one of the earliest friends of the family in the new land, allows attention to shift to Graeme, now a young adult. While Graeme is central, the novel involves itself as well with the romances and marriages of all the other children. Graeme's life is decided only when the others are settled and, close to thirty, she can marry the man she loved much earlier, now a widower. The return of a youthful love, widow or widower, is a favourite ploy of Robertson's.

In the new land America's classless society seems the most difficult cultural obstacle for Janet and the family. As Janet expresses it, "She never could make out 'who was somebody and who was naebody;' and what made the matter more mysterious, they did not seem to know themselves" (86). Janet resolutely keeps to her place as a servant, to the indignation of the New England townspeople, who wish to place her on a plane of equality. Addressing her as Mrs Nasmyth, they invite her to tea with the clergyman she serves. She refuses. Invited to tea with the family, the New Englanders are indignant that Janet does not sit with them and that tea is poured not by her but by the fifteen-year-old daughter. It is only with strong assurances from the family that they can manage without her that Janet remains in New England to marry her widower.

Characters in *The Bairns* are well drawn. The children – four boys and three girls – are sharply individualized. The reader observes them maturing, lovingly supporting one another. One son goes to the American midwest, where he becomes a successful businessman; another prospers in Montreal, as does the eldest in his law practice; the youngest returns to Scotland to study for the ministry, returning on completion of his studies. For the first third of the novel Janet is the mainstay of the family; then that role is passed on to the eldest girl, Graeme. Both Janet and Graeme confront problems with honesty, compassion, and determination. The first break in the family is the death in early adolescence of the middle daughter of consumption. Like that of Christie and Hamish, it is a holy one. Perhaps most notable in its handling is the vivid description of the family's grief. To her own rhetorical question a few days after the death, "And was the worst over?" Graeme responds, "There was the gathering up of the broken threads of their changed life; the falling back on their old cares and pleasures, all so much the same, and yet so different. There was the vague unbelief in the reality of their sorrow, the momentary forgetfulness, and then the pang of sudden remembrance – the nightly dreams of her, the daily waking to find her gone" (188).

If the women are strong, unifying elements in the family, the clergyman father is a remote, respected figure, showing little initiative, being tenderly cared for by the women of the household. On the move to New England, for example, he stays in the comfortable house of one of the community's most distinguished members while Janet and the children work to make their new home comfortable before he joins them. While, as in earlier novels, religion is an important element of everyday life, there is little reference to the father's mission to the townspeople, but many examples in the life of the family of generous and self-sacrificing acts by the brothers and sisters for one another and for others. The home rather than the church appears as the spiritual centre. There are several examples of the benefit derived by those brought into the family's orbit. The one case of conversion comes largely through Janet's influence. And while the Elliott sons prosper, the novel reports their business activities only in the most general terms; influences and interaction in the home are central in making them into the men they are in the outside world.

This novel probes a woman's questioning of her role more deeply than do Robertson's other novels. Graeme, and later her younger sister Rose, when disappointed in love, experience restlessness and dissatisfaction with their lives and question what is termed throughout the novel "woman's lot." Graeme observes, "I think it must be delightful to feel that one is 'making one's living' … I *should* like to know how it feels to be quite independent, I must confess" (332). A debate on marriage versus single life pits Graeme against Janet, with Janet the traditionalist urging Graeme neither to marry for passion nor to wait for an ideal man who may never come, but to marry a man for whom she has friendship. "The wild carrying away of the fancy" does not always bring happiness, says Janet. "Mutual respect and the quiet esteem that one friend gives to another who is worthy, is a far surer foundation for a lifetime of happiness" (425).

Graeme argues the value of the single life, angrily defending single women from the ridicule she has observed to be often their lot: "I have no patience with the nonsense that is talked about old maids. Why! it seems to be thought that if a woman reaches thirty, still single, she has failed in life, she has missed the end of the creation, as it were; and by and by people begin to look at her as an object of pity, not to say of contempt" (426), adding further, "women who would be spoken of by the pitying or slighting name of 'old maid,' who are yet more worthy of respect for the work they are doing, and for the influence they are exerting, than many a married woman in her sphere" (428). Robertson, though, despite her own choice of a single life, rewards her protagonist with a happy marriage at the end of the novel.

The novel also explores the marriage of unequals, as instanced in the marriage of Arthur, eldest of the family, to a superficial, spoiled young woman who, while socially and financially superior, is morally and intellectually beneath him. The family is dismayed, but Arthur is as blissfully unaware of his bride's shortcomings as he is of the manipulation that brought him to engagement, then marriage. The narrator digresses to comment in a general way on the results of such marriages, presenting the views as those of a friend: "One who has made good use of long opportunity for observation, tells me that Arthur Elliott's is by no means a singular case" (310), she begins. Her considered view is that a man may so divorce his home life from his other activities as to come to accept quite contentedly a wife unable to share his intellectual life. For a woman such a marriage is more difficult, for she is more dependent on a husband for her intellectual as well as her social life. After lengthy consideration of the topic, the narrator continues: "But this is a digression, and I daresay there are many who will not agree with all this. Indeed, I am not sure that I quite agree with all my friend said on this subject, myself. There are many ways of looking at the same thing" (313).

While this narrative by-play seems to suggest a reluctance on the part of the narrator to take responsibility for these observations, it is made clear that, in Arthur's household, the frivolous wife makes life difficult for all, from the servants to Arthur's sisters. Ostensibly in

charge of household affairs, she has no interest in accepting responsibility but much in asserting her rights. Graeme skilfully continues
her role as administrator while allowing her young sister-in-law to
accept credit for a well-run house. Arthur remains cheerfully unaware
that it is not his inexperienced young wife's doing that all continues
as efficiently and serenely as when Graeme was in charge. Everyone
else is aware of the true state of affairs, however, which is underlined
when occasionally the wife insists on taking decisive action, and
disaster follows.

The Bairns was one of Robertson's most popular novels. In the first
eight years at least eight editions were published. Now, only four
years after her first novel, Robertson was well established. While the
Religious Tract Society (London) and the Sunday School Union (Philadelphia) continued to publish her more overtly didactic works,
Hodder and Stoughton in London and Thomas Nelson in New York
published most of her novels, which thus reached a wider, more
general audience. The shift to secular publishers shows that these
publishing companies were responding to the swelling popularity of
novels blending romantic plots with presentation of the new theology.
Emphasizing religious development in the home, this new kind of
Christianity implicitly glorified the mother, or mother figure, whose
realm *was* the home, and by extension the motherly preaching novelist.

With *The Inglises; or, How the Way Was Opened*[43] Robertson continued in the tradition of the family chronicle, in this instance
recounting the struggles of an impoverished clergyman's family of
four to keep afloat after the father's death. This family, the Inglises,
is contrasted with their wealthy cousins, the Oswalds. The novel's
plot makes clear that money does not bring happiness; rather, it adds
to problems and temptations. Children of the two families mature
through the difficulties they confront, which include for the Oswalds
loss of their wealth.

Not as successful as *The Bairns*, the novel does continue the author's
interest in the unmarried woman. Robertson introduces Miss Bethie
Barnes, plain and well past middle age, who becomes something of
a fairy godmother to the fatherless Inglis children. She buys the
father's library, which is virtually all he has left his family, as a way
of keeping it for the children, and invests the proceeds for the later
education of David, the eldest boy, who has taken on the paternal
responsibilities. Brusque, but with a heart of gold, Bethie Barnes
becomes much loved by all the family, and her involvement with
them gives purpose to her declining years. On her death she

bequeaths her home to the Inglises' mother and the invested purchase price of the library to David, who is about to begin his studies for the ministry.

While Robertson was to turn to the family chronicle again later in her career, she moved now to several shorter, more overtly didactic novels. The first and most unusual of these is *The Perils of Orphanhood; or, Frederica and Her Guardians* (1874), a complicated story of a Roman Catholic priest's attempt to convert a wealthy Protestant family. It is the only Robertson novel to criticize a specific religious persuasion. The absence of religious training for the children, only nominally Protestant, and of religious practice in the home provide the opportunity for the priest and his accomplice, placed in the family as housekeeper, to influence the family. As well, the wealth of the family provides an opportunity for the author to criticize worldliness. All is eventually resolved satisfactorily, with everyone esconced in Protestantism and Father Jerome thwarted in his attempt to gain a wealthy family for his church.

Young Frederica, fifteen when the novel opens, is a bright and spirited protagonist who gradually comes to comprehend Father Jerome's deceit. She is largely responsible for the resolution of the family's problems and the rescue of the young children from the various Roman Catholic schools in which they have been immured. Father Jerome is presented as something of an evil genius. With its atmosphere of intrigue, its characters' use of disguises and their continual plotting, this novel is the closest Robertson comes to the gothic. Never again does she create such a menacing atmosphere or antagonist.

Robertson then turned her attention from materialism to another major concern of religious writing and, later, of social-activist women's groups, temperance. Women writers and activists such as Marshall Saunders and Nellie McClung were to fight against alcohol as a major cause of social problems, especially among the working class. Some years earlier than these women Robertson set out to dramatize this issue, and to suggest as well possibilities for rehabilitation, with two temperance stories, both appropriately published by the Religious Tract Society, *A Year and A Day: A Story of Canadian Life* (1874–76?) and *Stephen Gratton's Faith* (1876).

A Year and A Day imbeds the problem of alcoholism in an involved story of family life. It is a Glengarry story of two sisters in a situation familiar to Robertson readers. The mother dies and the seventeen-year-old becomes a teacher, taking on responsibility for her two-year-old sibling. Some years later, as the elderly sister's health fails, the situation reverses, and the younger tends and cares for the elder. The novel then shifts to another problem, the drinking and gambling of the women's young stepbrother. The young man reforms through the love of a good woman, whose agreement to marry him when he has been sober "a year and a day" is the source of the novel's title. The one original twist in this conventional plot is that the woman who inspires sobriety is niece of the local tavern keeper, recently arrived to assist her uncle in the tavern. *A Year and a Day* is one of Robertson's most obvious Sunday-school stories.

Stephen Gratton's Faith, subtitled *A Temperance Story*, a short novel of only sixty-four pages, treats the problem of alcoholism very differently; from the beginning, this is the novel's focus. Gratton, a reformed drunkard who had earlier been responsible for the deaths of his two children while he was drunk, befriends John Morely, an alcoholic, who has similarly caused the death of one of his children. Gratton helps Morely to overcome his addiction and reunites him, rehabilitated, with his family. The most interesting aspect of this story is its appreciation of the difficulty for an alcoholic to overcome his addiction, the lengthy struggle involved, and the need for long-term psychological support once the initial acute stage is over. The novel implicitly recognizes alcoholism as a disease. And Morely's recovery through the support of a reformed alcoholic acts out the procedures that in this century Alcoholics Anonymous have adopted as the most effective means to cure alcoholism.

With *David Fleming's Forgiveness* (1879) Robertson returns once again to the Glengarry family chronicle. In the essentials of its plot and the detailed description of community events this novel recalls *Shenac*. Action centres on feuding between Yankee and Scots settlers in adjoining communities, and between two families in particular. As in *Shenac*, one of two New England brothers, more energetic and businesslike, prospers; the other does not. Robertson paints a panoramic scene, involving numerous characters and complicated relationships, through the lives of three generations. More obviously than with earlier chronicles, *David Fleming's Forgiveness* is the story of a community, but its diffuseness limits its impact.

It had become clear that Robertson must find new grist for her mill. All of her stories had been set in Canada. But in the nine years since *The Bairns* the energy and intensity of her stories had diminished. Looking elsewhere for inspiration, Robertson turned to Scotland and set her next three novels in the land she left at the age of nine.

The first of these, *The Orphans of Glen Elder. A Tale of Scottish Life* (1879), is a short novel, too obviously intended for the edification of young readers. Focusing on a young brother and sister taken in by a childless widowed aunt after their mother's death, the story contains a large cast of characters. Characters are stock and the story sentimental and overrighteous. For example, a once-prosperous neighbour impoverished by the dishonesty of others has become bitter and suspicious. She is described as "a pitiable example of the effects of unsanctified affliction, and a warning to all who felt inclined to murmur under the chastening hand of God" (61). Noteworthy, however, is the portrayal of Scottish village life and the use of Scottish dialect in the speech of the characters. Robertson is feeling her way in this different culture, showing the influence of literary sources as well as personal memories.

In her next novel, *The Twa Miss Dawsons* (1880), character is more effectively drawn, particularly in the portrayal of the first Miss Dawson. Once again, the central characters are orphans. Jean Dawson is fifteen and her brother George thirteen when their widowed mother dies. Their mother had been a gentlewoman, reduced to supporting herself by sewing when her husband, mate of a whaling ship, was lost at sea. Jean continues to sew to support her brother through school. George then enters business, is soon successful, and is joined in his enterprises by his sister as his equal and partner. For Robertson, whose women tend to maintain their traditional roles, this career woman is a departure. The narrator assures the reader, however, that Jean never becomes "a mere hard business woman"[44] but remains femininely quiet, reserved, and kind. When at twenty-nine Jean has her one romance, with a sailor younger than she, intellectually and morally beneath her, George, although younger than Jean, takes it upon himself to intervene in protective paternal fashion. The young man accepts George's challenge to prove himself on one last sea voyage, and drowns proving his worth. Jean remains unmarried. So much for a younger brother's officiousness.

The novel then shifts to the second Jean Dawson, the younger of George Dawson's two daughters. While her elder sister is inclined to be selfish and thoughtless, Jean in contrast is much like her aunt in personality. She intelligently refuses a marriage proposal from a penniless, dull-witted, blueblooded Englishman who has all the faults of a spoiled young aristocrat, reminiscent of Sara Jeannette Duncan's satirically portrayed young Englishmen in *The Imperialist* and *The Simple Adventures of a Memsahib*. Jean marries a Scottish sea captain she has known for years, thus continuing, like her grandmother and aunt, the family link with the sea.

In the elder Jean Dawson, as in *The Inglises'* Bethie Barnes, Robertson creates a sympathetic portrait of the unmarried woman, capable and successful in business while retaining "feminine" qualities. Jean's brother asserts that her life is more useful than that of many married women, that in fact she would be missed more than many mothers. What greater praise can a woman in a patriarchal society receive from male relatives?

As in *The Bairns*, Robertson uses Scottish dialect to distinguish the less educated from the better – hence, the elder Jean speaks in dialect; her educated nieces do not. The setting for the novel is the coastal town of Portie, close to Robertson's birthplace, Stewartville. In narrative this novel differs from earlier works in deviating from strict chronology; it begins with George Dawson, now a successful merchant, banker, and shipowner, then shifts to the past, to the childhood of George and Jean.

While Robertson left Scotland at the age of nine, it becomes increasingly evident with her Scottish novels, even more with the later and best, *By a Way She Knew Not: The Story of Allison Bain* (1888), that her knowledge of the Stewartfield area was more extensive than a nine-year-old could have had or retained for more than forty years. Robertson's acute awareness of Scottish town life and the attitudes of the inhabitants, of the speech patterns and expressions of the region, and her detailed description of the changing seasons all point to a more recent familiarity with the region, and led me to speculate that Robertson must have visited Scotland in adult years. I found that this was so. Robertson's brother Joseph visited England in 1874 to float a provincial loan of four million dollars.[45] Margaret went with him and visited her home town with her brother. She "astonished her brother by giving the name of the occupant of every house in Stewartfield when they left in 1832."[46] Her remarkable memory stood Robertson in good stead when she turned to Scotland, shortly after this visit, for the settings and characters of her novels. Unlike May Agnes Fleming or Rosanna Leprohon, who set novels in an England they never saw, Robertson confined her novels to the locality and the way of life she knew, the village life and surrounding countryside of Aberdeenshire, and, from time to time, Aberdeen itself.

Allison Bain's realistic portrayal of the fictious Nethermuir, its detailed description of daily life and of the natural surroundings of the village, far exceeds that in the earlier Scottish novels, and in fact leads me to postulate that Robertson may have made another extended visit to the area after 1874.

Structurally, this novel recalls *Shenac*. Unlike the more diffuse family chronicles, *The Bairns*, *David Fleming's Forgiveness*, or *The Inglises*, for example, Robertson in this novel focuses on one character. Allison Bain remains central. Her personality and behaviour, her way of coping with problems and temptations are the focus of the narrative. The protagonist's central dilemma emerges early in the narrative. Allison Bain runs away from a marriage to which she had agreed only to save a young brother from an undeserved jail sentence. Her mother's illness and, following her mother's death, her father's illness, have allowed Allison to postpone moving into her husband's house; duty and devotion require that she care for her parents. But on her father's death she can no longer forestall the inevitable. Rather than consummate her marriage to a harsh, rough man old enough to be her father, she runs away.

Allison's new life is the core of this novel. Under an assumed name she becomes a servant in a poor missioner's family. The novel is set in 1843, at the time of the formation of the Free Church of Scotland as a missionary church. Choosing this period allows Robertson to discuss in her novel the history and beliefs of the breakaway church, which she praises, especially through her portrayal of the missioner's family, for practising the love it advocates. The novel also suggests something of this church's more democratic attitude, referring, for example, to women being allowed to speak at meetings, which was not permitted in the established church.

In describing the daily round of village activities, Robertson, always the teacher, pays particular attention to schooling. She notes that each student pays the schoolmistress a penny a week, and the teacher lives in the school building. She also describes the girls at school, steadily knitting – part of the family's cottage work. Her own penchant for knitting would account for her picking up on this historical detail. Never wanting to be idle, but with poor eyesight preventing her from doing other close work, Robertson became known for her obsessive knitting. "The knitting work seemed never out of her hands, and her fingers flew like lightening," said a friend.[47]

Allison's dilemma is that of a married woman who, having left her husband, must live in a society in which the duties of a wife are clear and unequivocal. In her new life, as various neighbours begin to learn or suspect her identity, a debate about her situation develops. Because she is much liked and respected, her running away is accepted, if half-heartedly. It seems clear that if her husband discovers her he can compel her to return. Those who come to know her identity consider that they cannot tell her to return, although some believe she should do so voluntarily regardless of the unhappy life she would face. The narrator makes it clear, however, that Allison cannot achieve happiness in her present, unresolved situation, with no possibility of annulment or divorce. A marriage proposal from a young man to whom Allison is attracted makes her situation even more untenable.

The dilemma is resolved finally when, hearing of her husband's serious injury, she returns to care for him and to be forgiven. Some suspense develops at the possibility he may live paralysed for years, a burden to his young wife. This situation does not occur, however. Robertson provides a happy ending. The husband dies, freeing Allison for a suitable marriage. None the less, the point is made that Allison achieves happiness by accepting her duty to her husband, a happiness she could not achieve at Nuitherfield, despite her devoted service to others.

The variety of well-drawn characters of all ages adds to the interest of this novel. The setting, home of an evangelical clergyman, provides the opportunity to discuss sermons, church meetings, and the zeal of the missioners in some detail. The missioners preach a forgiving religion that offers support, the courage to endure trials, and hope for betterment. Love and understanding are shown to be the keys to a satisfying life. Dialect once again effectively conveys the social level of the characters.

Margaret Robertson's Scottish novels are important forerunners of the vastly popular "Kailyard novels" of the 1880s. Scottish women writers such as Catherine Sinclair, Mrs Oliphant, and Annie B. Swann kept the Scottish tradition alive in the 1840s to 1870s, after the death of Scott and before the rise of a new school. Then J.M. Barrie, Ian MacLaren, and S.R. Crockett emerged, enormously popular.[48] All combined romantic stories with local-colour realism and, in the case of MacLaren and Crockett, pious messages. Robertson's work was part of the movement opening the way for these later Kailyard writers. The Canadian novelist was among those who popularized a new wave of fiction, acceptable even among the most strait-laced Presbyterians, thanks to the easing of strictness in the 1870s. Her connection with Scottish scenes, Scottish publishers, Scottish audiences, and, ultimately, Scottish writers is part of the international history of fiction.

Throughout her writing career Robertson relied heavily on personal experience for material, using settings with which she was familiar in Quebec's Eastern Townships, Montreal, Glengarry, Aberdeenshire, and to a lesser extent New England. The closely knit Scottish families she creates parallel the family in which she grew up, as does the frequent presence of a clergyman father. One assumes that the loss of her mother in childhood had a profound effect on Robertson, so frequently do her novels begin with that event. When a mother is present, she is a weak, shadowy figure, such as the mother in *Shenac*, so bereaved by the loss of her husband that her children must take on all responsibilities. In Robertson's fictional families the eldest sister is the effective mother figure. The father, if present, is usually a remote figure, kind, often severe, to be respected and served but not central to the novel. Boys in Robertson's families are as dutiful and hard-working as their sisters, except, of course, when a weaker young man succumbs to the temptation of drinking or gambling and requires the concerted efforts of the family to redeem him.

Gender roles are clearly defined by Robertson. Young women like Shenac or Jean Dawson face crises with courage, determination, initiative, and responsibility, but once the crisis is over they relinquish their independent role. Robertson's most memorable young women have a fiery spirit, and her single women Jean Dawson and Bethie Barnes are capable, independent women who argue for the single woman's life, the life that Robertson herself had chosen.

Class remains as defined as gender roles. Dialect identifies the Scot of less education and concomitant lower-class standing. There is no indication that such an individual will rise in social status, or indeed has any desire to do so. Janet in *The Bairns* refuses invitations to be accepted on an equal level with her American neighbours because this would place her on the same level as the family she serves. Those of higher social class retain their status, even if poverty places them materially on the level of their former servants. Thus Jean Dawson, although she must support herself and her brother by sewing, retains her bearing of gentility, and once her brother is educated, both rise quickly to their former comfortable middle-class status.

For the most part Robertson wrote for a young audience, often referring in her narrative to "my young reader." With her young woman or adolescent girl protagonists her stories would attract a primarily female audience. Since her novels were published in the United States and Britain, her descriptions of farm life and seasonal activities in Canada are detailed, more so than in her novels of Scotland (with the exception of *Allison Bain*) or in her rare incursions into New England for background. Romance plays a limited part in the novels, which centre on family life rather than the ups and downs of courtship. But Robertson's protagonists do meet and marry suitable men, often a teacher or a clergyman, always a man of strong character and moral worth. The most frequent complication of the courtship is a lengthy separation from the suitor because of some obligation he has undertaken, but her lovers are patient and loyal, and eventually reunited.

All Robertson's novels stress the necessity of religion in everyday life. Families pray together, read the Bible together, attend church services regularly. Lengthy sermon-like speeches of religious encouragement are worked into conversations. Individuals are sometimes converted to a deeper, more loving faith that is a source of happiness and satisfaction and, in times of trouble, of strength and consolation. Children grow up and mature through hard work, responsibility, and suffering, bolstered by their strong religious faith and the love and support of the family. Right living is the source of true happiness. While material gain is to be disdained in Robertson's world, honesty and hard work bring material as well as spiritual prosperity.

The sentiment in these novels usually includes at least one deathbed scene, of a father or mother or, more movingly, of a child or adolescent. Christie Redfern's death after her maturation into a loving young woman and that of the loving, gentle Hamish (Shenac's twin) are among the most moving.

Liveliness, humour, a keen sense of observation, an intense interest in human nature – these qualities in Robertson's writings make it easy to credit those who speak of her as "a brilliant conversationalist" whose social skills "brought the brightest and best" in any gathering to her side, and of her reputation as a teacher loved and revered by her students. One friend recalled Robertson as "one of the truest women I ever knew," continuing, "she was so downright Scotch – her yea was yea, and her nay was nay. She was Scotch through and through. And, oh, she was the loyal friend. Never to any one could I go for help in any perplexity as I could to her."[49] It is these characteristics – loyalty, integrity, kindness, reliability, generosity – that Robertson advocates through the characters she creates in her novels.

Sentimental, didactic, moralistic, at the same time colourful, entertaining, filled with memorable characters, Robertson's novels were widely read and frequently reprinted in Britain, the United States, and Canada during the late nineteenth century and into the twentieth. Although she was known in her day primarily in religious and juvenile writing circles, we recognize today how effectively Robertson defined a specific area of nineteenth-century Canadian life. A strong, independent woman, Robertson knew what she wanted to achieve and set about quietly and effectively to do it. In so doing, she shifted the sentimental romance into a more realistic, domestic mode.

Within the specific ideological framework she chose as her own, she was successful. Writing moralistic stories for young people, she created women characters who are lively rather than prissy, intelligent rather than self-righteous, imaginative rather than prudish. Forgoing the melodramatic, the gothic, the sensational, and only occasionally, as in *The Orphans of Glen Elder*, slipping into a too overtly polemical mode, she made the acceptance of the challenges of everyday life sufficiently exciting and worthwhile. In Robertson's novels the most significant events occur in the home. Here, where women are in charge, a woman is the strong, unifying element. Happiness results from carrying on everyday activities in a spirit of loving co-operation, a co-operation that stems from Christian love. The religion that pervades life and comes into everyday conversations and activities is the source of that love. When it is not present, dissension, jealousy, and anger can come into the home and, by extension, into society. Showing the woman as the centre of activity and crucial upholder of religious and moral values in the home implies that she is crucial in the development of a loving, co-operative society, of which the family is the microcosm.

The society Robertson advocates, with love at its base, mutual respect and co-operation its mode of operation, is a society guided by women, unlike the exploitative, materialistic, hierarchical world of patriarchy. Robertson's brothers may have been distinguished lawyers and politicians, but her sister in her Glengarry home was the more influential. One wonders whether Robertson's Sunday-school admirers were quite aware of the consequences of accepting the ideology implicit in these novels.

Susan Frances Harrison ("Seranus"): Paths through the Ancient Forest

CARRIE MacMILLAN

One of the most active women in the literary and musical life of Ottawa and Toronto in the late nineteenth century was the poet, novelist, and musical composer Susan Frances (Riley) Harrison (1859–1935). A contemporary of Charles G.D. Roberts and the rest of the Confederation generation of writers, she participated in the exciting spirit of national optimism that characterized the Canadian cultural scene in the 1880s and 1890s.

She wrote with insight about post-colonial attitudes towards the English in Canada; but her imagination was more particularly engaged throughout her writing and performing career by the songs, speech, history, and general cultural traits of French Canada. As a member of the Confederation group of writers who sought to promote Canada and Canadian literature, to take pride in their culture, and to seek an international audience for Canadian accomplishment, Harrison found in Quebec the distinct Canadian image she required to achieve these ends.

Yet for all that Harrison worked hard to achieve a distinctive voice, and particularly a Canadian voice, she was not fully appreciated at home. In 1895 she wrote: "I may say here, that I really was the first writer in Canada to attract general attention to the local colour, so to speak, of the French. Fully eight years before Lighthall, MacLennan, D.C. Scott or any others attempted the subject, I had brought out – in Ottawa, therefore wasted – a little book of short stories dealing with the *habitant*. In fact, I have always looked upon this as my special subject, yet – you know how sometimes the pioneer is forced to fall behind."[1] By 1916 Harrison had come to feel out of tune with the younger world and bitter that her work was not recognized as it might be. Indeed, by 1933, a fellow writer, Marjory Willison, noted that all Harrison's books were out of print, that they might be read only in the libraries, and that "such a condition of affairs reveals how little care is taken of productions which should be treasured, and not forgotten." Willison offered her opinion: "given some leisure and the benefit of fostering opportunity, such as may be found in older countries, Mrs. Harrison would have taken in all probability a high place as a novelist far beyond her own country."[2] Considering Harrison's remarkable musical and literary activity in late nineteenth-century Canada, it does seem peculiar that her name – and her once-famous pen-name, "Seranus" – are virtually unknown in Canada today.

Harrison was born Susan Frances Riley in Toronto in 1859, the daughter of John Byron Riley, an Irish innkeeper, proprietor of the Revere House on King Street West.[3] Her mother, whose maiden name was Drought, came from Dublin, and the family had connections with the clans Burton, Plunkett, and Netterville. The young Frances also claimed the romantic tradition of a connection with Louis de Jeune, son of the Countess Montmorenci.[4]

Frances Riley was educated at private schools in Toronto and Montreal, to which city she moved in her mid-teens. In Montreal she developed the interest in French Canadian culture that would characterize much of her poetry, fiction, and music.

She was for a time a student in Professor Clark Murray's mental philosophy class at McGill.[5] A noted Scottish educator who studied at Glasgow, Heidelberg, and Gottingen, Professor Murray had taught for ten years at Queen's University before taking a position on the faculty at McGill in 1872.[6] Frances played and sang for McGill students at the home of the university's principal, Dr Dawson,[7] and was also an active member of the Montreal Ladies' Literary Association. On prize day at her ladies' school she read her poem "The Story of Life" to a supportive audience. A precocious and ambitious young woman, she began to publish reviews, essays, and short stories at the age of sixteen, either anonymously or using her first pen-name, "Medusa."[8] She wrote verse for the *Canadian Illustrated* and the *Canadian Monthly*. Apparently she returned to Toronto in the mid-1870s, for in 1876–77, when still a young girl, she trained the choir of the new Church of the Ascension in that city.[9]

On returning to Montreal, Susan Frances Riley met the man who would become her husband, John W.F. Harrison, a respected musician. Raised in Bristol, England, Harrison was an organist and choirmaster who had studied music under various eminent European masters, including Esain, Lubeck, and Riseley, and had been choirmaster at the English Church in Naples before coming to Canada at the age of twenty-four. He was organist at St George's Chapel, Montreal. After his marriage in 1879 he moved, with his twenty-year-old wife, to Ottawa. Here he became musical director of the Ottawa Ladies College and organist and choirmaster of Christ Church Cathedral.[10]

Although very little documentation of the marriage exists, it seems safe to speculate that it was happy and fulfilling, given the shared musical interests of the couple. Harrison refers to her husband in her letters with respect and affection. Being married to an Englishman no doubt sharpened her awareness of the interplay between Canadians long settled in Quebec and Ontario and newcomers from Britain – a relationship that would become one of the main themes of her work.

Young Mrs Harrison was very active in the musical sphere during her Ottawa years, when she wrote the words and arranged the music of the "Address of Welcome to Lord Lansdowne," presented for the new governor general, His Excellency the Marquis of Lansdowne, on his first public appearance in Ottawa.[11] She also wrote other songs that were published in periodicals in the United States under the name "Gilbert King," wrote music reviews for the *Detroit Free Press*, and wrote the full orchestral score of a three-act comic opera in the manner of Gilbert and Sullivan, entitled *Pipandor*. The libretto was composed by F.A. Dixon of Ottawa.[12] In Ottawa too she was able to pursue her interest in French-Canadian music and culture. John Harrison was noted for his contribution to the musical life of the city, especially for some major musical productions, including the first Canadian performance of Mendelssohn's *Antigone* in 1874 and the only Canadian production before 1912 of the companion piece, *Oedipus at Colonus*. He was also a composer.[13] Life must have been busy for the young couple, for Frances found time, among her other creative activities, to have two children.

In Ottawa Harrison kept up her literary activity by serving as an Ottawa correspondent of the *Detroit Free Press* and contributing to such periodicals as *Stewart's Quarterly* and *Belford's Magazine*.[14] An article on Harrison published in 1933 would state that in her early years she published "many unsigned reviews, essays, etc., in ill-fated Canadian magazines."[15] Some time around 1882 she travelled to England in a vain attempt to place her work with a publisher there.[16] She also visited New York early, presumably with the same object. In a later letter to the American editor Clarence Stedman, Harrison writes of having been in New York in the early 1880s and of how difficult it was to meet people and to have one's talents recognized. She describes how she lodged on Twenty-third Street near Sixth Avenue "and *starved* one night."[17]

Discouraged in her efforts to find a British or American publisher, she eventually collected her stories and arranged for them to be published in Ottawa. Under the title *Crowded Out and Other Sketches*, the collection was printed at the *Ottawa Evening Journal* office in 1886 in an inexpensive paperback edition.

Crowded Out is an uneven volume, of interest for what it reveals of the early thematic and stylistic qualities of Harrison's writing, both strengths and weaknesses. The first trait is a strong interest in the presentation of Quebec characters, mostly habitants, and settings. She fiercely claimed these as her own, and she was indeed one of the first English Canadians to see the possibilities for literature in French Canadian local colour and folklore.[18] The constancy with which she pursued the Quebec theme in her writing suggests the special meaning it held for her. This emphasis characterizes Harrison's poetry as well, where she favoured the villanelle, a form of French verse that she likely felt particularly suited her subject matter.

Another feature of the stories is that they are almost always narrated in the first person by an Englishman. This tells us something of the audience Harrison expected for her work and of the forces working on the writers of the day. There is little doubt that Harrison had hoped to publish her sketches in England and make a name for herself there, the seal of success for the later nineteenth-century Canadian writer. Presumably she felt that an English narrator would make the stories more accessible, less "exotic" or "foreign" to the English audience. "Crowded Out" does employ a Canadian character, a writer seeking a publisher and audience for his work in London. Although the story is autobiographical, Harrison uses a male narrator, apparently to lend authority to the work. These were the constraints on the woman writer in Canada in the 1880s, still unsure of the Canadian and the female voice. The central characters in Harrison's two later novels would also be male, although Canadian. Nevertheless, the use of the outsider figure did allow Harrison some opportunity to present cultural contrast, to compare the English type with the Canadian type, a popular pursuit in the days of the international novel.[19]

Thirdly, Harrison reveals herself in these stories to be fond of the rural setting, one that both suited the demographic condition of Canada in her time and reflects her allegiance to the romantic and picturesque tradition in English literature. Although the flora and fauna of her stories are Canadian, they are often seen through the aesthetic or spiritual sensibility of romanticism. Sometimes there are actually favourable comparisons with the English landscape, as if to legitimize, once again, the Canadian terrain, to make it palatable to her (hopefully) English, or English-minded Canadian audience. However, even given these weaknesses (as they appear today), there are redeeming qualities to Harrison's settings. One is that, as with the presentation of Quebec, she is striving for a landscape that is worthy of recognition, of taking its place in a legitimate tradition. Also, there are quite fine passages in the stories in which she does achieve convincing realistic description of small-town and rural Canadian life.

There is no doubt that the stories in *Crowded Out* are almost all undermined, to modern and post-modern taste, by an emphasis on sentimental and melodramatic plots and the stereotyped characters and situations that accompany them. Here Harrison is conforming to the popular taste, the demands of the publisher and the audience of her day.[20] However, recent feminist criticism suggests that there can be redeeming qualities to melodrama and the sensational, that these are legitimate forms of literary expression that capture cultural attitudes and conditions, and attempt to redefine the social order.[21] Harrison's stories do convey much about the emergent Canada, its historical figures, its social structure, its culture, its artists, its women, and its relationship with England.

A closer look at the stories reveals more of Harrison's qualities as a writer and about the questions being addressed in late nineteenth-century Canadian fiction. "The Prisoner Dubois," for instance, features a leader of a Métis rebellion in western Canada – a thinly disguised portrait of Louis Riel, whose 1884–85 rebellion was very fresh indeed in the minds of Canadians when *Crowded Out* was published in 1886. In this story Harrison wrestled directly with an important Canadian issue of her time, as it still is of ours: relations among Canada's native peoples, its French, and its English. Riel's rebellion and the political turmoil it engendered in Canada must have had particular significance for Harrison, with her interest in and sympathy for French Canadian history and culture.

In Harrison's story a young society woman named Cecelia returns to Ottawa from her "finishing" in Europe to discover that the Métis leader Pierre Dubois has been captured and awaits inevitable hanging. Cecelia recalls a Pierre Dubois whom she met and became fond of in Port Joli, where her family spent summers when she was young. She remembers a boy with solemn eyes and beautiful brown hair, who knew the flowers of the woods and the French Canadian folk songs, and talked passionately of his people, land, and culture. She remembers him too as loving his country and hoping one day to be able to aid and advance it. She feels sure that this young man loved the English but could not help loving the French more, given his ancestry. She says about him:

He was born to be a leader and to bring them away from the home into battle and make war for them, and where in that does he differ from other heroes we are taught to love and admire? If you had ever heard him talk, and had seen the people all gathered round him when he spoke of all these things – as for the Church and the Virgin and the priests, it would be well if you and all of us thought as much about our religion and loved and revered it as he did.[22]

The young woman asks whether, if the incarcerated Pierre Dubois is mad, hanging him will "bring peace and friendliness, and right feeling, or will it bring a fiercer fire and a sharper sword than our country has yet seen – a hand-to-hand fight between rival races, a civil war based on national distinction?" (94)

When Cecelia actually meets the prisoner, she discovers that he is the same Pierre Dubois, the boy from her childhood, but that he has changed dramatically. He does not remember her and treats her coming as a boost to his male ego, making insinuating glances at the jailers. He arrogantly takes a chair that has been brought for her, and when she speaks of trying to save him, he tells her that the French people will never let him hang, that he is their king, their prophet, their anointed: "their fat priests acknowledge me, their women adore me."

Cecelia leaves, realizing that she has been talking to a madman and accepting the fate that awaits him. But on the day of his execution her mind is filled with uncertainty about Pierre: "Is he a lunatic, or a fanatic, a martyr or a friend, an inspired criminal or a perverted enthusiast? Perhaps he is a mixture of all these." Her questions about Pierre Dubois are those that have vexed Canadian historians concerning Louis Riel from the time of the rebellion.

Harrison's portrait of Pierre Dubois shows her grappling, through fiction, with a controversial figure at the centre of contemporary Canadian life. By enclosing a description of the young Dubois within a sentimental plot, she attracts sympathy for him. In his passionate love of his country and his poetic soul Harrison sees much to identify with. And her rendition of the prisoner Dubois, while it presents a very unattractive image of the older man, tends to excuse him on the grounds of insanity. Cecelia's ambivalence at the end likely reflects Harrison's attitude to Riel, an attempt to sort through her own ideas about Riel and French Canada. By presenting a rather sympathetic portrait of Riel, she was also likely attempting to dissipate some of the inevitable anti-French feeling pervading English Canada in those dramatic days. No doubt Cecelia's concerns about the wisdom of executing Riel, given the effect this would have on French Canada, were Harrison's as well. With French Canada playing such a strong mythic role in her definition of the Canadian character and culture (and with her general affection for French Canadian culture), she could not wish to see the French and English cultural fabric of Canada torn apart by a bitter civil war.

A story of Quebec, ironic rather than tragic, is "The Story of Etienne Chezy d'Alencourt." This tale is narrated by an Englishman who has come to the Ottawa region in quest of the true French Canadian type: the habitant. He discovers this type in "Netty," the nickname of Etienne, who works as a labourer in a paper-mill on the Gatineau River. The Englishman befriends the illiterate Netty, who secretly starts to study reading and writing after work at the mill so that he can better converse with his new friend. During a holiday in the north, on Calumet Island, the Englishman finds Netty ill with consumption, hastened by overwork in the evenings on acquiring literacy. Eventually Etienne's hard-won literacy, the product of his friendship with the Englishman, helps him to decipher an old missal that confirms he is the descendant of a French officer who came to New France in the eighteenth century at the time of the Governor Bigot. The Englishman's own research in parliamentary archives confirms this discovery. The irony is that Netty's literacy, which helps him to find a proud and noble identity, also costs him his health and his life. Netty's hope of some day visiting France, the home of his ancestors, is scuttled by his death. Harrison appears in this ironic story to be content to attribute a proud heritage to her habitant characters without disturbing the romantic cultural distinctness of their humble rural lives. In this story Harrison legitimizes Quebec, and by extension Canada, by bestowing on it a proud past.

Englishmen in Canada are more clearly in focus in two sentimental tales, "Descendez à l'ombre" and "As It Was in the Beginning." In both the Canadian setting is a backdrop for the resolution of actions that have begun in England. In "Descendez à l'ombre" two Englishmen are in Canada to indulge the restless need for adventure of one, an aristocrat, who frequently leaves his family and goes off to exotic foreign parts, in this case French Canada. His companion is a more sensitive and penniless relative who chivalrously worships the aristocrat's wife and accompanies the aristocratic traveller in order to watch over his well-being. In the Gatineaus the nobleman refuses to be vaccinated for smallpox, in spite of his worried companion's urging. The companion, concerned that the aristocrat's wife and children not lose their husband and father, rather improbably manages to vaccinate him in his sleep. However, he is then unable to muster the courage to treat himself. Predictably, the sensitive companion dies of smallpox within a day of the travellers' arrival at the picturesque cottage of a habitant. The poorer Englishman is laid beneath a pair of trees that he had admired from afar as being shaped like a lyre.

The trees and the rest of the French Canadian setting are here simply instruments for "dressing up" a very improbable and sentimental tale. However, even in this unlikely story and in "As It Was in the Beginning," in which a years-old rivalry between two English brothers is resolved in the Canadian bush, Harrison presents Canada as a setting that deserves treatment in literature, and does what she can, within the conventions of her day, to bring it to literary life.

Further, there is a moral message imparted in these stories, in which Canada offers insight into or resolution of ills that have started in England. In "Descendez à l'ombre" the aristocrat learns in the Canadian bush that life is not a game to be taken lightly, and he may be more considerate in future. In "As It Was in the Beginning" one brother learns to set aside the rivalry of the past and to forgo the busy world of affairs for the nobility and serenity of nature. There is a moral imperative in these and others of Harrison's stories, one in which Canada acts as a setting of peace and integrity, far from the crowded and busy worlds of Britain and the United States.

A more mythic use of the Canadian landscape and character occurs in "The Idyl of the Island," where a visiting Englishman happens upon a beautiful island while boating and discovers a woman asleep on a thick bed of soft moss. She wakens and initiates him into the outdoor world of camping: building a fire, and cooking breakfast. This Odyssean idyll is brought to an end by the imminent return of her husband. The Englishman leaves, but he never forgets the woman of the island. Through use of the poetic language of nature, Harrison spins a myth in this tale of Canada, like the mesmerizing woman and her dramatic setting, as beautiful, wild, self-reliant, honourable, and elusive.

When the Englishman first sees the woman, her abode, encircled with wild grape vines and cushioned with moss, strikes him as a perfect union of art and nature. As he gets to know her, he becomes convinced that she is not happy with her husband. One senses in the story an imprisoned poet-princess longing for escape and thinks of the unrecognized writer Harrison longing for admission to the literary world of England but hampered by prevailing attitudes to women and colonials. It is a story that resembles Joanna E. Wood's later *Judith Moore* (1898), in which Canada is looked at mythically as an environment for the artist.

Another story suggesting mythic qualities in the Canadian national character is "The Bishop of Saskabasquie." Here Harrison implies a contrast between the English clergy, evoked early in the story by reference to a popular satirical play that presents them as generally cynical and lax in their vocation, and an English colonial bishop on whom the Canadian landscape and people have worked marvels by sharpening his faith and duty. He emerges as a dedicated cleric who has mastered native and French Canadian languages in order to tend his flock; he is also a good father and husband. His wife laughs at the hardships of life in his northern see and makes do with very little. The jolly good nature of the bishop and his heroic carrying out of his duties in a vast and dangerous landscape mythically bespeak the wholesome character that is built in the Canadian wilderness, in contrast to the brief images of a more enervated clergy that appear at the beginning of the story.

A story that satirizes post-colonial attitudes to the English in a small Ontario town is "How the Mr. Foxleys Came, Stayed and Never Went Away." Although it starts, like many of the other stories, from the perspective of the outsider Englishman, favourably comparing the beauties of the Canadian countryside with those of England, it goes on to give a wonderfully realistic and quite humorous picture of the social structure and lifestyle of rural Ontario. The extent of its intended closeness to life is evident from an inscription in the copy of *Crowded Out* in Special Collections in the Ralph Pickard Bell Library at Mount Allison University. This is a copy given to the biographer of Charles G.D. Roberts, Elsie Pomeroy, by Harrison. On the first page of the story is written, in Harrison's hand, "Lambton Mills," the name of the town on which Harrison based her story.

The focus of the story comes to rest on what seems to be the dominant trait of this small town: its passionate allegiance to all things English. This is not surprising, given that many of the inhabitants (the doctor, the minister, the innkeeper, the farmer) are from England. When two English brothers, sons of an aristocrat, become enamoured of the area and settle for a time at the local inn, a romantic farce ensues that is both funny and revealing. One of the brothers harmlessly (or so it would seem to him) pays periodic visits to the rector and his unmarried daughter and to two impoverished but genteel maiden sisters, middle-aged daughters of the deceased doctor. When it becomes obvious that the Englishman is not going to propose to her, the rector's daughter marries in spite a rich American (described as generally lacking taste and sensibility). The elder of the maiden sisters dies of a broken heart, and her sister, who also "loves" the Englishman, hearing he is to marry the innkeeper's hired girl, purchases vitriol and throws it in his face, blinding him. After this dark and hasty action, she discovers it is the Englishman's brother who intends to marry the servant girl.

The point of the story, which emerges with delightful irony, is the ridiculous extent to which the local people pin their hopes on the English aristocrats. To underline this, Harrison has a wealthy and respectable farmer propose marriage to the younger sister, not knowing she is on her way to town to buy the vitriol. She is overcome with horror at the audacity of a mere farmer making such a proposal to the daughter of a doctor. She can think only in more rigid British terms of class distinction. It does not occur to her to consider the comfortable, warm, prosperous home that the Canadian offers, away from her present pinched, cold, frugal life, or his genuine concern for her sad condition. In this story Harrison reveals a finely critical and ironic eye, capable of detecting the shortcomings of her society. In addition to presenting the positive aspects of Canada mythically elsewhere (its romantic past, beautiful landscape, and moral superiority), Harrison was capable, as "How the Mr. Foxleys Came, Stayed and Never Went Away" tells us, of seeing its colonial traits in realistic terms.

Another category of story in *Crowded Out* contains gothic elements – either of mystery or of horror. One of the most interesting in this respect is "The Story of Monsieur, Madame and the Pea-Green Parrot." What makes it memorable is the vivid image of the parrot, with its haunting refrain, "But for goodness' sake, don't say I told you." This refrain pervades the story, giving it unity and heightening the theme. The incomplete, mysterious ending is a tantalizing relief from the generally overdone, nailed-shut plots of the other stories.

Again the story is told in the first person by an Englishman. He is a would-be writer who has left a civil-service post in Canada to go to New York. One evening in a pleasant Italian restaurant, he and a friend are amused by an interesting domestic situation. The restaurateur keeps a brilliant pea-green parrot that he coddles and talks to, displaying more affection for it than for his wife, whom he ignores, and whose jealousy and unhappiness are apparent. The parrot's reiterated line implies some guilty secret. The narrator learns that the restaurateur has been married before, also unhappily.

After dinner, sitting in New York's Union Square, the friend casually remarks to the writer that here is material for a book or a play: "Put them – the three of them – Monsieur, Madame and the Pea-Green Parrot – into a book ... There's your title ready for you" (16). The writer admits he has been thinking the same thing but claims he does not understand the wife's mental and moral condition sufficiently: he has not enough to go on. He hopes something will happen to clarify the drama. At that moment people start to run across the square to the restaurant. The two men return to find the wife in a state of nervous collapse, the husband absent, and the parrot shrieking its habitual phrase. The first part of the two-part story ends enigmatically with the two men unsure whether anything has actually happened.

Harrison's story has up to this point raised, in addition to the question of the husband's disappearance, some fascinating questions about the artistic process and the relationship between art and life. How much does art conform to life (the writer wanting to study the "characters" more closely before he can write about them) and life conform to art (the writer and friend wanting something to happen, and life obligingly seeming to respond)? The parrot's insistent cry ("For goodness' sake, don't say I told you") heightens the theme of telling, as well as emphasizing the elusiveness of art (what is it that is not to be told?).

The teasing interplay between life and art continues ironically in the final part of the story. Years have passed, and the writer is back in Canada. He visits the Grey Nunnery in Montreal, researching French Canadian local colour for his writing. Here he happens into a room that contains a grey parrot sleeping in a cage. As he is about to leave the room, the parrot suddenly wakens and shrieks, "For goodness' sake, don't say I told you." The drama of the past returns. He is convinced the parrot has seen something, that something has happened. He learns that the parrot belongs to a nun, Sister Félicité, but that she lies ill and dying. He sends a message to the dying sister: that he was in the restaurant that night years ago and that, if there is anything she wishes to divulge, he will visit her tomorrow. The next day he returns to find that the nun has died but has left him a letter. He identifies the dead woman as the wife of years ago. But the piece of paper on which the dying nun wrote a message to him is discovered in tiny pieces at the bottom of the parrot's cage. The mystery of the restaurateur's fate remains just that. The narrator keeps the bird, which remains grey: he speculates that it was painted vivid green in days gone by and has returned to its natural colour.

The story is very intriguing. One forgives it its use of coincidence and improbability for the interest Harrison builds around the mysterious couple and their bird. The bright bird, which readily suggests a symbol of art, the enigmatic telling referred to in its repeated phrase, and the Sister's adopted name, Félicité, or Happiness, all suggest the elements that are involved in the creative process. The enigmatic ending is appropriate in a story about a function, the artistic process, that is impossible to define or to understand fully. It seems fitting that the writer should be left with the bird and the puzzle at the end of the story, the tantalizing elements requiring the fire of imagination to realize them in a completed statement. Further, the story that the writer contemplated writing in New York's Union Square is the story that the reader has just read, complete with the same title. In this age of fascination with self-reflexive literature, the reader is struck by the subtle subtext concerning the creative process in "The Story of Monsieur, Madame and the Pea-Green Parrot."

"The Story of Delle Josephine Boulanger" is a melodramatic and sentimental tale, memorable for its effective use of the Canadian setting in an evocation of Poe-like horror. An Englishman has taken a room in the little house of an elderly French Canadian milliner in a town near Montmorenci Falls, Quebec, which he has come to sketch. On the night of a heavy snowfall he secretly discovers the old lady, attired in a bizarre red hat and antimacassar, talking to her image in a mirror. The next morning he finds the lady dead in front of her mirror, still strangely attired. To his horror, he cannot get out of the house to seek help because it is snowed in. Eventually he is released and learns the sad past of Mlle Josephine, left mad by an accident in her youth.

What makes the story memorable is the briefly realized atmosphere of horror Harrison achieves through madness, death, and entrapment (burial). Ironically the Englishman, who has come to sketch an awe-inspiring setting in nature, has got more than he bargained for – an awe-full glimpse of the human condition.

The most memorable fiction in *Crowded Out* is the six-page short story that gives the book its title. The story is remarkable for its intensity and its psychological realism. It is the only story in the collection narrated by a Canadian, and is the most autobiographical. It is told in the first person by a writer living temporarily near Oxford Street in London. Again the Pomeroy copy of *Crowded Out* in the Bell Library at Mount Allison University provides a clue to the realism and accuracy of the story. Harrison has written at the top of the first page: "42 Bolsover St. London England." Bolsover Street is in central London, near Oxford Street. One surmises that this is the address at which Harrison stayed when she went to London as a young woman with her opera, poetry, and sketches. In an article published in 1888, two years after the publication of "Crowded Out," Ethelwyn Wetherald states that there is a general belief this story is based on Harrison's own experience in London, "whither she went some years ago with her heart full of ambition, and in her hands poems, songs, operas … which failed to find a publisher."[23] The fact that Harrison employs a male character in such a personally significant story illustrates the constraint she felt as a woman writer in a world that took writers seriously only when they were male.

The narrator in the story has been in London for some time and has not been successful in placing his work, like Harrison's "a comedy, a volume of verse, songs, sketches, stories." The story enacts the psychology of failure and rejection, beginning with the sentence "I am nobody" and ending with the writer's death. All of the images of the story, particularly details of the narrator's third-class room, up three flights of stairs in a London lodging-house, are those of failure. In his room

the square central table … is rickety and uncomfortable. Useless to write on … the fireplace is filled with orange peel and brown paper, cigar stumps and matches. One blind is pulled down this morning and the other is crooked. The lamp glass is cracked, my work too. I dare not look at the wallpaper nor the pictures. The carpet is kicked into holes … my clothes are lying all about. The soot of London begrimes every object in the room.   (5)

He has come with ambition, hope and love, to woo London, to possess her, but she rejects him, is cold, blind, cruel; and therefore, again, "I am nobody. I am crowded out." His condition of failure and unhappiness is heightened by short, sparse, repetitiously structured sentences, frequently beginning with "I," which focus on him and his sense of failure. The absence of stylistic variety and expansiveness illustrates his loss of the muse.

The story consists entirely of night thoughts, as the narrator watches from his third-storey room the people of Oxford Street go about their business and pleasure, seeing "Irving, Wilson Barrett, Ellen Terry." He wonders: "What line of mine, what bar, what thought or phrase will turn the silence into song, the copper into gold?" (6–7)

If London rejects him, so has Canada. He recalls that there he loved a woman named Hortense, at Beau Séjour; but because he did not belong to her social level or religion, the priests kept her from him. All that is left is to write of her, and perhaps to win her by gaining recognition in London. But "who in this great London will believe in me? Who will care to know about Hortense or about Beau Séjour? ... a northern river ... its impenetrable pine wood." "Sing, Hortense, will you?" he cries:

Sing now for me,
Descendez à l'ombre
  Ma jolie blonde.

The story ends with the long grey fingers of dawn stealing into his room, but there is no ink left, and his heart fails. Once again the refrain of the French Canadian boat-song is heard, and the story ends.

"Crowded Out" confirms the mythic significance of Quebec in Harrison's writing. French Canada – its distinct history, culture, and setting – provides the images of the Canadian nation and character, as it has in many of the stories in the collection, explaining the reason for its pervasiveness in her writing, and her nationalistic intent. The story also illustrates a theme close to Harrison's heart, the difficulty the Canadian writer has in finding recognition at home or abroad. Canadian society and its lack of interest in artistic pursuits, its preference for church and political concerns, and its colonial attitude are represented by the narrow-minded, tradition-ridden priests. The Canadian muse, or inspiration for the Canadian writer, is embodied in Hortense, locked up and inaccessible to him. The Canadian landscape, the pine wood, the ancient estate of Beau Séjour, as well as the songs of the habitant, are redolent of Canadian history and culture, which the writer has attempted to capture in his writing. He has come to London to prove himself, the familiar necessity for the colonial artist, but his homespun themes and wild settings hold no interest for the publishers and producers here. Unsupported at home and abroad, his ink dries up, and he dies.

The intensity and effectiveness of Harrison's "Crowded Out" make one regret enormously the constraints of place and time that influenced her not to explore more deeply the real conditions of life for Canadians in her day. And one regrets as well that she did not feel confident enough in this story to present the situation of the female artist struggling in London, a perspective that would have intensified further an already memorable story, a classic in defining the condition of the Canadian artist in the early 1880s.

Thus, in her stories written before 1886 Harrison proclaimed the right of Canada to take its place in the larger cultural world. In order to support this theme, she focused on Quebec to illustrate a distinct

Canadian character. She also viewed the Canadian landscape and society through the eyes of itinerant Englishmen to awaken her (hopefully) British readership to Canada's significance. And she dealt with the difficulty of being a Canadian artist in a country that seldom appreciates its own and in the larger world that is not interested in Canadian matters.

Harrison's *Crowded Out* does not appear to have drawn much critical response in the journals of the day. Published, perhaps at the author's expense, at the office of the *Ottawa Evening Journal*, it would not have had the promotion and circulation that an established book publisher would have given it.

Crowded Out and Other Sketches was published "By Seranus." This pseudonym had presented itself accidentally when a friend misread her signature, "S. Frances."[24] It was to become very familiar to Canadian readers in the next few years.

In 1886, the year *Crowded Out* was published, the Harrison family made its major move, after seven years in Ottawa, to Toronto. Here John Harrison took a position, which he would maintain until 1920,[25] teaching piano and organ at the Toronto Conservatory of Music, and also became organist and choirmaster at the Church of St Simon the Apostle. In Toronto the family home was first at 13 and later at 21 Dunbar Road in Rosedale.[26] It was in Toronto that Frances began to use the pen name "Seranus" consistently. In Toronto too she increased her literary activity, serving as a music critic for the *Week* in 1886–87 and for a period of nine months as editor of that magazine.[27] Many poems, articles, and short stories by Seranus also appeared in the *Week*.

Her patriotic pride in her country is expressed in her publishing, in 1887, two years before Lighthall's *Songs of the Great Dominion*, an anthology of Canadian verse, *The Canadian Birthday Book*.[28] This 415-page anthology of Canadian verse contains a Canadian poem for each day of the year. In 1891 Harrison collected and published her most significant collection of poetry, the 208-page *Pine, Rose and Fleur de Lis*.[29] She was highly enough thought of as a poet that two of her poems appeared in 1895 in the American literary critic Clarence Stedman's *A Victorian Anthology*, which included a short Canadian section.[30]

The slim documentation of Harrison's life leaves as many questions unanswered as answered. One would like to know more about her family relations and how she managed a home and a musical and literary career before the advent of the household conveniences that make life somewhat easier for today's working woman. It would be nice as well to have a more personal glimpse of the author. Her picture in Garvin's *Canadian Poets* reveals a tiny, rather bird-like woman, with large, soft eyes and straight nose, in Victorian dress, her hair "fringed" and worn up and topped with an assortment of ribbon and lace – perhaps the kind of costume Frances would wear to one of her evening musical performances.[31] Ethelwyn Wetherald in 1888, when Frances was about thirty, describes her as *"petite,* very dainty in style, manner and attire, with a noticeably intellectual cast of face, which is finely chiselled, and quite classical in character."[32]

In her mid-thirties, in 1893 this inventive and ambitious woman offered classes in English literature in her home in Rosedale[33] and kept up her musical interest by becoming a recognized authority on French Canadian folk songs. In the 1896–97 season she offered a public recital, "The Music of French Canada," a combination of lecture and musical illustrations, which was delivered to musical clubs in Montreal, Toronto, and London, Ontario.[34] The reviewer for *Saturday Night* who heard her program in Toronto at a meeting of the Canadian Society of Musicians stated: "I doubt very much whether a more interesting paper has ever been read in the history of the society."[35]

She travelled to New York again around 1897, where she was "looking after my literary interests."[36] One reward for the constant professionalism of her attitude towards writing came when she placed her first full-length novel with a major British firm, Arnold of London. At that, however, the novel had been written almost a decade earlier, in 1890, according to a letter from Harrison to Wilfred Campbell.[37]

In *The Forest of Bourg-Marie* (1898) Harrison comes closest to finding a genre that expresses in a sustained and effective manner her most deeply felt concerns. On one level her novel simply tells the story of Magloire, a French Canadian who has run away from home at the age of fourteen to pursue the promise of success offered by that Eldorado of so many Canadians of the day, the United States, and who returns home nine years later to a grandfather who rejects him. On this level the novel, which is also characterized by rather two-dimensional characters, coincidence, and the supernatural, may be described as a romance with elements of realism. It does deal with sensitivity to the "problem" of "going down the road," and contains as well some good descriptions of late nineteenth-century habitant life.

But *The Forest of Bourg-Marie* is also redolent of larger meaning, its characters, landscape, and action those of a sustained allegory in which Harrison explores the theme of Canadians who are lured to the United States by the promise of financial reward, and the cultural deracination, corruption, and estrangement from home that can result. Harrison's characters are like archetypal figures from fairy-tales and folklore, appealing to memories of the unconscious, feeling, intuitive mind. It is interesting to note also that whereas the stories, published in 1886, are pervaded with Canadian-English relations (the narrators so frequently Englishmen experiencing Canada for the first time), this novel, published more than a decade later, is concerned with Canadian-American relations, reflecting the powerful drain by the 1890s to the United States of Canadian labour and talent. Not only were Canadian domestics and nurses finding work in the "Boston States" (for the Maritimers), but writers like Charles G.D. Roberts, Bliss Carman, May Agnes Fleming, Marshall Saunders, Basil King, Arthur Wentworth Eaton, Graeme Mercer Adam, E.W. Sandys, Gilbert Parker, and P. McArthur found it worth their while to live near the lucrative publishing houses and periodicals of Boston and New York.[38]

The plot of *The Forest of Bourg-Marie* concerns three central characters. Mikel Caron, the wise old man, forest ranger, and trapper, is the only person in the region to have explored all the dark, deep, dense forest, and one of the few in memory to have entered it at all. The forest is his ancestral home, part of a nine-hundred-*arpent* grant made to his ancestor, the seigneur of the region, in 1668. Old Mikel has learned from the forest: high thoughts from the eagle, pluck from the bear, and accurate observation and a quick eye from the small forest creatures. He is referred to as the "old fox" and the "old man of the woods."

The forest is full of ghosts of the past. Here roam "spectral shapes of trapper, voyageur, Algonquin, Iroquois, Briton, Highlander, Saxon and Celt," while "the imaginative peasantry say spirits of the past roam here." The narrator describes it as "fitting soil for fable and legend."[39] Mikel is the only person in Bourg-Marie to know of one mysterious place, the old turreted stone "manoir," his ancestral home, that overlooks the forest. It is Mikel's dream some day to restore the old manor house to its former glory.

In the manor are three rooms where Mikel has secretly been hoarding treasure to this end. The first room is hung with furs of all kinds, trapped by Mikel himself over time. The second room contains a banquet table laden with the family's ancient silver and crystal. The third room contains original weapons brought from Rouyn – shields, sabers, rapiers – as well as old Indian relics of battle. Mikel, in his knowledge of the land, the wildlife, and the human history of Bourg-Marie, is the keeper of the past, the accumulated treasure of the people.

To Mikel all these things are sacred. His visits to the manor house and the three rooms are like visits to a shrine, where he appears almost to worship the artifacts. As the plot of the novel will illustrate, however, Mikel may worship his proud, noble past and illusions of restored grandeur too much, to the point where he is unable to deal effectively with the present, particularly his own family. Mikel is perceived as a remote, solemn, and aloof figure by the other inhabitants of Bourg-Marie. But although Mikel has yet to learn humility and a faith that goes beyond past glories, there is no doubt of the stature of the man in the text.

Magloire Caron, Mikel's grandson, is the second principal character in the novel. The son of Mikel's impish and irreverent second son, who cares not at all for the past and speaks out from an early age against the church, Magloire has followed in his father's footsteps. In spite of his grandfather's attempts to instil respect for the values of the past in him, Magloire has not responded at all to Mikel's plans of sending him to Laval for a classical education and some day becoming the learned and respected "seigneur" of the region – in modern parlance, a member of Parliament. Instead, Magloire has run away from home to the United States at the age of fourteen and worked at menial jobs, as barber's assistant, bartender, and driver in various cities, winding up in Milwaukee.

Magloire is so impressed with the outward manifestations of wealth in the United States that he thinks he has found his Promised Land. He uses his wages to buy cheap, flashy clothes and jewels and to take out flower girls and dancers. When he returns to Bourg-Marie he still owes money on a watch bought on credit. He has come to regard Bourg-Marie as a poor, backward, ignorant place, its people slaves to priests and government, and talks with great confidence of the "emancipation" he has found in the United States. This emancipation includes, ironically, anglicizing his name to "Michael Carter," as he has found that Americans respond better to English names. In his betrayal of his birthright, identity, and culture, Magloire illustrates the effect of deracination that Harrison sees overcoming Canadians who move to the United States, a more culturally dominant, wealthy, and confident country.

Eventually Magloire falls in with a bad crowd in Milwaukee, which includes a "business partner" who owns a bowling alley and a shooting gallery. This "go-ahead" friend has taken Magloire as a partner after hearing Magloire boasting, untruthfully, that he has money. In fact the little money Magloire has is made from gambling. The expatriate Magloire becomes enamoured of his associate's wife, a flashy Irish woman out for what she can get. In the United States Magloire has also become a member of a rather murkily described order, the Universal Levellers Club, based in Chicago. Socialist in character and dedicated to the overthrow of church and government, it essentially proclaims anarchy.

Magloire returns to Bourg-Marie, as the novel begins, to try to get money from his grandfather to keep his lady and her husband happy. On his way to his grandfather's he whistles a refrain picked up at an American oyster bar. He offends his grandfather Mikel by his trivial and impertinent character and by his attempt to pass himself off as an English fur trader before revealing his real identity. After his nine-year absence he perceives the forest as lonely and gloomy, not sensing what the omniscient narrator describes as its "primeval majesty and the beauty of the solitude." Magloire is an unattractive character, one on whose rebellious nature the expatriate experience has bred vanity, arrogance, and dishonesty.

The third major character in *The Forest of Bourg-Marie* is the poor woodsman and trapper Laurière, who respects the stern and aloof Mikel but is thrown into confusion, on Magloire's return, by the picture he paints of the attractions of the United States. Very much impressed by the flashy clothes and descriptions of easy wealth to be made in the States, Laurière is nevertheless uncomfortable with the temptation Magloire offers. He is "being tempted to forfeit his nationality and forego his country ... 'A something' struck at his heart and mental vision so that he could not answer its solemn questionings" (26). It is only when Magloire makes a socialist speech, attacking the tyranny of the church, that Laurière realizes he cannot subscribe to this way of life. Laurière has a strong faith, supported by his sister's having experienced a miracle at the shrine of Ste Anne.

The difference between Laurière and Magloire is apparent in Laurière's reaction to a beautiful diamond Mikel shows him. Instead of envisioning wealth in the jewel, he sees in it images of nature and his own land – sunsets and waterfalls. Laurière, unlike Magloire, is concerned about Mikel. He pledges loyalty to the old man, using images of the seasons to affirm it.

Mikel recognizes the qualities of Laurière and adopts him as his heir. Through his love of Laurière and recognition of his good qualities, particularly his faith and affection, the proud old woodsman rediscovers his emotions, lost since the early death of his wife and disappointment in his son and grandson. The alliance of Mikel and Laurière, that of culture and faith, combines the positive qualities of French Canada, which Harrison celebrates in this novel.

The tensions inherent in the return of the prodigal are compounded by Magloire's resorting to unscrupulous methods to gain his grandfather's fortune. Magloire goes into league with Pacifique, a habitant whose physical deformity (he is a hunchback) and purely evil character seem well suited to Magloire's greedy, evil scheme. Disguised in a bearskin (symbolically usurping nature for his own ends), Pacifique hides outside Mikel's forest cottage, becoming Magloire's spy. Here he sees the friendship developing between Mikel and Laurière; and here he catches a glimpse of the huge diamond that is part of Mikel's treasure.

The novel comes to a dramatic climax on a stormy night when Magloire and Pacifique go to the manor to take what they can from Mikel's three precious rooms. Laurière has been left at the manor, recovering from a broken leg sustained when he fought the "bear" (Pacifique). Hearing Magloire and Pacifique approach the manor, he hides in the first room, behind some animal skins. When he hears the two robbers quarrelling fiercely over the treasures in the second room, Laurière emerges to save Magloire. Magloire is able to flee with enough treasure to keep him and his mistress happy in several mid-western American cities for some time; Pacifique, who has found the huge diamond and fled with it, is killed, fittingly, given his previous use of nature for unnatural ends, by a giant bear in the forest, calling out at the moment of his death: "I believe in God! I believe also in the devil" (281). Mikel arrives in time to see his beloved manor towers blown to the ground by the storm, and lightning start a blaze that levels what remains.

Mikel also finds the mortally wounded Laurière, who has fallen into an old cistern on the ancient estate. Reaffirming his love for him, Mikel mourns the loss of Laurière as greatly as he regrets the loss of his dream of restoring his ancestral home. Laurière dies, confirmed in his faith by his vision of a blaze of light. He tells Mikel, "Bury me in Bourg-Marie. There can be no sweeter place, nor nobler soil to lie in" (304). So Laurière lies, deep within his beloved native soil, on the site of the old manoir, formerly the focus of Magloire's complete devotion and affection.

Harrison has chosen a somewhat ironic ending for her novel. The unattractive and unscrupulous Magloire goes unpunished; the pure Laurière dies, and the old woodsman loses his dreams of a restored family estate. But in fact the important components of the ancient forest are still intact: culture and faith. The old folk-songs are still sung; hunting and trapping continue (Mikel is again the most successful trapper of bear in the next season), and Bourg-Marie remains much as it was before the return of Magloire. The ancient manor is gone, but Mikel still knows and walks the forest paths. And human affection and faith, learned from Laurière, have replaced the former selfish desire to reconstruct the glories of the past. The positive prospect for Bourg-Marie is confirmed in a letter of the curé to the bishop that describes a vision he has had of a cloud in the sky in human form, resembling the Virgin, surrounded by a blue mist. The age of miracles, he proclaims, is still with us.

In her novel Harrison has affirmed the sovereignty of the Canadian landscape, inviolate and pure, and condemned those who would deny their birthright. By using a forest dense with legends and archetypal figures and events, she has produced a Canadian legend for her time, and perhaps for ours.

Unlike *Crowded Out*, which evoked so little critical response, Harrison's *The Forest of Bourg-Marie* was reviewed generally and favourably. The discriminating American periodical the *Nation*, in a review article of five novels, including Charles G.D. Roberts' *A Sister to Evangeline*, had several very kind things to say about it.[40] It is fortunate that the Canadian novels were reviewed together, as this offers an opportunity to compare the critical responses to Harrison's fiction with reactions to the work of the most important Canadian literary figure of her day. The unnamed reviewer is very critical of Roberts' novel, observing that the author is a better writer of descriptive verse than of prose romance and that he knows and feels more about the landscape of "Acadia" than about its people. He notes that any hack could capture the "imperishable pathos" of the Acadian deportation but that Roberts "has managed to miss it with astonishing completeness":

He has no faculty for characterization, apparently no intuitions about human nature. His people are ineffective and superficial in ordinary life, and more markedly so in crises. He has at his command no clever mechanical devices by which a more serious deficiency might be concealed. His plot and paragraphs are as unsubstantial as his characters. His English is not the natural English of any period – closer, perhaps to the seventeenth-century Puritan phrase than any other; a form which does not go trippingly on the tongue of his eighteenth-century Frenchmen. The burden of the drama is borne by a purely artificial and incomparably dull pair, Grul, the idiot, and La Garne, the Black Abbé ... They are perfect bogies, and unless he can shake off their fascination, it will prove fatal to his aspirations as a novelist. (167)

The critic goes on to discuss Harrison's novel, admitting that he was prepared to find in it all the same deficiencies. And he was confirmed in his suspicions by the first page, which describes the northern Canadian landscape in predictable and not necessarily apt images from classical Greek mythology. But his doubt quickly changed to admiration as he recognized "work done from the life by a keen, truthful observer with a hand surprisingly bold, yet sincerely sympathetic." He describes Magloire as a "type of the Americanized Canuck ... drawn to the life with a frankness no more cruel than he deserves." Further,

Besides the Carons, there are half-a-dozen types vigorously sketched without exaggeration or sentimentality, and with no notion of working them up to an utterly false conception of a picturesqueness inherent in their race and condition. The picturesqueness of the *Canadien* is largely imaginary, but nobody who meets a humble *habitant* bearing the name of a seventeenth-century gentleman of France can help surrounding him with the atmosphere of romance ... In the make-up of her novel, Mrs. Harrison betrays inexperience. The passages of the Caron family history are cold interpolations; some of the conversations wander unduly, and the catastrophe at the Manoir is too full of sound and confusion. But these defects should be easily overcome by a writer who can give us a book so very much alive. (167)

While the reviewer sees the weaknesses in the novel, he feels that Harrison does have a talent for characterization and that she resists the temptation to sentimentalize and idealize. He does not apprehend the larger thematic aspects of the novel, discussed here, which would have been harder for an American to recognize.

The book was well received at home as well. The nationalistic Robert Barr, writing for the *Canadian Magazine*, described it as a "work of genius ... superb in character drawing, noble in diction, thrilling in incident." He makes the additional perceptive point that it "dispenses with conventional love-making without losing an atom of interest" and that it does not have a heroine.[41]

After the publication of *The Forest of Bourg-Marie* Frances Harrison herself struggled heroically to continue a literary career. She wrote for the *Mail*, "obtaining marked commendation from Mr. Charles Belford," and for the *Globe*.[42] She contributed short stories and articles to numerous Canadian and foreign periodicals, to the extent that, by 1912, she had published in the *Strand*, *Pall Mall Magazine*, *Temple Bar*, *Atlantic Monthly*, *Cosmopolitan*, *New England Magazine*, *Canadian Courier*, and *Saturday Night*.[43]

She was described by the London *Spectator*, in what was meant to be sincere praise, as a "Canadian Longfellow," and by the *Saturday Review* as a "deep-hearted patriot whose series of songs are veritable caskets of precious New World conceits."[44] In a letter written in 1904 she declares her desire to have journalistic work so she can "move about a little more" – travel.[45] The remarkable variety of her journalism also pays tribute to a lively, curious, intelligent, but also practical character, a woman able to contribute to the family income as well as move in the more rarefied spheres of music and poetry. One finds in journals like the *Week* and *Massey's* articles by Seranus on such diverse subjects as "Flaubert's Salammbo," "Rembrandt House" (an art gallery), "Statue of Dr. Ryerson," "An Educationist in Music" (Dr Edward Fisher, principal of the Toronto Conservatory of Music), "The Chopin Centenary," and "William Dean Howells" – all titles that reflect her interests but that in their well-researched backgrounds and lively

commentaries reveal an author with an ability to impart her enthu-
siasms to others. She became principal of the Rosedale branch of the
Toronto Conservatory of Music for twenty years, and contributed to
the *Conservatory Quarterly*.[46]

Harrison also occasionally translated French poetry, including that
of Théophile Gautier, into English for the journals. She brought out
a little book of her own poetry in 1912, a twenty-page volume titled
In Northern Skies, and Other Poems: By Seranus. In recognition of all
these activities, Henry Morgan included her biography in his prestigious *The Canadian Men and Women of the Time* (1912).[47]

In 1914 Harrison published her second novel. *Ringfield* came out
simultaneously in New York from Hodder and Stoughton and in
Toronto from the Musson Company. In *Ringfield* Harrison returns to
the Quebec forest, though it is less isolated, dense, and mythic than
that found in *The Forest of Bourg-Marie*. In this novel there are once
again forces of change emanating from outside Quebec, this time the
spectre of industrialization, which creeps up, as did Magloire in the
earlier novel, from the United States. There are also strong images of
decay, emanating from the old Clairville manor and manifest in the
moral decline of most of the novel's characters, including its hero, the
Methodist minister Joshua Ringfield, and its heroine, Pauline Clairville. If Harrison's first novel may be described as legend or folk-tale,
her second and last novel more properly belongs to the category of
tragedy. The unhappy outcome is anticipated effectively in the opening
pages, in which the dark, cold water of the St Ignace River and Falls
is described. The last, tragic action of the novel will take place at the
same falls, providing a satisfying structural unity to the novel.

The influences of industrialization, and the accompanying forces of
cultural change, are apparent at the beginning of the novel, when the
reader is introduced to the local St Ignace hotel and mill owner Poussette, who has learned American "go ahead" from friends of his who
have gone off to the United States. As the novel opens he is trying
to convince a young Methodist minister, Ringfield, to remain in St
Ignace and become the rector of the Methodist church he is building.
Poussette freely admits that he is building a Protestant church because
he wishes a divorce from his wife and can only obtain it by embracing
a faith that can accommodate the dissolution of marriage. Poussette's
language is laced with irreverent oaths and Americanisms; there is
whisky on his breath, and he later reveals his vulnerability to the
fairer sex. While Poussette is as much a comic character as a villain,
given to genuine efforts of reform and then very human lapses into
wine, women, and song, the general malaise that overtakes the central
characters in the novel emanates from his hotel. It is Poussette who

convinces Ringfield to come to St Ignace, initiating the fatal relationship with Pauline Clairville that is at the novel's core.

At the outset of the novel Ringfield is a paragon of virtue and innocence, born and raised in the Maritimes and completing his theological studies in Toronto. He originally has no intention of taking the St Ignace church, but fate, in the shape of a Hardyesque misdirected letter, intervenes, and he finds he has no option but to do so. He is also attracted to the position because he feels that Poussette is not a bad fellow and may be reformed, and by his attraction to Pauline Clairville, a beautiful and mysterious woman who lives at Clairville Manor.

Ringfield's attraction to Pauline will lead to his downfall. Never having experienced love for a woman before, he becomes passionately obsessed with Pauline, who is much more experienced in the ways of the world. Educated at a Protestant school, she is not a captive of the precepts of the Catholic faith of her ancestors. The last, with her idiot brother, Henry, of the proud, aristocratic line of Clairville, she has taken a job on the stage in Montreal to support her brother and a mysterious child, Angèle, also mentally handicapped. By the time Ringfield discovers that Pauline is an actress, he is too far gone in passion to eschew a woman involved in a profession that is anathema to his church. Ringfield justifies his relationship with Pauline by convincing himself that she has no recourse but to perform on the stage because she must support dependents and therefore can be excused. Similarly, when he discovers that in the past Pauline has had a relationship of some kind with Crabbe, an Oxford man turned St Ignace guide and drunkard, Ringfield overlooks the details of the situation to put Pauline in the best possible light. Even a terrible intimation of Pauline's possible character, his first glimpse of the large-headed Angèle, whose face bears a remarkable resemblance to Pauline's, does not deter him from ardently pursuing the woman he loves.

Pauline, it turns out, is desired and pursued in various ways by most of the men of St Ignace. These include Poussette, Crabbe, and the curé in addition to Ringfield. As the novel unfolds it becomes clear that Pauline does not have much of a theatre career left. Her temper has made her an unreliable actress. So she is not impervious to the ardently expressed love of the innocent minister, as unlikely as their relationship may be. Like Poussette, Pauline is a sympathetic character, although flawed. The reader is made to feel her very limited options as a woman with dependents, and her frustration at her situation. She has learned to use her feminine qualities to her advantage and at this point in her life will choose for her husband the man who can best offer her a better life. When Ringfield declares his love, in a very passionate scene, she promises herself to him.

However, once again fate steps in and influences the young minister's life. Crabbe sends some poems to a British journal, which publishes them. On the night of a theatrical entertainment at Poussette's, where Pauline has been living since her brother contracted a serious infectious illness, Crabbe appears, dressed as in his Oxford days. He explains to Pauline that his name has been recognized in the English journal by his family's lawyers and his address traced by them to inform him of a large inheritance. He asks Pauline to accompany him back to England to live as a lady and as his wife. Pauline instantly agrees, totally forgetting Ringfield.

Ringfield's jealousy of the Englishman Crabbe grows to be as gargantuan as his obsessive love for Pauline. He follows Crabbe to Montreal, where he has gone to arrange a marriage licence, and plots to make him return to drink, which Crabbe had given up on hearing of his inheritance and winning Pauline. The image of the formerly innocent and fine young minister stealthily tracking Crabbe down in his Montreal hotel and leaving him with the liquor, knowing he will not be able to resist it, is a dramatic one.

Crabbe recovers from his Montreal debauch and returns to St Ignace in time to take Pauline away. However, the story ends in a violent scene at the St Ignace Falls. Here Crabbe informs Ringfield that, contrary to Ringfield's belief, Angèle is not his child with Pauline but her brother Henry's with a servant. Ringfield, angered at Crabbe's proprietary knowledge of Pauline's life, violently pushes him away; the result is Crabbe's accidental death. The scene at the waterfall is well done, Crabbe being lured (unintentionally) over the footbridge across the falls to bid Ringfield farewell by the sight of Ringfield's red carpetbag. The red carpetbag in the snow is a vivid emblem of the hatred and jealousy that have overcome the minister, of his total resignation of faith to passion, of the utter moral deterioration that has accompanied his love for Pauline.

At the end of *Ringfield* Crabbe is dead, Pauline is an invalid at Clairville Manor,[48] Ringfield has gone to live with a Catholic religious order, and Poussette lives happily with an actress friend of Pauline, his wife having joined a nursing order in Montreal.

Ringfield contains a subtext, heightened by symbolism and melodrama, that dramatizes the moral degeneracy that derives from Poussette's turning his back on his traditional faith and family and embracing the "good life" and comforts emanating from south of the border. It is Poussette who brings Ringfield to St Ignace, and it is in his American hotel that Ringfield woos Pauline, occasionally visiting her room. Crabbe is employed by Poussette, and they drink together. Poussette originally wishes to marry Pauline, triggering Ringfield's jealousy, but when she becomes engaged to Crabbe, he willingly substitutes an actress friend of hers who has come to stay with Pauline in his hotel.

The hotel is the setting of theatrical entertainments that Ringfield should condemn but participates in. Its primary purpose is to provide accommodation to visitors to St Ignace, mostly American. Harrison is at the vanguard of writers like Thomas Chandler Haliburton and Hugh MacLennan who portray the effects of American and English Canadian influence on Quebec, the breaking down of the traditional French Canadian way of life to make way for a cultural amalgam. Such an amalgam did not, it would seem, appear to Harrison a particularly felicitous one.

Ringfield is also a novel that explores the dark side of male-female relations, particularly passion and obsession in a demi-world of decadence. As Poussette, prey to money-getting and external cultural influence, betrays his church and family, so does Ringfield, in a sense in Poussette's employ, become obsessed with the fatal Pauline, confronting the sexuality he has been taught by his church to avoid. Pauline's home is an emblem of the dark passions that will overwhelm Ringfield. Described in gothic terms of isolation, darkness, and decay, and inhabited by a madman, it is an apt image of decadence. A splendid white peacock that struts in the grounds of the old estate and that fascinates Ringfield becomes an image of his sexual obsession with the beautiful, dark, and tempestuous Pauline. While Ringfield's physical relationship with Pauline does not go beyond a kiss, the toll the relationship takes on his religious principles, the extent to which thoughts of her supplant those of religion, the jealous scenes in which he observes other men desiring her, and the desperate measures he resorts to to keep her, all spell a dramatic sexual obsession. Harrison has used the exotic and distinctive "other" world of Quebec to delineate the dark world of sexuality, a topic not easily or politely discussed in Canadian fiction in her day, particularly by women authors. The crumbling manor house, the haughty white peacock, and the dark, pounding falls all mirror the passions that churn, scarcely contained, beneath the proper surface of the novel.

Ringfield, like *The Forest of Bourg-Marie*, found favour with the critics. A reviewer for the *Bookman* (London), who unfortunately had the gender of the author of the novel wrong, noted:

In his description of the hamlet of St. Ignace the author of "Ringfield" gives quite the best picture we have seen of one of these primitive lower Canadian settlements, and his characterization of local types is done with an uncommonly sure touch, whether he is depicting the prolific Tremblays, with their families of eighteen or twenty-four, or Monsieur Amable Poussette, owner of the local sawmill and proprietor of the summer hotel, "in clothes, opinions, and religious belief a curious medley of American and Canadian standards."[49]

After describing the plot of the novel, the reviewer concluded that "*Ringfield* is a strong novel told with unusual skill and sincerity."

Harrison was hurt and angered when a critical study of the literature of Montreal published in 1916 in *Saturday Night* by E.J. Hathaway did not make mention of her pioneering work in this field. She wrote to Hathaway making a case for her inclusion in the article, observing that "both in poetry and fiction and in many *many* articles I have been picturing French Canada now for a good many years and I can assure you, if you choose to consult our most eminent critics and others interested in our entire literature, they will, in their turn, say a good word for me."[50] One surmises that Hathaway may have justified his exclusion of her work on the basis of his inability to recognize specific Montreal sites, or of her writing's not being realistic enough, for a second letter from Harrison to Hathaway, laced with a scarcely contained anger, itemizes different settings in *Ringfield* that qualify for inclusion:

You will find in Chapter V page 38, an attempt to describe the home of the *Cercle Littéraire*, taken from life some years ago, a little bit satirized, perhaps, but only enough for purposes of fiction. The "back street in the purely French quarter of Montreal" was, I suppose, not sufficiently intwined with the plot for you to read about it, but there the building and the characterization of the particular French-Canadian literary circle and afterwards the Théâtre des Nouveautés are drawn from actual knowledge as I know them both. It makes three good pages I think. In Chapter 24, page 235, you will also find the third-class French hotel depicted, with some degree of fidelity and in Chapter 25, page 248, there is allusion to the peculiarly French chaps on the Rue Notre Dame ... I am a realist, a modern of the moderns. My Montreal is not the easy historical one of some writers. You are quite right, it is a splendid field of fiction and I have long hoped to make more use of it, but Canada always wants to be written up as such a splendid country, etc. I see other things of the people.[51]

One senses that by 1916 Harrison was feeling out of tune with the younger world, and somewhat bitter that her work was not recognized as it might be.

During the next decade, Harrison's literary accomplishment declined. Besides *Ringfield*, she wrote and published poetry, but the vitality of the earlier years is no longer there. Nevertheless, she was anthologized in John W. Garvin's important collection *Canadian Poets* (1916), where nine short lyrics appeared.[52] She herself paid for the publication in 1925 of *Songs of Love and Labor*, issued as "By Seranus." Another little volume, *Penelope and Other Poems*, "By Seranus," is undated.

The late 1920s and the 1930s were marred for Harrison, by now in her seventies, by illness and death. A visit in 1929 to her son, who worked in the insurance business in Winnipeg, was followed in 1932 by his death.[53] She must have been pleased, however, that the Insurance Institute of Winnipeg established a prize in his name. That year too Professor Harrison had "an attack" and could not talk for a day. Finances must have been straitened, for Frances tells Lorne Pierce in a letter in 1928 that she cannot pay for the publication of a small volume of her poems, as "Professor Harrison and I have a very slender competence indeed and even out of that have to support several dependents."[54] The sixteen-page volume consequently came out in 1928 under the Ryerson imprint; it was entitled *Later Poems and New Villanelles*.

No doubt the advent of modernism in the 1920s did little for Harrison's reputation among the more serious and younger literary figures of the day, although a biographical appreciation that appeared in the *Canadian Bookman* in 1933 must have provided some compensation. Marjory Willison in that article commends Harrison's verse for its "vigor, color, firmness of outline, skill in technic and ... original freshness of conception" and claims for her short stories "a certain ironical detachment, a robustness of intelligence, sharp drama, no sentimentality, passionate feeling, and the gift for portraying portentous scenes and terrifying characters which bears a not unjust comparison with the work of Poe."[55]

In spite of illness and age Harrison kept up some literary activity to the end of her life. In 1933 she published at her own expense an eighteen-page collection, *Four Ballads and a Play*. Marjory Willison in her 1933 article notes that Harrison has a "number of unpublished manuscripts in her possession"; these are referred to as well in the Lorne Pierce Collection at Queen's, but they are not known today. Harrison's letters to Lorne Pierce, editor of the Ryerson Press, in the late 1920s and early 1930s, propose various publication projects, including a life of Marie de l'Incarnation, a collection of short stories, and collections of poetry.[56] She recommends her granddaughter, Nancy Lord, a student at the College of Art and Central Technical School in Toronto, for illustration work to Pierce as well. A period of three years follows her last letter to him, in 1932, and her death in 1935 at the age of seventy-six.

While many details of Harrison's life are lacking, there are clues in what material we do have to her character. The first impression one has is of her enormous energy and enthusiasm for music and literature, and the remarkable diversity of her talents and activities. Harrison was an accomplished musician, composer, authority on French Canadian folk music, poet, novelist, editor, and music and literary critic. There is evidence that she responded to the spirit of the day not only in her writing and musical achievements, already noted, but also in the sphere of travel.

No doubt she received impetus from the exciting period in which she lived, in which her generation actively and optimistically searched for a Canadian literature, a Canadian culture, and a Canadian national character. She would have been supported too by the spirit of the times for women, a period in which the "leading edge" of women received a higher education, engaged in independent travel, and worked beyond the home. Although it may not be quite accurate to describe Harrison as a "New Woman" – she does not appear to have advocated actively the women's cause – there can be no doubt from her writing, editing, reviewing, and performing that she pursued her work seriously.

A further feature of Harrison's character is her support of fellow women writers. While she did not necessarily seek out or favour them, writing on men as well as women, she recognized the talents of and praised women when she had the opportunity. An early example of this is a two-column article on Isabella Valancy Crawford published in the *Week* in 1887, shortly after the poet's death.[57] In it she ranks Crawford's poetry with that of the best English and American poets. A letter from Elsie Pomeroy, who wrote the first biography of Charles G.D. Roberts[58] and was active in the literary life of Toronto in the 1930s, to Lorne Pierce in 1939 informs him that one of her most prized possessions, recently acquired, is an autobiographical sketch that Crawford wrote for Harrison.[59] In her 1887 review of Clarence Stedman's *Victorian Poets* Harrison gives considerable space to Stedman's praise of the poetry of Elizabeth Barrett Browning and notes that Stedman suggests that other women could be as fine poets if given a classical education.[60] The Lorne Pierce papers at Queen's contain a "Birthday Book" presented to Marshall Saunders on the occasion of her seventieth birthday, on 13 April 1931, at a party attended by the Toronto literary community in the Royal York Hotel. The Birthday Book includes a poem by Seranus that celebrates Saunders' achievements.[61]

Another facet of Harrison's character, one shared by many Canadians of her day, was her pride in Canada. One of her earliest books was *The Canadian Birthday Book* (1887), and her earliest stories, collected in *Crowded Out* (1888), have for the most part Canadian, and more particularly Quebec settings.

Quebec is also an important source of imaginative inspiration in Harrison's novels, and her poetry celebrates French Canadian settings, characters, activities, and forms. One senses that Quebec and its images provide for her an opportunity to identify and examine an indigenous Canadian culture and character, one that is dramatically distinct from the English and American traditions and in which she takes great pride. She used the landscape, folk, and culture of rural Quebec to create a distinctive national voice in her fiction, one that she hoped would find its place in the larger international literary community. There is no doubt that Harrison simply loved the lively and colourful Quebec folk tradition. It is true that she tended to idealize this culture and resisted looking beyond the stereotype, but her reason for doing so is valid – to find a distinct Canadian "type," even a "myth," to present to the world.

For all that Harrison celebrated Canada in her writing, she also sought recognition beyond her country, claiming, one suspects, not only a place for herself but also for Canada in international literary circles. Her letters to Clarence Stedman, preserved at Columbia University, while not as sycophantic as those of Charles G.D. Roberts and some other Canadians, reveal her attempts to break into the New York literary scene through introductions to other writers, and by offering a program of readings from her poetry and lecturing on French Canadian music to whatever groups might wish to hear her.[62] Her early story "Crowded Out" reveals the frustrations of an artist trying to make a name for himself in a large, impersonal city.

Although Harrison published in periodicals abroad and her novels were published in London, *The Forest of Bourg-Marie* with Arnold and *Ringfield* with Hodder and Stoughton, she never gained a strong reputation abroad, perhaps because of her distinctly Canadian settings and concerns.

She populated her fiction too with themes that she felt were important in Canada, particularly those of identity, of the artist, and of the dangers of cultural dominance, at first from England and later from the United States. Her work is often characterized by contrived and melodramatic plots, used to heighten a subtext of mythological meaning that gives her work unity and makes it significant within the canon of the literature of the developing nation.

Margaret Marshall Saunders: A Voice for the Silent

ELIZABETH WATERSTON

Marshall Saunders lingers, half-remembered, as the author of *Beautiful Joe*. This story of a dog, written for children and published in 1894 by the American Baptist Publication Society, was the first Canadian book to become a world bestseller, the first to sell over a million copies, and the first to achieve multiple translation: in eighteen languages it carried the views and values of this Nova Scotia woman to an incredibly wide audience. Like all children's books, this novel reveals by indirection the adult tensions, assumptions, and conventions of the author and her times.

Marshall Saunders wrote nine other books with animal protagonists – *Golden Dicky the Canary*, *Bonnie Prince Fetlar the Shetland Pony*, *Jimmy Gold-Coast the Monkey*, *Pussy Black-Face* – and the list goes on to cover a whole menagerie. The string suggests sentimentality, cuteness, and maybe an obsessive substitution of animal concerns for human ones. But lovers of *The Wind in the Willows* and *Charlotte's Web* have theorized about the deep value for children of books that cater to the child's identification with animal life; Marshall Saunders at her best helps us to understand more accurately the way animal stories work not only for children but also for a grown-up audience.

In five other novels by Marshall Saunders animals appear, but interest centres on the children who look after them. A book like *Princess Sukey: The Story of a Pigeon and Her Human Friends* deserves to be considered not as an animal story but as a novel in the central stream of children's literature. Such a book, like *Alice in Wonderland* or *The Adventures of Tom Sawyer*, deserves critical attention as a form of romance, a mythical adventure that releases fears and desires in young readers and facilitates sublimation of troubling emotion. Reading such books is for children a form of vicarious initiation into modes of behaviour acceptable in the adult world. Again there is an adult audience for this kind of book – the huge audience of grown-ups who will read stories to children even when other literary adventures are no longer a part of their imaginative lives.

For adult readers of a more critical bent, examination of children's books such as Saunders' can restore memories of the powerful emotions they themselves felt during that initiation period. Marshall Saunders, like many of the other important writers of children's books – Louisa May Alcott, Lewis Carroll, J.B. Tolkien – knew best the child she herself had been. Her novels, like theirs, successfully catch some of the real turbulence of a remembered childhood.

The turbulence came partly from Margaret Marshall Saunders' passionate commitment to causes. Animal rights inflamed her imagination when she wrote *Beautiful Joe*. In her books about city children she reveals other commitments – to abolition of child labour, to slum clearance, to enlargement of playground facilities, to vegetarianism. These commitments also shine through many of her novels of a third kind: adult romances. In such a book as *The Girl from Vermont*, animals and children barely appear. The young teacher from Vermont operates as a force for social change as well as playing out an unusual role in a courtship story. In this book and in eight other adult romances Saunders draws puzzling sketches of strong-minded women trying to breach the conventions of propriety so as to allow for the urgent desire to effect social change.

Many of Saunders' novels – both animal stories and "social-problem fiction" – are set in the United States rather than in her native Canada. The choice reflects her sharp interest in sales and in copyright. Her publishing history constitutes another claim on our interest.

Here then is an author of animal stories, of children's books, of problem novels, a cosmopolitan Canadian recognized in her own time with honorary degrees and a CBE as well as by huge world-wide sales. Since her death her work in both genres – adult romance and children's stories – has been bypassed by serious Canadian critics. Yet searchers for signs of Canadian identity, tracers of Canadian intellectual history might well pause to peruse the works and consider the life of this odd, opinionated, compassionate woman.

Childhood experience made Saunders aware of the complexity of her native province, Nova Scotia. Near the Atlantic coast, in Milton, one of the villages based on shipbuilding and maritime commerce, lived her mother's people, the Freemans, West Indies merchants. Here Margaret Marshall Saunders was born, in 1861, while her parents were visiting in the big family home. But her father came from farmland, from the Annapolis Valley on the Bay of Fundy side of the province, and Marshall Saunders spent her early years in this pretty agricultural area, once part of French Acadian settlement. Her father was the Baptist pastor of a church in the small town of Berwick. The Saunders family moved from this pleasant countryside to Halifax in 1867; here the little girl adapted to the city environment of a historic fortress and naval centre.

Margaret was the second child in a family of six. Over and over again she would tell stories of large families, and some of the tensions as well as some of the joys of a sibling community appearing in these stories presumably reflect her own first memories. At the fringes of Saunders family life was an awareness of two other groups of people, the Acadians of north-shore Nova Scotia and the Micmac Indians, each with its own history and legends. Another presence in the Saunders family circle, again characteristic of Nova Scotia, was Ellen, a black woman who helped with housework and provided a fund of negro spirituals, to be quoted often in Saunders' novels. Finally, home life included a tumble of animals – dogs, cats, pigeons, rabbits, horses, a goat – very dear to all members of the family.

The Reverend Edward Manning Saunders was his daughter's first teacher. A studious man of German derivation, he received a bachelor of arts degree from Acadia when he was nineteen and finished a master of arts degree there in 1863, when he was already hard at work as pastor, father of a young family, and part-time farmer. He began teaching his little daughter Latin before she was six; he encouraged all the children to read. In a reminiscence written forty years later Marshall Saunders particularly remembered a set of Walter Scott's novels, in yellow paperback, brought by her father from an 1870 trip to Edinburgh with his friend Dr Theodore Harding Rand.[1]

To Edinburgh the fifteen-year-old "Maggie" Saunders was sent, for boarding-school training in conversational French and German as well as in standard subjects such as history and English literature. The diary she kept during 1876 and her letters home reveal a dutiful determination to study hard and do well at lessons, but show no special self-confidence or literary ambition.[2] Both diary and letters show a devastating homesickness. The teen-aged girl writes to her mother, "Sometimes I get in a perfect agony thinking of you, and it seems to me that my heart will break ... I cry all the time when it does not interfere with my lessons ... I do not believe a child ever loved her mother as much as I love you."[3] In another letter she says that if they would only let her come home, "I would be willing to sleep with the rabbits [there were sixty of them] in the loft of the carriage house."[4]

The diary records daily life at Miss Deuchar's school; it lingers over the pleasure of walking Miss Deuchar's little dog Prince, and shudders at the excitement of a break-in next door to the school – "the thieves got in by the attic and destroyed a great deal. Nearly every house in this neighbourhood has been visited by thieves during the past summer and autumn."[5]

Young Maggie Saunders made friends with several Scottish families in Edinburgh, including the Blaikies, a family well connected with religious, educational, and literary groups. After the school year was up she went with the Blaikies' daughter to Orléans, for a year in a French pension to work on her languages. Then, her formal education apparently finished, she went home to Halifax.

Among the Scottish writers most admired at this time was George Macdonald, author of *At the Back of the North Wind* (1871) and *The Princess and the Goblin* (1872). Saunders records feeling "quite breathless" when she heard an Edinburgh friend remark casually to his wife, "George Macdonald writes that he cannot come to see us now."[6] The allusion reminds us of the popularity of books for children at this time and the respectful acceptance of their didactic powers. Anna Sewell published *Black Beauty* to great acclaim in the year that Saunders was in Edinburgh (1877). Like Macdonald's *At the Back of the North Wind*, this story about a gentle horse uses animal adventures to purvey moral lessons, and in both cases the animals are imagined as offering warmth and admiration to human friends. Macdonald and Sewell would be among Saunders' most important models when she herself became a writer.

For the next eight years of her life there is little direct record of her doings. Between the ages of seventeen and twenty-four she lived at home, taught school, helped with housework, and supported her energetic mother in good causes – such as a campaign to prevent baby-farming in Halifax. While she was away her father had published his first brief book, a *History of the Granville Street Baptist Church* (1877). In 1882 he gave up his ministry in order to become a full-time writer and editor, proprietor of the *Christian Visitor* and author of religious biography and histories. Perhaps the presence of a working writer in the house set a model for his daughter. She was not of course considered qualified to do any "serious" writing, but her father's friend Dr Theodore Rand urged her to try her hand at literary work – to "describe a bit of woodland ... the track of a rabbit in the snow."[7] By the time Dr Rand left for Toronto in 1885 (he eventually became chancellor of McMaster University) his young friend was launching herself into writing – although for the time being she avoided rabbits and aimed at more robust stuff.

An anecdote tells what it took for a young woman to set out on "an author's life": "For three weeks sister Rida did the house-keeping, and I scribbled."[8] The sisters did not show the results to "our hero, Dr. Rand," but they sent off the manuscript of a blood-curdling story, set in Spain and titled "A Gag of Blessed Memory," to *Frank Leslie's Magazine*, "and to our mingled delight and amazement a cheque for forty dollars came flying back from New York." *Leslie's* rejected a follow-up story, but *Godey's* published it in 1886 and paid twenty-five dollars for it. Egged on by Rida, and supported tolerantly by the rest of the family, Saunders expanded her efforts, and in 1887 completed a novelette, which she titled *My Spanish Sailor*.

In attempting a shipboard story Saunders was following one of the popular modes of her day. Best-selling books, including Robert Louis Stevenson's *Treasure Island* (1884) and *Kidnapped* (1886), were set largely aboard ship, while Mark Twain's *Huckleberry Finn* (1885) and Rider Haggard's *King Solomon's Mines* (1886) added to the interest in adventurous travel. Saunders made a brave effort to utilize her own travel experience, while modelling her heroine on the sprightly young women in novels by Henry James and W.D. Howells.

In Saunders' tale names, settings, and plot twine a provincial girl's thin experience into the rich romance of myth. The heroine, Nina, lives near a bridge in "Rubicon Meadows," Nova Scotia, and seems ready, as the story begins, to cross into maturity. Raised by a local couple, she has come to suspect that they are in fact foster-parents only. There is a third adult in Nina's life – the Spanish Esteban, a ship's captain who has visited her intermittently over the years and acted as director and adviser in her education. He is middle-aged, self-controlled, and solemn: Nina calls him "Mr Owl" and "Dear Monster." Unexpectedly, Captain Esteban announces his determination to marry his young protégé and take her with him aboard his ship to England. A bargain is struck: the marriage will be in form only, to turn into a real marriage whenever Nina chooses.

The story of Nina's dread of accepting the "Monster" as a husband is a strained and skittish reworking of the old stories "Beauty and the Beast" and "The Princess and the Frog." Like those fairy-tales it tells of the slow acceptance of worth, hidden beneath a menacing or ugly appearance.[9] But the little red cape that is part of Nina's trousseau carries the implication that, like Red Riding Hood, the young woman may find her "Monster" not really a gentle prince in disguise but a devouring wolf. Nina enjoys shipboard life – an opulent cabin, a place at the captain's table, and a rich variety of new friendships – all the while craftily holding the captain at bay. "Fold your arms," she says firmly. "I don't want them twining around me like the tentacles of an octopus."[10]

No doubt Saunders' memory of her trip to Scotland furnished details of the elegance and comfort of a steamer, and also the sense of frightening confinement. But the crimson furniture of the dining-saloon, the white berths and red couch of Nina's cabin, the ruby-red curtains and rose-shaded lamps of the captain's bridge, all become parts of an effective symbolic setting for the drama of reluctance to accept passionate marriage.[11] An undercurrent of real fear of sexuality runs through this section of the story.

Once ashore in England, Nina comes under the care of a kindly shipboard acquaintance, Lady Forrest. (Variants of this name will recur throughout Saunders' novels.) As a New World libertarian, Nina takes fiery and funny exception to the condescension of the aristocratic British and their snobbish patronage of Captain Esteban. The mystery of Nina's real parentage emerges as a major plot thread: her long-lost, wily, attractive father turns up in the person of a con-man bearing the name of Stenner (a name that will also recur, in variants, in later novels). Nina is able to reject his meretricious charm.

The ending is idyllic: Nina returns to Esteban, who fits out a little cabin boudoir on his ship, in blue satin, with "a cast of the Milo Venus, behind not a red drapery like the one in the Louvre, but a blue velvet one to match the room." What a nice late Victorian touch of titillation combined with prettiness and propriety! The final dialogue of the reunited couple has an arch and innocent charm. A family tradition held that Marshall Saunders had two "loves" – a Scottish friend, and her cousin Reginald.[12] To judge from the treatment of Nina's love scenes, neither of the author's experiences progressed beyond the realm of dreams.

A Cinderella ending thus concludes a plot that has invoked many archetypes of terror: the Whale, the Beast, the Wolf. Similar powerful archetypes appear in the work of many women writers: frightening dreams tamed into a sentimental mélange, a standard romance of initiation. Saunders also reveals some personal obsessions: the sense of being rejected by parents; the attraction of an older, serious man; the presence of thieves and con-men even in respectable circles; and the value of the natural manners of people in the New World, compared to European sophistication. There is no trace at all of what would become her other major themes: the lives of animals or children, or the need for social reform.

When the novel was finished, the young author's family arranged for her to return to Scotland and France; she visited old friends from school days and came back under the chaperonage of Sir Charles Tupper, a Nova Scotia politician who was at that time Canada's high commissioner to Great Britain. She had needed the refreshment of the trip: her nerves were strained with the combined efforts of teaching, writing, helping her mother with Sunday school, visiting the poor and the sick, and meeting all the other calls a Baptist conscience imposed. At this time too the family suffered the loss of seventeen-year-old Laura – a first blow to a close family circle.

John Blaikie of Edinburgh, who had published with Longman's of London a book on geometry, found a publisher for Margaret Marshall Saunders' first novel. Ward and Downey of London brought out *My Spanish Sailor* in 1889. It was reviewed kindly in the Edinburgh *Scotsman*, thanks also perhaps to the influence of the Blaikies, the Cruikshanks, and other Edinburgh friends. The author's name appeared on the title-page as "Marshall Saunders": the schoolgirl "Maggie" had been replaced by a de-feminized novelist.[13]

In the winter of 1889–90 Saunders took some courses at Dalhousie University, which had been accepting women students since 1881. She was trying to upgrade her qualifications as a teacher, for many years her back-up profession in the precarious life of a freelance writer. In the late 1880s and early 1890s she sold short stories to *Our Home*, the *Union Signal, Dumb Animals*, and the *Writer*, all accessible, respectable magazines flourishing in a magazine-hungry era.[14]

Several of these stories were collected and republished by Banes of Philadelphia in 1896, under the title *For the Other Boy's Sake*. They show the author's apprenticeship in the mode that would bring her world-wide popularity when *Beautiful Joe* appeared (1894). In "Poor Jersey City," for instance, the spotlight is on a dog, a runaway bull terrier, star trick-dog who has "skedaddled" from the circus. After incredible adventures, Jersey City finally settles on a farm "on the shores of the beautiful Bedford Basin of Halifax harbor, Nova Scotia."

"Poor Jersey City" implies that animals not only sympathize with humans but can intervene in their lives. Such intervention would remain a central feature of Marshall Saunders' animal stories. Work in this genre had been growing in popularity and complexity in the century since the pioneering John Newbery began publishing work specifically for children. Saunders' earliest animal stories are indistinguishable from the mass of popular work of her own period, a time when animal stories were beginning to expand into book-length form, as in Louise de la Ramée's *A Dog of Flanders* (1872) and Anna Sewell's *Black Beauty* (1877).

Others of Saunders' magazine stories show a second developing interest. In "Jessie's Debt" and "Proud Tommie," both about little girls suspected of theft, in "Her Excellency's Jewels," about a little gypsy girl who thwarts a theft, and in "For the Other Boy's Sake," about a young Irish maid accused of stealing by her rich old employer, there is a curious emphasis on crime. Perhaps it was triggered by memory of the excitement aroused in her schooldays when thieves broke into the house next door to the school.

Third, into these apprentice stories Saunders introduces national and regional colour. "When He Was a Boy" presents an idyllic Christian childhood in a German-speaking community. Fritz and his cousin Emma, Aunt Lotta and the others perhaps reflect memories of the German connections in Mr Saunders' family. "The Two Kaloosas" introduces Micmac Indians: the first Kaloosa lived in happy days before white men took over the Micmac lands; the second Kaloosa, present-day abandoned child of a drunken mother, is separated from her by social workers. In her recognition of the plight of the contemporary Canadian Indian, caught in a cultural transition, Saunders parallels such a poem as D.C. Scott's "Onandago Madonna" (1893, republished in Boston in 1898 in *Labor and the Angel*).

Happier child life appears in "Ten Little Indians," which introduces specific details from scenes along the Saint John River in New Brunswick. Ernest Thompson Seton's *Two Little Savages* (1903) perhaps picked up some ideas from this short story. In it, ten-year-old boys, little brothers of men who have formed an "Indian Club," go in three boats, the Orimocto, the Jinseg, and the Canawita. (This third name, Canawita, will recur throughout Saunders' works, always signalling Indian values.) The boats move from Fredericton to Lower Gagetown, past hay islands, potato farms, a horse ferry. Far from being a disadvantage in reaching an American audience, the local details about Canadian regions fit into a general interest in local-colour stories. American bestseller lists of the 1890s were dominated by stories about Indiana "Hoosier" country, Kentucky backwoods, upstate Vermont, all carefully recording regional dialects, customs, and scenery. Among Canadian writers, Duncan Campbell Scott published a collection of short stories, *In the Village of Viger* (1896), that delineates life in a Quebec community, typical of the extension of local colourism to a Canadian setting. Scott's friend E.W. Thomson, as an editor since 1891 of the American magazine *Youth's Companion*, made sure that Canadian scenes were presented to young audiences as well as to adult ones. Saunders found a ready audience in the United States for the Canadian short stories collected in *For the Other Boy's Sake*.

Canadian in a different sense, as it introduces a political note, is "The Little Page." In this short story a boy in Ottawa becomes parliamentary page just before the leader of the government dies. This death and the state funeral that follows were undoubtedly suggested by the death of Sir John A. Macdonald in 1891, at a time when Saunders was visiting Ottawa. A most interesting note in the story is the cry of the little page: "I am proud that I am a Canadian boy ... When I grow up I will be a politician and work for ... my country." Saunders, of course, as a woman could not hope for direct political life. Her increasing frustration at this situation would reappear in her 1898 novel *Rose à Charlitte*.

Meanwhile, in Ottawa Saunders kept a diary (1891–92), recording her developing friendship with her brother's fiancée, a young woman from Meaford, Ontario. In Meaford Saunders heard an interesting tale about "Beautiful Joe," a big, rough-looking Airedale. She decided to expand the tale: the American Humane Education Society had offered two hundred dollars for a novel that could repeat the appeal of *Black Beauty*. That sentimental story of a mistreated horse had enjoyed renewed success since its first American edition in 1890. Saunders spent six months collecting material, submitted the story of *Beautiful Joe*, and won the prize. Her canny writer-father advised her to keep the rights rather than turn the manuscript over to the Humane Society. It was 1893 before the manuscript was finally placed with the American Baptist Publication Society of Philadelphia, to be published in 1894, with Charles H. Banes acting as editor.

Beautiful Joe begins very violently. Joe's first owner cruelly crops the puppy's ears and tail, beats his horse, mistreats an older dog, Joe's "mother," and brutally flings against a wall all the puppies in the litter except Joe. Even after Joe escapes to the kinder hands of Miss Laura and the Morris family, he is surrounded by cruelty. Animals are cruel to each other – dogs chase rats, kill pigeons, fight each other ferociously. Joe's friend Dandy, the tramp-dog, has no good qualities. But humans are not merely instinctively cruel; many are malicious, evil, merciless, and self-destroying. Such is the darker side of *Beautiful Joe* – a book that introduces young readers to a very harsh vision of life. The other side enters the book with the coming of Miss Laura (named for the Saunders sister who had recently died). Joe's devotion to Laura grows as he sees her fearlessly trying to improve the world – to stop drunkards from their folly, to add mercy to the justice meted out to criminals like Joe's first owner.

Presumably parents – who are after all the choosers of books for children – found Saunders' preaching on social problems palatable when presented in the whimsical form of a dog's "autobiography."

Perhaps the adult response to Joe stems from the subtext of universal suffering. It has also been suggested that the animal story flourished at this particular time as a form of literary avoidance of the problems of human beings. Animal suffering deflected sympathy from abused humans – child labourers, dominated non-whites, unenfranchised and intellectually undernourished women – whose exploitation posed more difficult economic and political problems.

For children, the appeal of *Beautiful Joe* is harder to explain. It is certainly easy for children to learn necessary lessons about suffering, weakness, and death from a story about animals, and adults may be right in assuming that the pain of such lessons will be less poignant than when the protagonist is a fellow human. But many children identify very strongly with animals and consider pets part of a real circle of acquaintance, often more beloved than human friends. A story of animal suffering like *Beautiful Joe* can be deeply disturbing, its fearful appeal having the dubious power of any work filled with terror and violence.

At any rate, *Beautiful Joe* came out at a propitious time. Rudyard Kipling's first *Jungle Book* appeared in the same year, 1894, and the *Second Jungle Book* in 1895. Charles G.D. Roberts was just beginning to write stories of wild animals, and his *Earth's Enigmas*, a collection of these, would appear in 1896, published in Boston by Lamson and Wolffe; Ernest Thompson Seton's first collection of realistic sketches, *Wild Animals I Have Known*, would be published by another major American firm, Scribner's of New York, in 1898.

The "realistic animal story" has been dubbed the first literary genre initiated in Canada. Most critics would exclude Saunders' work from this genre because she imputes to her animal characters a human rationality and an unrealistic power of complex communication with each other. Beautiful Joe talks to his readers and to his fellow animals. But although Saunders falsifies the capabilities of pets, including dogs, cats, monkeys, parrots, and canaries, and also of horses, cows, goats, sheep, and other domesticated non-pets, there is a documentary exactness in her detailing of their habits and needs.

Another kind of realism in *Beautiful Joe* is in the portraits of humans "as others see us" – "others" in this case being our pets. This device has a gentle didactic force: children accept Joe's vision of their own shortcomings and bad habits because it rings true.

Joe's emotions also reveal the real though hidden reactions of his creator to her life and times and society. Joe is a small, mutilated being. The woman who created him chose as her narrator a persona "cropped" by cruel owners. Her choice of persona represents the self-image of many women in this period. As the voice of conscience in a harshly utilitarian age, women felt similarly restrained and restricted. Women organized movements such as the Women's Christian Temperance Union, directed not only against alcoholism but against its attendant child and wife abuse. They worked for other social reforms also, trying to soften cruelties of the workplace, of domestic employment, and of a punitive judicial system. But Saunders, as a member of many of these reformist movements, felt the hampering of their efforts by the real powers of society – usually male.

At a deeper level, as a writer she faced the restraints of the conventional treatment of "scribbling women," as applied by the kindly, paternal editors and publishers who dominated the world of books. She had changed her writing name from Margaret to Marshall; now she took as narrator the name Joe. Interestingly, Joe – gruff, self-deprecating, loyal, impetuous – has many of the characteristics of another "Jo," the troubled protagonist of *Little Women*. Louisa May Alcott's rebellious, anti-romantic heroine glories in her boyishness, and her author has the vicarious pleasure of playing a role usually assigned to a male. The release felt by a female artist when she lets the male "animus" of her personality express itself contributes in a similar way to the force of *Beautiful Joe*.

Force it certainly had. The first American edition sold out in ten days and by 1900 had sold 625,000 copies. The Canadian edition had sold 558,000 copies by 1900, and the British 146,000 by the same date. It was a good time for a Canadian writer. American publishers were eager to find a succession of good producers of popular books and were already including many Canadians among their authors and editors. British publishers felt benign towards the imperial children – as well they might, given the enormous success of Kipling from India, Olive Schreiner from South Africa, or Gilbert Parker from Canada. Canadian publishers stood ready to profit from the national pride in local authors that was part of late imperialism. Saunders, though in some ways the most provincial of local-colour writers, had an international perspective because of her schoolgirl travels and an international connection because of her father's position in the Baptist network. Her book came opportunely into a good market and did very well indeed.

The build-up to success was slow, however. Letters to Saunders, now at Acadia University, show the problems of getting international publication, the publishers' failure to advise her on protecting her copyright, and also the pressures exerted by editors on both sides of the Atlantic. Writing from the American Baptist Publication Society, Charles Banes noted that the second half of the book "falls off badly" and that there are scientifically incorrect statements in it.[15]

He did not mention that by failing to arrange simultaneous publication in Canada or Britain his author was losing her chance at British copyright. Her Scottish friend Mr Blaikie advised her that she should revise the book and change its title in order to protect British sales against piracy. Blaikie's own publisher suggested that she change American details back to Canadian ones, cut out the chapter in which an "Englishman" played a depraved part, and omit Joe's philosophical meditations, which "spoil the 'go' of the narrative." Blaikie also advised that she request a letter of endorsation from Lady Aberdeen, wife of the governor general, and delete the letter from Hezekiel Butterworth, editor of *Youth's Companion*, that adorned the American edition.

This advice taken, the book was published by Jarrolds in London. In Canada, where it was brought out by the Standard Publishing Company owned by the Baptist Convention, it contained both Lady Aberdeen's letter and Butterworth's, plus a letter from Saunders herself, as "Superintendent, Department of Mercy, and Assistant Superintendent Loyal Temperance Legion, W.C.T.U., Halifax, Canada." "The hearts of men and women are careless and cold," says the author here: "let me appeal to the children."[16]

To profit from that appeal, and from his author's popularity, Charles Banes published two booklets, *Charles and His Lamb* and *Daisy*, in 1895 and brought out the collection mentioned above, *For the Other Boy's Sake and Other Stories*, in 1896.

Marshall Saunders now spent almost two years (1895–97) in Boston, writing, and reading at Boston University. Her next work, *The King of the Park*, shows a sharp perception of the big city, particularly its underside – back alleys where cats flee from drunken women, and boarding-houses where an orphaned boy could live for months without anyone's noticing. Such a child is the central figure in the new novel. Eugene, a little boy from France who idolizes the memory of the mighty Emperor Napoleon, develops a new bond with Police Sergeant Hardy, the gentle veteran who patrols the park on the Boston fens where all the homeless cats in Boston gravitate. Boozy, biggest of the abandoned cats, is "king of the park." He helps to unravel the plot by alerting Eugene to the perils of the boggy fen.

This charming and interesting story shows Saunders' good ear for talk – the pompous phrasing of the French boy; the funny and convincing baby talk of a little girl: "I'll ask Bridget not to forget me about it"; the comic dialect of a curé from a French village who comes to rescue Eugene from Boston; policeman Hardy's advice to Eugene: don't "get priggish."

Saunders did not find a Boston publisher for this story, nor did Banes of Philadelphia pick it up. Years later she would speak whimsically of "humbly suing" at the gates of New York at this period.[17] *The King of the Park* was finally placed with the New York firm of Crowell and Company in 1897.

She offered her next and much longer novel, *The House of Armour*, to Banes, but he felt this romance was not on a subject "legitimately belonging to our line of publications" and sent it back to her with criticisms of her phraseology, and advice to set it aside and revise very carefully – as Dickens, Longfellow, and others always did.[18] *The House of Armour* was passed along to Rowland of Philadelphia and brought out in 1897, within months of *The King of the Park*.

A modern reader would agree that the novel still needs revision. The plot repeats one motif from *My Spanish Sailor*: a daughter discovers that her father has been a destructive and cunning scoundrel. It adds a new motif that will recur in many later novels: a strange, intense relationship links a brother and sister. The names of the characters are markedly odd: the hero is Valentine Armour, the heroine Stargarde, and a newcomer from across the seas, neither hero nor heroine, is the strong-minded Vivienne de la Vigne. Their lives are as melodramatic as their names, but the dialogue is realistic and the sense of place, particularly the indoor scenes in an old Halifax house, is strong.

Saunders now attempted something more ambitious and more stylish. There had been a flurry of publications on the Acadians: Charles G.D. Roberts' *The Raid from Beauséjour* (1894) was followed by his *The Forge in the Forest* (1896); his *A Sister to Evangeline* was also completed and would appear in 1898. Saunders probably knew Roberts: he had been teaching at King's College, Windsor, from 1885 to 1896, in an area close to Acadia University, with which Saunders' father was closely connected.[19] Saunders also knew and frequently quoted from J.F. Herbin's *The Marshlands* (1893), poems describing the Acadian landscape, and *At Minas Basin* (1897), composed by her old family friend Dr T.H. Rand, who in his days with the Department of Education in Nova Scotia and New Brunswick had been a strong supporter of the Acadian revival of the 1880s. Saunders herself had grown up in Berwick, near Acadian country. In 1897 she set out from Boston to spend five months among the Acadians, gathering local colour. She set her new novel, *Rose à Charlitte*, published in 1898 by the L.C. Page Company of Boston, on the Bay of Fundy shore of Nova Scotia and dedicated it to Dr Rand, suggesting a new seriousness of intention and ambition.

Once again Saunders chooses to tell her story from the viewpoint of a male protagonist. This time, however, the voice is not that of a victim but of a man involved by heredity in the process of victimization. The Bostonian Vesper Nimmo, sadly aware of the evil part played by his ancestor in the expulsion of 1755, sets out on a quest for modern-day descendants of those Acadians. (His surname is that of a Scottish friend from Saunders' schooldays; his strange first name suggests the twilight, tentative quality of the man.)

Vesper is diverted from his quest into courtship of Rose, abandoned wife of Charlitte de Forêt. Rose and her little boy Narcisse show Vesper Acadian life. Old folks tell stories of the "dérangement" and reveal oddities of the Acadian patois – "checque choose" for "quelque chose," "le dogue" for "dog," and so on. Narcisse, a hypersensitive child, responds hysterically to his father's disappearance and later, in a strange scene at the Cave of the Bears, where Indian legends of Glooscap linger, to the presence of his mother's new suitor.

In contrast, a little Acadian girl named Bidiane attracts Vesper with her vigorous, headstrong ways. Bidiane provides the answer to his quest: she is the direct descendant of the Acadian victimized by Vesper's ancestor. Her growing up dominates the second half of the book. She becomes a fighter in the Acadian cause, working indirectly, because she is female, coaching a male cousin who runs for Parliament and rallying the other women to manoeuvre the men into voting for him.

This young woman's political activities appear unique compared to women's roles in other novels of the period. (Duncan's Advena in *The Imperialist* leaves politics to her brother.) In other ways Bidiane stirs surprised recognition. Red-haired, impulsive, and voluble, she tumbles from one scrape into another: she anticipates L.M. Montgomery's Anne. It is hard to imagine that the younger Montgomery failed to read this novel by a fellow Maritimer, writer of an enviable bestseller. When, eight years later, Montgomery finished her own novel about tempestuous, headstrong girlhood, she sent it off to L.C. Page, the Boston firm that published *Rose à Charlitte* in 1898.

Rose à Charlitte was brought out simultaneously under British copyright as *Rose of Acadie* (1898). Perhaps few readers on either side of the Atlantic who relished the sympathetic treatment of the Roman Catholic Acadians realized what an achievement this represented for a Baptist writer. Appropriately she chose the Bostonian Vesper as narrator, not only to attract American readers but also to reflect the wider perspective that her time in Boston had given her.

Clearly the Boston publishers were pleased with their new writer. L.C. Page brought out a new Marshall Saunders book every year for the next five years. The subtitle of the first of these next novels, *Deficient Saints: A Tale of Maine* (1899), promises the salty, eccentric, true-hearted stereotypes of the then-popular State-of-Maine novels. Elderly Miss Jane Castonguay satisfies these expectations, with her cropped hair, man's jacket, riding-whip, and her outspoken opinions. Miss Jane acts as adviser to two young women: Chelda, who wants to deflect her fiancé from accepting a missionary post in an Indian settlement; and Derrice, the bride (like Nina in *My Spanish Sailor*) of a judicial older man. Beautiful Derrice (again like Nina) discovers that her father is a man from the criminal underworld. This evil character turns out to be the long-lost brother of kindly Miss Jane.

Saunders now poses questions about criminality untouched in the earlier novel. Is the criminal instinct innate? Is it fostered by the kind of tenderness Miss Jane lavished on her orphaned young brother? How much did the grim old prison in which the youth was incarcerated contribute to his depravity? Miss Jane, puzzled by these questions, and by the recognition that the dessicated religious strictures of the village also shaped her brother's fate, finally recognizes one alternative to the "sneaking Puritanism" of her world: the dignity of the old-time Indians. She is proud to claim an Indian chief, Kanawita, among her own ancestors.

Deficient Saints is good adult fiction, its double plot of romance and crime neatly dovetailed, its Maine setting clearly realized. To keep Saunders' name before the public, the publisher L.C. Page now revived her first novel, *My Spanish Sailor*, expanding it by adding some American details and retitling it *Her Sailor*. In 1900 the same company also brought out, in its Cosy Corner Series, a little book for children, consisting of two stories Saunders had published earlier in *Youth's Companion*. The title story in *For His Country* is particularly interesting to Canadians. A young Canadian woman working in France meets a little American boy desperately homesick for California. He tells "Miss Canada" how terribly he misses his own country: he is willing to die rather than forget his own country. The story of course was designed to please American readers, but there is an odd poignancy in "Miss Canada's" recognition of a homesickness parallel to Saunders' own past experience as a schoolgirl in Scotland, and a subtle irony in the portrait of a patriot true till death painted by a Canadian who had just changed all the Canadian details in her first novel and set her latest novel in Maine in order to satisfy American interests.

In *'Tilda Jane: An Orphan in Search of a Home* (1901), a little American girl shares the spotlight with her dog Poacher. The book is representative of a large group of popular novels of the time. Why did little orphan girls so dominate books around the turn of the century? There was *Rebecca of Sunnybrook Farm* (1903), *Lovey Mary* (1903), Judy in *Daddy-Long-Legs* (1912), *Polyanna* (1913) – not to mention Dorothy in *The Wizard of Oz* (1900), and of course, in 1908, *Anne of Green Gables*. Did this focus rise from new concern about child life, new theories of child development that emphasized environment over heredity? Did it reflect a growing sense of alienation among the mostly non-orphan readers of these books? An emphasis on the loneliness, the possible independence of females in an age just beginning to open up new fields of work? The experience of isolation felt by the individual child in the predominantly large Edwardian families? The availability of domestic help that freed the middle-class girl from domestic chores and released her into fantasy life? Social concern over the real plight of the many children actually orphaned in a time of persisting childbed mortality? All these factors probably helped to develop the burgeoning taste for "orphan-girl stories," to which *'Tilda Jane* contributed.

The story of 'Tilda Jane had appeared in serial form in *Youth's Companion*. In keeping with the fashion of local-colour stories in that magazine, it includes a good deal of dialect – too much for modern taste. Where *Huckleberry Finn* or *Anne of Green Gables* suggests a localism by cadence and phrasing, *'Tilda Jane* presents a phonetic rendition of dialect forms. The result is distracting, a diminution of involvement. Otherwise, scrappy, impulsive 'Tilda Jane could hold high interest.

"Elfish ... impish ... a diminutive witch," 'Tilda Jane has run away from a "'sylum" in Maine. Going north by train, she is too confused to realize she is crossing the border into Canada. Thanks to a mix-up at MacAdam Junction, the child is returned for detention as an illegal immigrant. Saunders creates a real atmosphere of border-crossing. She also gives her readers a convincing picture of a poor French-speaking family near the border, using the kindness of these people as a contrast to a mean old man for whom 'Tilda Jane briefly keeps house. This grumpy old cripple tries to kill her dog. In shock over the presumed death of her one friend, 'Tilda Jane revenges Poacher by burning the old man's crutches while he helplessly watches. Again it is impossible not to see 'Tilda Jane as a precursor of Anne of Green Gables, but Saunders' heroine, in such an action as the vengeful burning of the crutches, reveals a hostility that would be alien to Anne.

Even if 'Tilda Jane comes partly from the currents of the Zeitgeist noted above, she comes partly also from a disturbing time in Saunders' own life. The choice of an orphan girl, trailing with her dog across the American-Canadian border, feeling no one wants her, reveals much. Marshall Saunders was now thirty-nine. Since 1897 she had been wandering, looking for new material, making a two-years' journey through the United States, ending with a prolonged visit with her sister Rida in California. When Rida married, Marshall returned to Halifax. Here she found her mother busy with reform causes, her father very much absorbed in his own research (1902 would see the publication of his massive *History of the Baptists of the Maritime Provinces* – 502 pages of careful text). Marshall Saunders set out again, travelling between Boston and Halifax, participating in meetings of the Humane Society, the WCTU, and other benevolent groups. She trailed with her the continuing immense popularity of *Beautiful Joe*, but she was caught essentially in the role of "an orphan in search of a home."

'Tilda Jane had considerable success. It was published by Jarrold's in London, went into many reprintings, and as a story of a "pitiful and charming runaway" was well reviewed. From this point on Page listed *'Tilda Jane* along with *Beautiful Joe* as works by the author when they set the title pages of successive books. But *'Tilda Jane's* sales were moderate compared to those of its successor, *Beautiful Joe's Paradise* (1902).

Four years earlier, Saunders' father had suggested that she weave a further story of Joe into a book she wanted to write on the possibility of immortality for pets. The idea boiled up when she herself lost a very dear pet, the setter Nita. (She would publish a little memorial pamphlet titled *Nita* three years later.) This loss coincided with the creation of *'Tilda Jane's* beloved and battered Poacher, and followed closely news of the death of the original Joe, back in Meaford. Perhaps too the separation from one sister, when Rida married, stirred memories of the earlier loss of another sister, when Laura died.

All these incidents might make us expect the appearance of a sad and sentimental book. On the contrary, *Beautiful Joe's Paradise* is lively, funny, and bubbling with inventiveness.

Once again Saunders chooses a male narrator. This time it is a San Francisco boy named Sam Emerson, a quick-tempered, cheerful, teasing, boy. Like Beautiful Joe, Sam has been wounded – not with physical multilation but by the death of his dog, Ragtime. Sam, because he has been kind to all animals, is given a chance to visit the island where animals go after they die. He travels to the island in a wicker basket slung beneath a "very snug little white balloon."[20] The beautiful aerial view of San Francisco that follows is a tour de force imagined and composed in a time before actual air flight.

(Maybe the idea was picked up from the balloon flight of L. Frank Baum's wizard when he escaped from Oz?) The entranced Sam takes this fantastic voyage in the company of a wise old chimpanzee, two handsome swans, and a black cat called Her Necromancy.

On the island Sam finds Ragtime and all other lost pets, including Beautiful Joe, who, after his life with Miss Laura was over, has become president of the happy community. All are alive again, and all have acquired the power of speech and can greet Sam enthusiastically. Says Sam to the chimpanzee, "Are you dead?" and the chimpanzee replies jauntily, "As a door nail!" (23) This zestful, humorous book serves the same function as E.B. White's *Charlotte's Web*: it helps young readers confront and accept the fact of death.

The story is packed with jokes, adventures, games, races, and jolly meals. The animal isle is indeed a paradise for a healthy boy. Sam rides Jumbo the famous Victorian elephant, and Palo Alto, the late, well-remembered racehorse. A goat waxes poetical:

> A hunk of bread, a brook of drink, and me,
> Running and prancing, and singing diddle-dee!"   262

Sam laughs so hard at the animals' antics that at one point he is reduced to "a gasp of a squeak ... I had used my laughing apparatus so hard, that it was all out of gear, and I felt sore!" (320)

Saunders had come a long way from the didacticism of 1894. She still used her story to preach kindness to animals and to add some new digs against vivisection, blood sports, meat-eating. But preaching dissolves in energetic fantasy and is humanized by the ordinary voice of a boy. His name, Sam Emerson, suggests that Saunders means to blend the powers of two great American writers, the comic Sam Clemens and the mystic Ralph Waldo Emerson. Sam's imaginary voyage takes her into the range of such literary creators. It appears that when Joe died – that is, when the "real" dog who had allowed Saunders to enter her major phase as a writer died – she was able to release a new voice.

Besides being an excellent animal story for children, *Beautiful Joe's Paradise* offers another revelation of the author's vision. She now tilts the balance of virtue towards male values. Sam, Beautiful Joe, and all the good and kindly animals are male. The sad and sinister cat, Her Necromancy, rules in an underworld of deception and suspicion. The goat's owner, Widow McDoodle, adds a second caricature of frightening female. Sam's mother, left behind when he takes his magic flight, welcomes him back – but doesn't believe a word he says. She proffers a neat, rational explanation of his story, offering a useful exit from the fantasy world but adding to the reader's sense of a female lack of perception. This anti-feminism may represent what feminist theorists see as a common "victim position": identification with the victimizer and scorn of fellow-victims.[21]

The nature of Saunders' concern over the attitudes and attributes of women becomes clearer in her next published work, *The Story of the Graveleys* (1902). A would-be independent young woman with the rather male name of Berty Graveley begins the story by refusing to live with her married sister. Instead she proposes to "keep the family together" and move with her grandmother and young brother to River Street, near the fishmarket, in the worst slum of a small Maine city.

On River Street Berty becomes newly aware of the corruption in her city. She finds and supports an honest though unpolished candidate for mayor. Through him she gets some action on parks for slum children, control of child labour by careful policing, and averting of strikes through listening to labourers' grievances. But Berty learns that although women and children and a few friendly men appreciate her, most of the men do not. She raises a sad double cry: "You men don't suffer ... You men all have votes."[22]

Berty's spirits – and the reader's interest – are maintained by the antics of her high-spirited suitor, Tom. It is clear that Berty will go on flinging herself into good causes, dragging the affable Tom with her, but equally clear that like her gentle grandmother she will have little direct effect on anything but her own family.

This novel, like its predecessor, was a reprint of a serial from *Youth's Companion*. It was dedicated to Grace Saunders, who had replaced Rida as "my faithful helper in literary works." Marshall and Grace had now ensconced themselves in the family home on Carleton Street in Halifax, where Marshall had used some of her royalties in 1901 to instal an aviary. Nevertheless, at the time the *Story of the Graveleys* came out, with its emphasis on the importance to women of the establishment of a home, the author herself was on the move, travelling in Europe with Rida and her husband. This would be the pattern of her life in the next few years: from the home base in Halifax to Boston, to Bangor, to Rochester (where Rida now lived), to Europe, to California, and back to Halifax. With Grace, in 1904, she bought a two-hundred-acre farm in the Annapolis Valley, but it was soon sold again. She spent the winter of 1905–06 in Rochester with Rida.

Her next book was *Princess Sukey: The Story of a Pigeon and Her Human Friends*, published not by Page but by the New York firm of Eaton and Mains, and in Canada by William Briggs of Toronto. Like

The Story of the Graveleys it is set in a fictional version of Bangor, Maine. Here we meet Titus, an orphan who lives with a stern grand-father, a pigeon fancier. Their household is soon enlivened by three other orphans: Dallas de Warren, the well-mannered son of an English actor; rich little Bethany; and Airy Tingsby, a fiercely ambitious child of poverty.

Each of the children has a problem or weakness, but each is a real character, well conceived, presented in lively, characteristic talk and unexpected but convincing actions and attitudes. The disparate group is pulled together by a need to frustrate a kidnapping plot directed against Bethany. The plot is foiled through the energetic intervention of Berty Graveley Everest, who reappears in this novel to muster the forces of goodness. Berty's sudden disruption of the kidnappers' plot constitutes one of three oddities in this quick-paced book.

A second oddity is the role of the grandfather. The judge's mel-lowing, through the impact of the children, is a central theme, but as the book ends he finds a good housekeeper for the children and withdraws with relief to his self-absorbed life of study and solitude. This may be a realistic report on the ultimate response of an older person to the tumult of young life, but it makes a curious ending to a story earlier focused on the revival of life and love in an old "fisher king."

The third puzzle is in the function of Princess Sukey, the pigeon. She loses our interest early in the book, once she has brought the judge and his grandson Titus together, and has nothing to do with the central kidnapping plot. Yet the book and the judge return to the pigeon, who presides over his study in the end, scornful and petu-lant. Perhaps she has a symbolic function, as a final comment on female vanity and empty-headedness, contrasting with the warm feminine presence of boyish, unconventional Berty. And of course Princess Sukey also gives the book a come-on title for readers hoping that an animal character would be a part of any new Marshall Saun-ders novel.[23]

The animal story was still the genre in which Saunders' reputation was strongest. This genre was now at its peak, and she faced stiff competition for readership from fellow Canadians. Page had signed up Roberts and brought out his *Watchers of the Trails* in 1904, and *Red Fox* in 1905. Seton had produced *The Biography of a Grizzly* in 1900, *Krag and Johnny Bear* in 1902, *Monarch, the Big Bear of Tallock* in 1904, and many more in the same mode. Jack London's *The Call of the Wild* (1903) and *The Sea Wolf* (1904) fed into the taste for stories of wilder-ness animals. Marshall Saunders joined the trend with her little 1906 book *Alpatok: The Story of an Eskimo Dog*. With this publication she returned to Page.

She also swung at this time to non-fiction. She put her ideas on criminal activity, so recurring a theme in her fiction, into an essay titled "Increase and Cause for the Growth of Crime." Prepared for an essay contest announced by the American Humane Education Society, her work again won a two-hundred-dollar prize. Yet, sympathetic as she was to working-class people, she in fact had little contact with them, had done no extensive reading in political or economic theory, and had picked up her ideas from the like-minded women with whom she worked for temperance, for playgrounds, and for peace. In a period when women had no direct voice on public policy and little access to substantive discussions of problems, Saunders made respectable entries into the field of discussion of humane concerns, but as her great-niece Karen Saunders has suggested, her notions essentially reflect middle-class values.[24]

In her private life she was not finding stability. She spent part of 1908 with Rida and her husband, and shared with them sorrow at the loss of their baby. *My Pets* (1908) reflects a life of increasing absorption in animal life in the Halifax house now devoted to the needs and habits of dogs, cats, parrots, birds. Her father was again preparing a massive work of "serious scholarship": *Three Premiers of Nova Scotia*, a 628-page tome published by Briggs of Toronto in 1909. Travels, with her mother to Boston and alone to Rochester, could not relieve a growing depression. At the age of forty-eight Marshall Saunders suffered a breakdown, and went into a rest home at Orono, near Bangor.

Nevertheless, in 1910 L.C. Page published a sequel to Saunders' "orphan story." *'Tilda Jane's Orphans*, like many sequels a string of anecdotes loosely centred around the still-vivid character of strong-minded 'Tilda Jane, uses distracting dialect again, and plot and style both seem tired.

Then Saunders' literary vigour revived. She came out the same year, in fighting order, with a strong new novel, *The Girl from Vermont: The Story of a Vacation School Teacher*. This story was published by the Boston firm of Griffith and Rowland – a reminder of the publication of *The House of Armour* by Rowland in Philadelphia. In her subsequent publications she would return only once to L.C. Page of Boston.

With *The Girl from Vermont* Marshall Saunders brought to a climax the phase of her literary work that was concerned with the possibility that women might confront social problems effectively. In *Deficient Saints, The Story of the Graveleys*, and *Princess Sukey* she had focused on urgent problems concerning crime, poverty, and homelessness. Although in the latter two novels she was writing to please a young audience, she was still clearly using her art to teach and persuade. The problems concerned humans: animals, for whom she had previously served as a voice, had virtually disappeared, or diminished to a pigeon's sardonic "Rockety-cahoo" at beginning and end of the story. In Jane Castonguay and Berty Graveley Everest she had created women determined to contribute to reform. Both these women, however, had to fit concern over social problems into the household duties that dominated their lives. All three novels include rather conventional scenes of courtship, involving attractive young men and women.

The Girl from Vermont dramatically highlights social problems. The opening incident concerns a battered child. Foster parents whose only interest is to collect insurance when the child dies are brutally and callously hastening that day. In a lively, convincing court scene, the judicial world is presented as shutting its eyes to this cruelty; the judge mocks the concerned women who have attended as witnesses and observers, calling them sentimentalists and sensation-mongers, and he returns the abused child to the respectable-looking man who has mistreated him.

The child's story is suspended, and the narration shifts to more common problems of poor children: economic exploitation in the workplace, where ten-year-olds still live a "little white slave life"; lack of play space or healthy recreational facilities for children, or for the after-hours of young workers; a bucolic school system that makes no adjustment for teaching undernourished, underprivileged, and over-worked city children. From children's problems through the problems of poor women, the novel moves to universal problems of violence, the escalation of armaments and of war.

The voice of protest on all these matters is the voice of Saunders' new hero, Patty Green. Patty observes the first incident of child abuse by chance and later involves herself in the battered-child courtroom scene. Later still, as pacifist, Patty makes a public speech against guns, urging her neighbours to fight with paper, with arguments and reason and willingness to compromise. As a feminist she protests against the judicial system where men impose their wills on recalcitrant women. As ardent worker for playgrounds she urges the development of green spaces as the real answer to urbanization. As teacher she experiments with educational methods adapted to the obstreperous slum children in her classes, and opens the classroom for after-hours assistance to parents, cleaning-women, policemen, the unemployed – and to the bourgeois managers who come to inspect and protest.

Patty scolds the men of the community, the poor men's employers, who ultimately cause the problems in her school, and mocks the false logic of those who try to patronize her and her ideas. She is a powerful figure who directly affects her community, a very different creature from the gentle teachers in Saunders' earliest stories, who help little children learn to be kind to pets.

She is given a romance, but it is an unconventional one. Patty rejects Victor Denner, her handsome young suitor, because she has fallen in love with his father, a middle-aged widower. Strong scenes between Patty and the senior Denner, before their mutual love has been declared, present them in earnest, sparkling argument, in an attractive study of growing trust and friendship between a man and a woman, transformed but not reduced into a love relationship.

In this unusual novel Saunders recalls the days when she herself as a teacher tackled with vigour and optimism the social problems in her community. She indicates her hope for young women who storm authority with pastoral ideals. The novel also catches the spirit of the day and reflects the movement towards the women's-rights battles of suffragism.

The dark shadow in this novel, however, is not social injustice but the recurring mystery of individual evil. Mr Denner has a malignant brother who, like Nina's father in *My Spanish Sailor* and like Miss Jane's brother in *Deficient Saints*, has "something wrong in his make-up." A melodramatic twist reveals that this evil man is responsible for the situation of the helpless battered baby of the opening scenes. The inexplicable bad streak has created irreversible consequences.

A year later Saunders spoke out in her own voice on many of the issues dramatized in *The Girl from Vermont*. In 1911 articles in the Toronto *Globe* pleaded for the victims of economic injustice; she made feminist speeches on the "women's cause"; and she published a series of articles in the Halifax *Morning Chronicle* that stirred her home city to the opening of two supervised playgrounds. She had become a member of the Women's Press Club and the local Council of Women, and of other activist groups such as the New York Peace Society and the National Child Labour Committee.

In 1911 Acadia University, which had earlier honoured her father, awarded her an honorary degree. At this point she shifted her customary travel itinerary and visited Winnipeg, Prince Rupert, and other centres in the Canadian west. The Canadian Pacific Railway Company, which was heavily involved in immigration schemes, commissioned an article by Saunders to publicize the new settlements, but the article was in the end not published.

Travels were suspended in 1912. Marshall Saunders was now very much involved in the care of her aging mother in Halifax. Rida was in Rochester, Jack Cramp in Ottawa, and another brother, Ned, in Toronto, so Grace and Marshall were left to cope with the parents, now both in their eighties. When Mrs Saunders died in 1913, Grace and old Dr Saunders moved to Toronto, and Marshall's home-base shifted with them. The Halifax home was sold in 1914.

Saunders managed somehow to write another "animal autobiography" in 1912, *Pussy Black-Face; or, The Story of a Kitten* (1913). This was to be her last publication with L.C. Page, which was acquiring a bad reputation for its treatment of popular women writers. Louis Page had published *Pollyanna*, *The Little Colonel*, and *Anne of Green Gables*, among other best-selling stories for young people, but he combined a nose for good manuscripts with a patronizing and exploitative attitude to his authors. These women began corresponding and comparing grievances. Canadian writers co-ordinated their efforts to improve their professional status by working through the Canadian Women's Press Club. When Saunders met L.M. Montgomery at this club a few years later, the two women shared horror stories about the exploitation of their talents by L.C. Page. Saunders took her next book, *"Boy": The Wandering Dog*, to the Grosset Company in New York; it was also brought out as *The Wandering Dog: Adventures of a Fox-Terrier* in the same year by Doran.

From the time the First World War broke out in 1914, travels were of course rigidly curtailed. Perhaps in consequence, wanderlust is the main trait of the hero of this new book. Boy's cheerful restlessness and his promiscuous friendships also show Saunders' reaction against a recent and very popular dog story from Scotland. Eleanor Atkinson's *Greyfriars Bobby* (1912) idealized a little terrier that refused to move from his master's grave. Boy, in contrast, slips in and out of the lives of many humans, including a waspish character named Stanner, an old negro woman, and a man nicknamed "Nap" for his resemblance to Napoleon. "I am an open-faced, wire-haired fox-terrier," says Boy,[25] and his creator obviously enjoys telling the story of his travels.

The first half of the story is set in the city of New York, described as a rather bad place for dogs, what with high licence fees, laws requiring muzzles, and rich owners "who give too many baths"[25] (58). A bad place in general, says one of Boy's acquaintances, "what with burrowing for the subways, sky-rocketing for the elevateds" (15), dreadfully dirty saloons in the Bowery, and women walking about dressed in fur coats, thanks to the "cruel seal traffic" (21). Boy also adds a dog's-eye view of the war – American dogs fight a daschhund and a German police dog.

The second half of *"Boy": The Wandering Dog* is a utopian idyll, projecting a world two years later when the war is over. This fantasy is no more improbable than the earlier accounts of Boy's ingenious interventions in New Yorkers' lives. Yet Boy's jaunty vitality reveals his author's pleasure in creating a wanderer, another energetic male persona in the tradition of Joe and Sam, a significant projection of a part of her self increasingly repressed as the war dragged on.

The Rev. Dr Saunders died in 1916. There is a touching small memorial of him in Saunders' own copy of the "New and Enlarged" edition of *Beautiful Joe* brought out in 1918 by the Toronto firm of McClelland, Goodchild and Stewart. The edition is enlarged only by the addition of two new pictures. The frontispiece of "Billie," the tiny terrier held in a man's hand, has an annotation: "My Father's Hand. – M.S."[26]

Another note inside this copy of the Canadian edition, now in the Osborne collection, Toronto, tells what has really been done to the book to bring it into accord with the taste of 1918: "25,000 words taken out of Joe. Present length 80,000." A further explanation, dated "March 21, Dayton Florida," adds, "Revised by Marshall Saunders." This note is in pencil, in a shaky hand, retraced in ink – and it is emended, in a stronger hand, to read, "Revised by Grace & Marshall Saunders." It is worth speculating how much Marshall Saunders had come to rely on her sister's judgment in making these extensive cuts, ninety-three changes altogether.

Seven chapters have been deleted, including "A Talk about Sheep" and "A Jealous Ox." These changes decrease treatment of animals other than pets. Other changes are those suggested long ago by Mr Blaikie: "The Englishman" has become "The Cruel Man." Strong language has been toned down: "rotten" vegetables become "decayed" ones. The opening description of the killing of the pups has been cut from "Some of them he seized by the legs and knocked against the stalls, till their brains were dashed out, others he killed with a fork. It was very terrible" to, simply, "It was very terrible." This kind of censorship reflects both a changed concern over the palate for violence in children, and also a new sensitivity to suffering, raw from the war years.

The revision of *Beautiful Joe* marks yet another major turning-point in Saunders' literary production. Joe seems to have had an uncanny power in his creator's life. Often in dreams or fairy-tales an animal acts as first guide into a deeply significant voyage. This seems to have been the pattern for Saunders, with Joe acting three times as herald of entry into a new field of creation. When, twenty-two years earlier, Saunders first let this small, mutilated animal wandering in search of a home into her imagination, she had found in this persona a way to release her sense of indignity against wrong. She had gone on to speak for other disadvantaged beings: the Acadians in *Rose à Charlitte*, the orphans in *King of the Park* and *'Tilda Jane*. Then, after returning to Joe to write *Beautiful Joe's Paradise*, she began a new sequence of stories with active protagonists who reach towards a better order and fight against social wrongs – first Sam, and then a series of women. Now, the experience of revision of *Beautiful Joe* seems to have taken her to a further stage. Once again she began to "speak" through the animal voice with increasing richness and complexity. In her next sequence of novels the animal "I" is again male: Dicky, Jimmy, Prince. Then, in her final novel, *Esther de Warren*, she would write for the first time in the first person, as a woman.

In this post-war series of books Saunders finds materials not in social theories but in personal memories. She comes "home" to those memories, using Canadian settings in her fiction for the first time since the 1880s.

The first and least interesting of this late series is *Golden Dicky: The Story of a Canary and His Friends* (New York: Stokes 1919). Most of the action takes place in a "bird-room," transcribed from her own aviary. After the death of their father Saunders and her sister Grace had established a permanent home of their own on a ravine in a then-new part of Toronto north of Eglinton. The stucco bungalow had been specially designed to house the many pets, particularly the birds that formed part of the household. Sixty or seventy birds were free to fly up and down from the basement to the sunroom by way of an "elevator shaft."[27] Canaries and other birds in *Golden Dicky*, as they become involved in rivalries and alliances, reflect the "personalities" of Saunders' pets.

Birds, as *Beautiful Joe's Paradise* suggests, always say everything twice, so *Golden Dicky* presents not only "Dicky-Dick" but also "Sammy-Sam" and "Lucy-Loo," until the modern reader wishes for some Hooded Fang to stop the flow of doubles. But the book excited the audience it was intended for. For instance, L.M. Montgomery recorded in her journals that when she read *Golden Dicky* to her little son Chester he was so overcome with suspense that she had to read the ending to reassure him.[28] Montgomery, placed next to Saunders at a meeting of the Canadian Authors' Association, found Saunders "a clever woman but a bit of a bore – talks too much and overloads her conversation with irrelevant detail."[29] The comment may reflect a touch of jealousy of a competitor, but also probably catches a real quality of nervousness and fussiness.

Of greater interest than *Golden Dicky* is *Bonnie Prince Fetlar: The Story of a Pony and His Friends*. This book was published in Canada by McClelland & Stewart, copyright for the United States being held by George H. Doran. The introduction of Canadian content is the first marked change. The scene is Muskoka, near the Lake of Bays. The six children in the story have all been named after Canadian heroes: Jeanne Mance, Tecumseh Hallowell, Marguerite Bourgeys, Samuel de Champlain, James Wolfe, and John Graves Simcoe.

Luckily for the reader, all are called by nicknames; but even these have a rather chauvinistic ring. The oldest boy, Tecumseh, is called Big Chief in deference to his physical strength; the oldest girl, Jeanne Mance, a tempestuous tomboy, is called Cassowary, the name of a wild running ostrich.

Big Chief is shorn of his pride of place through Cassowary's whisper that he is adopted. His anguish at feeling he is an outsider gives a cutting urgency to the old theme of the orphan child. But Cassowary, who is a misfit in a deeper sense – rebellious against the rules for decorum that govern girls, even in frontier places – discovers in the end that it is in fact she, and not Big Chief, who is the outsider, the adopted child. Ales Devering, the mother in this tumultuous family group, helps Cassowary adjust to her new knowledge and realize that she is valued for herself, not for her lineage.

The novel also dramatizes the toughening of a sheltered city boy named Dallas Duff, who comes to stay with the Devering family, bringing with him a little Shetland pony. Since this is an animal story, Bonnie Prince Fetlar intervenes in the human drama, frustrating Big Chief's miserable decision to run away from home and hence saving Cassowary from unbearable shame for her cruel taunting of her "brother." Pony stories are always popular with young readers, and this one introduces every kind of horseflesh: the Deverings own an Indian pony, a Hackney, an Exmoor pony and a Welsh one, big gentle work horses, and two thoroughbreds ridden by the parents. Pigs and the collies that guard them, a wild fawn, snakes, and even toads produce a rich sense of a full universe of animals. Sentimentalism has been modified however; the frontier attitude to hunting and to eating venison is justified: "precious as they [the deer] are, hungry people are more precious."[30]

An incidental pleasure is in the interwoven songs – happy songs that Canadian children really do sing: "I'm Captain Jinx of the Horse Marines," "Roll a silver dollar," "Pack up your troubles." The story comes to a great climax, with a fire, a ghost, and a final reunion in the woods. Saunders thus gives her readers a family story centred on real emotions, featuring at least three memorable children. For adult critics she sets off mythic overtones through the use of songs and archetypal summer-holiday scenes.

That was in 1920. It was four years before Saunders published again – the biggest gap in her long, long record of publications. Then she probed a darker store of memories, using details of her Nova Scotia childhood in *Jimmy Gold-Coast*. The Sandys (Saunders?) family moves to the city from a country valley where "nobody hurries," happy young people find work and games, singing clubs, good schools – and wonderful food. Breakfast is dulse and porridge and stewed pink rhubarb, and lunch is "parsley omelet, young radishes, hot potatoes swimming in melted butter, and saucers of preserved quince with cream."[31] Regional details pile up, fresh and appealing. Grandfather Sandys wears "his best beaver," picks a posy, and reads Greek while the children play at Trojan horse; grandmother feeds fat Spanish raisins to her pet parrot.

This idyllic life ends when "Nappy," a rascally sailor-nephew, is caught in a bank robbery and the family moves to Halifax to be near the jail where he is interred. The family trauma is offset by the chance to work for prison reform. At the end of the story there is some hope of rehabilitation for Nappy in a new-style prison-camp established outside the city, thanks in part to the efforts of Nonnie the black servant.

The story is told by Nappy's pet monkey. Jimmy, sad and cunning, from the dark heart of Africa, is the antithesis of the pony from Shetland, "Bonny Prince," narrator of Saunders' previous book. Saunders in these two books no longer makes a pat division of good/evil, female/male. Turbulent, rejecting Cassowary disrupts society, while mothering Nonnie unites it. The boy Dallas becomes a valuable part of a family, while the boy Nappy is outcast. Each story features a Scottish ghost, but even here there is no formula: in *Jimmy Gold-Coast* the "light of the clan" warns of death, while in *Bonnie Prince Fetlar* the "Old Highlander" brings peace and life. After a lifetime of writing, Saunders had achieved a vision of doubleness, of mixed innocence and experience, tied to each other by the sense of cyclic movement.

One suggestive point is that such a deep revelation of mythic universes is fairly commonplace in children's books. Perhaps the writing of a book for children frees the creator from inhibition and self-consciousness. She assumes that her visions will not be subject to complicated or cynical criticism. Children's literature has a sub-cultural aura, and subcultures have their own kind of freedom.

Writing for children – especially a lifetime of writing for children – can eventually free the storyteller for a sally into the realms of myth and fairy-tale.

"Fairy-tale" is a term that can be applied to the last and the most puzzling of Saunders' books. In *Esther de Warren* (New York: Doran 1927) she returned to memories of her adolescent voyage abroad and transmuted these into a fabulous Cinderella story. Lorraine McMullen, in her article "Marshall Saunders' Mid-Victorian Cinderella; or, the Mating Game in Victorian Scotland," has carefully collated the details of "real" life as outlined in Saunders' Edinburgh diary with the fantasies of romance as presented in *Esther de Warren*.[32] Now, at the end of a study of the whole series of Saunders' novels, more conclusions can be drawn about the way this novel fits in with all the author's dominant interests and idiosyncracies.

Esther de Warren, the oldest sister in a Nova Scotian family, is sent to Edinburgh to school when she is fifteen. On board ship she is initiated into adult social life. She forms a puzzled friendship with an odd, hypersensitive youth named David, and an admiring rapport with a beautiful young matron, Lady Cannaweeta Kelvie. In both cases a small animal speeds intimacy: David's red squirrel brings him and Esther together, and Esther's dream of a little lamb links her with Lady Kelvie. The use of an animal as narrator, however, has now disappeared. The voice is that of young Esther, writing letters home.

The relation between the young girl and a tutelary older woman represents an experience of guidance that feminists see as essential. Lady Cannaweeta's strange Indian name echoes that of the Indian princess Kanawita, whom Miss Jane Castonguay (the tutelary figure in *Deficient Saints*) claimed as ancestress. Lady Cannaweeta helps Esther to prepare to enter the "other world," the "old country" of Scotland.

There Esther gradually discovers that she and David are brother and sister. She learns to accept this difficult twin and also an alien parentage and a new name – not De Warren but Salas. In the end she must choose between three worlds: France, the home of David and the Salas family; Scotland, where a young man related to Lady Cannaweeta offers marriage; and Canada, home of the De Warrens, who have been her foster family. She chooses Scotland, but with the happy thought that the fostering De Warrens will visit her there.

Esther's change of name from De Warren to Salas makes us remember a long chain of linked names stretching back to Saunders' earliest novels. The name De Warren was first used, casually, in *The House of Armour*; it reappeared as the name of the central orphan boy, Dallas de Warren, in *Princess Sukey*. But Salas sounds like Dallas, and this new name of Esther's sounds like the names of many earlier characters: Dallas de Warren in *Princess Sukey*; Derrice in *Deficient Saints*; Dallas Duff, the boy who came into the Devering family in *Bonnie Prince Fetlar*; Ales Devering, the foster mother in that novel. All these names seem to echo that of "Alice" – the archetypal wanderer through wonderland and the world of mirrors.

The long, linked series of portraits of orphans perhaps mirrors Marshall Saunders' own sense of being "banished" from her family at fifteen; perhaps it reflects the more general story of a woman shut off from her full potential in a society unwilling to accept her true nature and powers. The series now culminates in the story of a girl who accepts and profits by her exile. The uneasy alternation between male and female voices ends with Esther's acceptance of the existence of a male twin, and her readiness to control and enjoy him.

The last novel Marshall Saunders wrote, like the first, thus tells of a young girl voyaging by sea to an older world. In the first, *My Spanish Sailor*, created by a young writer of twenty-four, the heroine is guided and guarded by her sailor-husband. She learns to live with him and to continue her voyage as seafarer, wife, and mother. In her last book Saunders, at sixty-six, still voices a dream of seafaring. But this time she dreams of power, control, and the acceptance of responsibility. The general tone is optimistic and vigorous: Esther is a hero who chooses her own destination.

The book obviously pleased its author. She wrote to her good friend Lorne Pierce, "Esther is my favorite book."[33] It was, at any rate, her last.

After her writing career ended, she went on giving speeches and illustrated talks, mostly about the birds and animals that still dominated her household. She addressed the Canadian Club, the Canadian Authors' Association, the literary societies of various churches in Toronto, and she continued to do club work – she belonged to twenty clubs at one point in her life. In 1934 she was awarded a CBE (Companion of the British Empire), and in the same year *Beautiful Joe* was brought out again, in a handsome, modern-looking edition.

The next years were increasingly difficult for her. Her travels and her lavish home-building had eaten up most of the royalties from her early books. In the mid-1930s she began to suffer recurring bouts of mental confusion. K.M. Saunders writes of her "estrangement from reality." From the normal reality of Toronto life she certainly had slipped away. This final sad period lasted until 1947, when she died at the age of eighty-six.

But how many realities she had illuminated in her productive lifetime! The reality of the animal kingdom, in faithful delineation of the habits of almost the full range of animal, bird, insect, and reptile life as observable in eastern Canada and many parts of the United States. The reality of children's tastes as readers – an uncanny sense of what children like to read about, the kind of children and speeches and actions they can identify with, the kind of adventures they can vicariously enjoy. The reality of social abuses, particularly social evils that affect women and children: alcoholism, overcrowding, unregulated working conditions, punitive judicial systems. The reality of dream – of a world where animals chuckle and converse and connive for our betterment. The reality of memory, a dim world from which an author could dredge up a golden world or a grey one.

If we look for a subtext in the whole oeuvre we may fruitfully connect the stories with Saunders' life as a creative woman rather than with her memories of a particular life experience. In her children's books Saunders learned to release the voices of animals, Joe, Alpatok, Boy, Dicky, and the rest. We remember that the shaman or seer in primitive societies similarly speaks deep truths through animal cries. Following the advice of her father, of Dr Rand, her editors, and other senior male mentors, Saunders early directed her shaman voice towards child readers rather than a more sophisticated audience.

A woman writer in a patriarchal society, she created in her fictions a series of fables of male/female relations, both between imaginary characters and within her central character – herself. The recurring twin motif can be seen as a working-out of any woman's puzzlement over the male/female elements in her make-up. In some of her novels the human males, boys such as David in *Esther De Warren*, Nappy McHadra in *Jimmy Gold-Coast*, and "Big Chief" Tecumseh in *Bonnie Prince Fetlar*, in spite of their kingly and powerful names, have a rogue quality: they lie, run away, cannot adapt to normal family life. Older men, including George Stenner, the evil father in *My Spanish Sailor*, and "Gentleman George," the equally worthless father in *Deficient Saints*, modulate into the kindly fatherly figure Mr Denner in *The Girl from Vermont*; yet Patty, the young hero in that novel, discovers that her kindly friend has a totally evil brother. Perhaps a psychologist could find a source of this rejection of older-generation males in Saunders' family life, so dominated by a beloved but daunting father. More likely it reflects the resentment of patriarchy in general on the part of a talented woman.

The recurring theme of orphanage, in these novels as in those of many of Saunders' contemporaries among women writers, is one mark of the widespread resentment and puzzlement felt by gifted women in the face of repressive familial and societal powers. Esther de Warren (Salas) in Saunders' last novel discovers that she does not belong in her putative family – the same discovery made by Nina in the first novel, by Derrice in *Deficient Saints*, and by Cassowary in *Bonnie Prince Fetlar*. This recurring motif represents the artist's discovery of the mystery of her own nature. But the author assigns to all three characters the discovery of "true parents" who are somewhat inglorious – a humble self-assessment. Should we now revise that humble opinion?

Marshall Saunders remained for many decades Canada's best-known and best-loved writer of children's stories. If she used her art not only to entertain and teach but also to release her deepest feelings about her own nature and the nature of creative experience, she was doing what the other masters of the genre – Lewis Carroll, Mark Twain, Rudyard Kipling, Louisa May Alcott – had also done. The conventional mannerisms of the time and the genre (use of phonetic dialect, comic racism, archness in baby talk, stereotyping of little girl/little boy interests) raise barriers between Saunders' children's books and the modern reader. Some of her children's books, however, still retain some value: *Beautiful Joe* remains available, and many children still enjoy the verve and variety of this story of animals told from the animal's point of view. Of her other children's books, *Bonnie Prince Fetlar* at least deserves to be revived and added to the shelf of classic books for young readers.

But the whole sequence of Saunders' work offers much more. In novel after novel she presents insight into a woman's dream-world, recognition of the power and darkness of the imaginative female vision. *Rose à Charlitte* for its blend of regional realism and romance, *The Girl from Vermont* for its affirmative mode and social honesty, *Esther de Warren* for its haunting reprise of fairy-tale motifs, all deserve rediscovery.

When *Beautiful Joe* first appeared, the Countess of Aberdeen, wife of the Scottish governor general of Canada, wrote in a prefatory note, "Canada has every reason to be proud that one of her daughters should prove herself so able a champion of the claims of the faithful servants of mankind who so constantly minister to our wants and pleasures." In her adult romances Saunders expresses the deeper claims of another range of "faithful creatures" – the women of her time.

Joanna E. Wood:
Incendiary Women

CARRIE MacMILLAN

Joanna Ellen (she was Nellie to her family and friends) Wood was acknowledged to be one of Canada's foremost novelists in the late nineteenth century. The *Canadian Magazine* described her as one of Canada's three leading novelists, along with Charles G.D. Roberts and Gilbert Parker.[1] Her first novel, *The Untempered Wind* (1894),[2] was described by *Current Literature* of New York as "the strongest and best American [sic] novel of the year 1894."[3] The *Week* in Toronto, not given to extravagant praise, declared the same novel to be "fully entitled to rank with the masterpieces of the century,"[4] and the *Canadian Magazine* pronounced it "perhaps without a peer among Canadian novels."[5] Her *Daughter of Witches*[6] was reviewed in Britain by the *Bookman*, the *Outlook*, the *Spectator*, the *Westminster Gazette*, the *Pall Mall Gazette* and the *Athenaeum*. The *Canadian Magazine* reported that Joanna E. Wood made several thousands of dollars a year from the publication of short stories in the "better" New York magazines, using such pen-names as "Jean d'Arc" or the names of some of her male friends.[7]

In the last decade of the nineteenth century and the first of the twentieth, Wood lived the life of a cosmopolitan, residing and travelling in London, Paris, Scotland, Boston, New York and Philadelphia, with frequent visits home to Niagara. She met the English poet Algernon Charles Swinburne's sisters in Paris and was introduced to the poet. A bracelet locket containing a lock of red hair and with the name "Algernon Swinburne" engraved on the back was among her effects when she died.[8] She was presented at court[9] and her portrait was painted by Miss Sermonda Burrell, "Lord Gwydyr's [sic] clever granddaughter."[10] She had her photograph taken in Paris, London, and New York.[11]

Today we know virtually nothing of Joanna E. Wood and of her five novels,[12] numerous short stories, and various magazine articles. There are several reasons for her having been lost to the literary tradition. With few exceptions serious Canadian literary critics of Wood's day tended to undervalue or dismiss Canadian literature generally and popular Canadian fiction particularly as having little merit in relation to British and even American literature. There was also a relationship between gender and judgment; women writers were not taken as seriously as men.[13] Very little Canadian literature was admitted to secondary-school and university curricula, which meant that a book could remain in print only as long as it had a popular audience.[14] Finally, even if contemporary books had enjoyed serious critical attention and inclusion in a canon, the reaction against romance and sentimentality ushered in by the Canadian modernists in the 1920s would have led to their deletion. Another factor that worked to Wood's detriment is that her best fiction was written at the beginning of her career in the 1890s; the later fiction, however fascinating it may be for its sensational qualities, is inferior. The falling-off of the quality of Wood's writing was not beneficial to her critical reception in our century.

It is true that a critical study of Wood's novels does not reveal a true "classic" of literature; even her best novels are flawed, to our modern taste, by an intrusive, didactic narrative voice or improbable, romantic characters and incidents or excessive sentimentality or sensation. However, there is much to be respected in her work, including some of the best early realistic and critical description of Canadian small-town life, mythic ideas on the state and possibilities of art and the artist in Canada, and unorthodox ideas about the condition of women. Wood is also of interest as an example of the Canadian writer in the exciting post-Confederation era, when internationalism and cosmopolitanism emerged. Finally, she is significant as one of the many interesting Canadian women who contributed to Canadian letters in the era of the first acceptance in this country of women into universities and careers in journalism and publishing.

Joanna E. Wood was born in Milton, Lesmahagow, Lanarkshire, Scotland, not far from Glasgow, on 28 December 1867, to Robert and Agnes (Todd) Wood, who had been married in 1844.[15] Robert Wood is described in a census found in the Scottish Register Office as a farmer. Relations included an uncle who was a clergyman and another who owned a coal mine.[16] Robert and Agnes Wood had eleven children, six of whom survived infancy: Gordon, James, William, Mary (Mrs Glennie), Jessie (Mrs Maxwell), and Joanna. Robert Wood must have been a man of some means, or who had access to financial backing of some kind, for in 1869, when Joanna was a small girl, he emigrated with his family first to New York and then in 1874 to Queenston Heights, Ontario, where he purchased a farm of two hundred thirty-three acres.[17] The farm occupied a picturesque and historic prospect on Queenston Heights, overlooking the Niagara River, within sight today of the Brock monument. The gracious and comfortable, large, wood-framed, central-gabled home, along the front of which ran a wide veranda, was called The Heights. Today much of the property is under the water of a hydro reservoir (an apt metaphor, it would seem, for Wood's "drowned" literary career), and the home no longer stands.

We know little of Wood's childhood except that she aspired at an early age to be a writer, which suggests a serious interest in literature. Certainly in later years she pronounced her favourite writers to be first the poets, Shakespeare, Shelley, Keats, Byron, Rossetti, Swinburne, and Elizabeth Barrett Browning, and next the novelists, Thackeray, Meredith, Hardy, and Barrie.[18] Quotations from the poets, particularly those listed here, are quite frequent in her novels, arguing a comfortable familiarity with their work.

Wood attended the St Catharines Collegiate Institute,[19] after which she travelled, in the late 1880s, to New York, where her brother William was embarked on a very successful career in the Metropolitan Insurance Company (he would become general manager), and to Europe, including Paris and London. The wealthy Scottish uncle who owned the coal mine provided financial support for the European "finishing" excursion.[20] In Paris she met the sisters of Algernon Charles Swinburne, who may have sponsored her when she was presented at court.[21] She also met the poet through his sisters, likely as an admirer of his writing and a young literary aspirant. The impression Swinburne made on her and her admiration of his writing and thought can be seen in an article she published in the *Canadian Magazine* entitled "Algernon Charles Swinburne: An Appreciation."[22] Particularly noteworthy in this article is Wood's championing of Swinburne's ability to paint "the beauty of flesh in words" in the face of his, as she describes it, puritanical society. Swinburne's influence, and that of the Pre-Raphaelites generally, is also evident in her later fiction, which has a definite *fin de siècle*, decadent quality in its fascination with the morally taboo, particularly behaviour that was taboo for women. It would be fascinating to know more of the details of the relationship between Wood and the Swinburnes, but at this time few have surfaced.

On her return to Canada, Joanna Wood achieved some success as a short-story writer. The American family magazine *All the Year Round* published "Unto the Third Generation" in 1890, for example. That she had exacting literary standards and modesty about her writing is suggested in an article that describes Wood's hesitation and reluctance to send her first manuscript to a publisher, which she finally did only at the urging of her brother William.[23]

The twenty-seven-year-old woman had brought back from her travels a very sharp eye for realities at home, and from her contacts with avant-garde writers such as Swinburne an emancipated reaction to traditional small-town mores. Her first novel, *The Untempered Wind*, published in 1894, describes Canadian village life; however, it does not conform to Desmond Pacey's description of the "regional idyll" prevalent in Canadian fiction in the late nineteenth century.[24] Rather, *The Untempered Wind* is a problem novel, a tragedy that presents sympathetically the unsuccessful struggle of an unmarried mother to survive in a narrow-minded and cruel small town, Jamestown, which is undoubtedly based on Wood's observation and experience in the rural Niagara area of Ontario. While English literature generally was familiar with the "fallen woman" (Thomas Hardy's *Tess of the D'Urbervilles* [1891] went into its twenty-sixth edition in 1894, and Hawthorne's *The Scarlet Letter* [1850] was a fixture in American letters), she was not a type well known in Canadian literature.

Wood's exploration of this problem character shows courage as well as sympathy. Wood sets her novel in the days before agriculture-related factories and workers' cottages had become a significant part of the Niagara landscape, but notes that the attitudes found in this recent past are just as strong today. They are now directed more against factory girls than against those in service. In particular, Wood offers a strong criticism of the rigidly moral and utterly uncompromising matrons of Jamestown who treat the "fallen woman" as a pariah and show her no Christian charity or forgiveness. In criticizing the "legislating matron," Wood is, of course, ultimately criticizing the patriarchal, fundamentalist, evangelical order that is responsible for her creation and relies on her for its existence. The legislating matron insures that women are kept in their place.

The novel tells the story of Myron Holder, who is "a mother, but not a wife," and presents Myron's life from the time just after the birth of her son "My" to her death a few years later. Myron's life, with the exception of the love she has for her child, is one of unremitting sorrow and penance brought on in large measure by the community and its "good women." Myron endures an unassisted and frightening childbirth, hard domestic work at far below the prevailing wage, poverty, hunger, cold, social ostracization, and cruelty. The one person in the community who has shown her any sympathy or support dies in the course of the novel, as does the one person who gives her love, her son. She is condemned utterly as an evil soul by the local minister, and her marriage at the end of the novel, at a cholera quarantine station, to the father of her child, an eminent bacteriologist, is followed almost immediately by her own death.

There is no doubt of Wood's sympathetic treatment of her central character. The strong sentiment apparent in the details of Myron's life is heightened by images of saintly resignation, madonna-like love of her child, and Christ-like suffering. We are introduced to Myron as she carries quilt frames through the town and out to her country employer, not unlike Christ carrying his cross, and the words "saint" and "madonna" appear frequently in the text. There are also promethean images of suffering, and of a classic, "Murillo-like" beauty. These images are enhanced by poetic quotations about noble love and valiant suffering from English classics, at the beginning of and occasionally within the chapters. In fact Wood's presentation of Myron Holder demonstrates the valorizing of patient resignation noted by Jane Tompkins in her study of early American fiction, *Sensational Designs: The Cultural Work of American Fiction 1760–1866*, a strategy whereby women writers of sensational and sentimental fiction created a kind of female hero.[25]

Wood also uses authorial intrusion to guide the reader in his or her assessment of Myron's actions or to plead for sympathy, particularly from other women. She makes her moral position clear at the beginning of the novel when she introduces Myron by observing that in giving herself before marriage Myron has broken a law, but that that law is social, designed for women's protection, and that Myron's action may not have been base but rather motivated by higher feelings, even by altruism. She also makes it clear that there is a double standard for men and women in the matter of pre-marital relations:

When under no more sacred canopy than the topaz of a summer sky – with no more bridal hymn than the choral of the wind among the trees – in obedience to no law but the voice of nature – and the pleading of loved lips – with no other security than the unwitnessed oath of a man – a woman gives herself utterly, then she is doubtless lost. But it must be remembered that the law she breaks is an artificial law enacted solely for *her* protection:

and it must be conceded that there may be a great and self-subversive
generosity that permits her to give her all, assuming bonds of sometimes
dreadful weight, whilst the recipient goes his way unshackled – uncon-
demned.[26]

From the beginning of the novel Wood affirms her contrasting attitude to those women who treat Myron with contempt: "Let those
who jeer with righteous lips at women such as this poor village
outcast remember that the meek maid-mother whom they adore
perchance shrank before the cruel taunts and pointing fingers of
women at the doorways and the wells (7)." Similarly, "but far far as
Myron Holder had fallen, deep as was her humiliation, black as was
her shame, inexcusable her error, she still shines in effulgent whiteness when compared with those women who refused her aid that
long night [of childbirth] through ... had Myron Holder died no
woman in all Jamestown would have been free from her blood-
guiltiness (17–18)."

But as much as *The Untempered Wind* is concerned with the particular suffering of Myron Holder a generation or so before, it is also a
larger plea to society to be more sympathetic to the fallen women of
any time. Wood makes this clear at the end of the novel when she
pleads with the women of her day to be more compassionate and
forgiving to the working girl in her struggle for survival:

The hearts of the Jamestown women, however, have not changed. The same
merciless virtue that hounded Myron Holder pursues the poor factory girl
who falters on her way. The same pointing fingers sting her soul. The same
condemnation, the same cruelty, the same scorn, greet her as were meted
out to Myron Holder ...

   But, O women, think well before you utter a harsh judgment? Your verdict
is the more sacred by virtue of being pronounced upon your own sex, for
woman is more nearly allied to woman than man to man. Each woman is
linked to her sister woman by the indissoluble bond of common pain ...

   It rests with women whether the bitter cup these unhappy ones drink be
brimmed to the lip or not. (195)

Wood clearly felt a strong mission to direct society's attention to the
condition of the working girl. In this respect she resembles the
contemporary Saint John, New Brunswick, novelist Maria Amelia
Fytche (1844–1926), whose 1895 *Kerchiefs to Hunt Souls* dramatizes
the plight of teachers, governesses, and women in service and blames
the education system and romantic literature for not equipping
women for the real world.[27] Joanna Wood's prescription for this

problem is compassion and charity rather than the "merciless virtue" of which she clearly found much evidence in her society.

To our taste, much of Wood's presentation of Myron Holder is overly sentimental, even at times melodramatic and maudlin, and the direct narrative intrusion, characterized at times by heavy-handed didacticism, is, to say the least, discomforting. However, in her day, before the dictum of showing rather than telling was so insistently adopted by literary critics and writers, her methods were acceptable, even expected and approved. But in other ways Myron Holder lives for us today. In addition to the methods of characterization already described, there is much that is good to contemporary taste and by contemporary literary criteria. There is, for instance, the close, accurate detail Wood uses to present Myron's day-to-day life as she walks the dusty road to the Deans' farmhouse where she does domestic work, or as she enjoys the few precious moments she has with her child at the end of the day. Details of precarious survival in the face of poverty, cold, and illness ring true. Myron is also psychologically convincing. Her sense of isolation, her feelings of shame, the hurt she experiences when the "good" children of the community tease or spurn her child, the respite found in the restorative sun on a beautiful Sunday after six days of hard work, all contribute to making her a credible flesh and blood character.

While Wood's presentation of Myron Holder does have strong elements of sentimentalization, her rendering of Jamestown society is ruthlessly realistic, even at times grotesquely gothic, and much more critical. In fact *The Untempered Wind* is one of the earliest critical studies of the Canadian small town and the moralistic, puritanical spirit so many novelists have found there; Sinclair Ross in *As For Me and My House* (1941), W.O. Mitchell in *Who Has Seen the Wind* (1947), Ernest Buckler in *The Mountain and the Valley* (1952), and Margaret Laurence in *The Diviners* (1974) are obvious twentieth-century examples. Wood achieves her essentially realistic presentation by close observation and detail. In the course of the novel she describes the history, customs, occupations, church life, social activities, seasonal patterns, and speech of Jamestown by taking us down its streets and into its homes. As Jamestown is set in time just before the recent industrialization of the agricultural industry, it is essentially a simple agricultural society with related occupations, unlike the more stratified and "modern" world of that other important realistic near-contemporary novel of small-town Ontario, Sara Jeannette Duncan's *The Imperialist* (1904). In fact it is a world not far in its simple rural society and pervading tragic vision from that of Thomas Hardy's Wessex novels, with which it was compared by contemporary critics.

Shortly after *The Untempered Wind* was published, Wood listed Hardy as one of her favourite novelists.[28]

The fulcrum of Jamestown society lies within the homes of the "good women" and moral arbiters of the community, Mrs Deans (for whom Myron Holder works), Mrs Wilson, and Mrs White, who are presented with a heavily ironic voice. Their shortcomings include narrow-mindedness, self-righteousness, hypocrisy, and lack of charity. These are particularly sinister traits because the women impose them on the whole community, sniffing out and exposing those who stray from the straight and narrow path. Their self-righteousness is competitive: each eagerly watches the other for some sign of wrongdoing and implies it even when it is not found. Both Mrs Deans and Mrs Wilson anxiously await the naming of Myron Holder's child, fearing it might be named after her own son, hoping it will be named after the other's. When Mrs Wilson's son Homer is kind to Myron, Mrs Deans implies that he is the father of her child.

The households of the women are wonderful illustrations of their mistresses' limitations. Mrs Deans' is almost grotesque, with her invalid husband and "stubborn young lout" son whose central form of pleasure is watching the discomfort of the bound girl (a young woman contracted into service) and Myron Holder as Mrs Deans harangues them with criticism and contempt. This pleasure is well founded because, if it weren't for these recipients of her venom, Mrs Deans would be making life unpleasant for the observers. The contagion that emanates from Mrs Deans is seen in her husband, who, "watching the girls [the hired help] as closely as he could ... sat blinking in the sun, like a malevolent lizard lying in wait for flies." The images of sadism, blindness, and evil are perfect reflections of the spirit of the Deans household.

The limited taste and houseproud qualities of the Jamestown matrons are ironically and humorously described in the homes of Mrs Wilson and Mrs White. Mrs Wilson lends quite an "air" to her place by landscaping the approach with whitewashed stones, rockeries, pendant coconut shells, and various tin pans and crocks containing a rich assortment of plants with such charming vernacular names, ironically recited by the omniscient narrator, as Live Forever, Old Man, Lemon Balm, Creeping Charlie, Wandering Jew, Jacob's Ladder, and Jerusalem Cherry Tree.

It is in her interior that Mrs White shines, as Wood reveals in a description laden with humorous irony. Domiciled in one of the older homes in the area, Mrs White has managed to cover up signs of unseemly age by dressing the windows at the front of the house in modern green shutters and strewing the floors with an assortment of "boughten" and homemade carpets and mats in a cacophony of colour and design:

trees with roses, daisies and blue flowers with names unknown, growing luxuriantly on every branch; bright yellow horses and green dogs stood together upon the same mat in millennium-like peace, undisturbed by the red birds and white cats that enjoyed the same vantage ground with them; but finer than any of the others was the black mat placed at the center of the floor, as being less likely to be trodden upon there; its design was a salmon-pink girl in a green dress. By what was little less than inspiration, Mrs. White had formed the eyes out of two large and glistening black buttons. (121)

The home serves as showcase for the young Miss White, a lady of accomplishment, as her numerous "tidies," which cover every pos-sible surface of the parlour, attest. These she has executed in a number of challenging patterns, including "Rose of Sharon," "Spider-web," "Sheaves of Wheat," "Double Wheel," and others where her imagination to name them has failed and which she simply calls her "One in strips," or the "Fancy patterning tidy." One cannot help but think of Anne Hébert's "House on the Esplanade" (1953), in which the mechanically produced lace doilies of Mademoiselle Bichette are also images of life in death.

Other "improvements" in the White home include the covering of an oak fireboard with wallpaper (pink roses on a white ground with blue border) and the bedecking of the mantel with a china vase containing paper flowers, a lamp in the oil of which is a red flannel cloth, "thought to be decorative as it showed through the glass," a cross cut out of perforated cardboard, and two clove apples. (Wood with tongue in cheek gives complete directions for making a clove apple, in case the reader should covet this prize.) Art tastefully enlivens the walls of the White home, including "a highly colored print representing a pair of kittens against a red velvet background, playing with dominoes; ... a glazed chromo of a preternaturally blond baby, sleeping in a preternaturally green field"; and "purple wools on a perforated cardboard asked again the piercing question, 'What is Home Without a Mother?'" (123) The poor taste and lack of appre-ciation of quality in these interiors are images of the closed, insular world that is Jamestown. For Wood, a writer with an appreciation of literature and art, they are images of the suffocation in this society of the artistic soul.

Other images of Jamestown are presented in a less entertaining fashion. Family life and relations are unpleasant and mean-spirited, even gothic. Myron's grandmother despises her granddaughter not only because she has brought "disgrace" to the family but also because she has always been jealous of her son's love for his wife, Myron's mother. Mrs Deans and Mrs Wilson trust in their sons very little, as we have seen. When Homer Wilson gives up his successful career in the city to return to his parents' jeopardized home and help pay off the mortgage, his brothers and sisters, who do not help, accuse him of robbing them of their birthright. When Homer, saving Myron's child, is killed by a runaway horse, his mother betrays her trust so far as to ask Myron if he was her son's father.

In Jamestown the motives for social visits are not friendly, nor are those for church attendance spiritual. Mrs Deans and Mrs Wilson visit to gossip and to plant seeds of doubt in their "friends" about their offspring. The good citizens attend spiritual revivals in order to testify and ensure their proper social standing. Matrons have the minister in to show off their good housekeeping and domestic finery. The pervading mean spirit extends into the work world, where farmer Disney tries to keep the good apples and give his sharesman the windfalls, or Henry Deans shuts down the local tavern owner by asking for a bottle of wine for church after hours and then reporting him for selling it.

The worst examples of Jamestown's cruelty are presented in the treatment of Myron Holder. No one dares to defy the rigid, puritanical attitude of Mrs Deans and her associates, so Myron is not talked to on the street, or is treated to pointed stares and rude comments when she goes by. She bears her child alone and is taken advantage of by Mrs Deans, who works her like a horse for hardly any wage, all the while declaring what a charitable gesture she has made in employing a girl of her character. When Myron's grandmother dies, the other women do not help Myron to keep vigil at the side of the dead through the night, as is the local custom, but leave her in her little cottage to face the shadows and darkness alone. The Methodist minister tells Myron, after the death of her son, when she is utterly alone, that she is a vessel of sin and, in order to avoid contaminating good people, must proclaim her sinfulness wherever she may go, even beyond Jamestown. Only one person in the community, Homer Wilson, helps Myron with wood during the cold winter or offers her a ride in his wagon on the long walk she has out to the Deans' farm. For being kind to Myron, Homer is ostracized by polite society and becomes the victim of malicious gossip. When he dies saving Myron's child, his paternity seems confirmed, for the town.

The most gothic image of Jamestown society is the character Bing White, a strange, terrible little boy who loves to see blood. Bing's arms are covered with self-inflicted "wolf bites," and he tortures birds and animals. The several brief appearances of the evil Bing in the novel well capture the malevolent spirit of the town. Wood makes the allegory explicit: "There was a strange and horrible parallel between his nature and the nature of the women who tortured so ceaselessly the woman whom fate had made their victim; a little difference in method, a little divergence of application, a slight change from the physical to the mental world – that was all save a dreadful difference in the victim; but the instinct of cruelty was the same (100)."

Whereas Wood uses her narrative voice to intrude and plead directly to the reader for understanding of Myron Holder, she adopts a coldly ironic voice for the rest of Jamestown's inhabitants, particularly the women: "Mrs. Deans had a modestly good opinion of herself. 'Thou art the salt of the earth' impressed her with all the directness of a personal remark" (27); "woman and mother as Mrs. Deans was, she was never moved by their [the bound girls'] needs" (29); "Mrs. Deans was a good woman, therefore she looked with unutterable contempt at Myron Holder" (29).

The grimness of Jamestown's treatment of Myron Holder is leavened somewhat by Wood's description of day-to-day rural life. Her detail lends humour and authenticity to the novel and is the strong point in all her best writing. She particularly has an ear for dialect and local expressions and beliefs. If a person is angry, he "has his ears back," or if a person is ambitious, he has "washed more than he can hang on the line." Local wisdom is reflected in weather prediction:

"The smoke is falling, the ducks and geese are flying about, the maple leaves are turned underside up, the cocks are crowing, the cat is eating grass, the gulls have left the lake and fly over the land, the flies sting, and the cement on the cellar floor is damp, I think it's going to rain ..." said Mrs. Deans. "Yes," said her husband, "it's a deal like rain, the moon had a shroud on it last night, and the frogs croaked terrible and my rheumatics has just been romping." "Yes," went on Mrs. Deans, "my corn has ached intolerable." (101)

Brief portraits of rural characters like the ragman's wife, who covers her clothes with the buttons claimed from her husband's trade, or the town drunk, Ann, who has lost her husband and child, add authenticity to the social scene, as do local stories of shrewd trading or trickery that have the quality of local legend and folklore. In her use of the vernacular, in her character portraits, and in her descriptions of the homes and seasonal activities of Jamestown, Wood achieves one of the most vivid representations of small-town Canada in nineteenth-century fiction.

Critical reception of *The Untempered Wind* was very favourable. Even before its New York publication, the *Week* announced:

"The Untempered Wind," a novel by Joanna E. Wood, a Canadian author, is now ready for publication by J. Selwin Tait & Sons. This is Miss Wood's first book and we are assured that competent critics declare it to be fully entitled to rank with the masterpieces of the century – with, for instance, Charlotte Brontë's first work and with the "Scarlet Letter" of Hawthorne. This book, however, is said to be unique in itself and that in its subtle analysis of village life and its vivid and accurate portrayal of character and also of the depths of cruelty to which the gentle sex will on emergency descend; it is unequalled in modern fiction.[29]

This is extravagant praise from the *Week*, which normally printed a simple announcement of an upcoming publication.

On the novel's publication, *Current Literature* of New York gave it a column of space, offering a plot summary, a brief profile of Wood, and the following critical remarks:

Miss Wood's book can be taken seriously. The story is simple, yet it is charmingly told. It is earnest and sincere. There are touches here and there that suggest a mind master of itself. There is a poetry of expression that suggests Hawthorne. There is a depth of thought and feeling that reminds us of George Eliot. There is a human element and a pathos that makes one think of Charlotte Bronte. Above all, there is a delightful style in simile and description that more than once pleases us as only Dickens can please. This may seem like an exaggerated estimate, but it is an honest one. This book deserves to live. There are one or two characters in it – notably a confirmed old reprobate – who will live ... It is safe to prophesy Miss Wood will make a literary success with The Untempered Wind.[30]

While we would deplore the comparison with major English and American novelists, which sets up impossible expectations of Wood's novel, the critic undoubtedly meant well in his or her attempt to suggest its merit. By January 1895, three months after publication, the interest in Wood had become strong enough that *Current Literature* dedicated a column to a character portrait.[31]

The Untempered Wind went through several editions in the United States, and the Ontario Publishing Company of Toronto issued the first Canadian edition in 1898. By that time the *Canadian Magazine* would pronounce the novel to be "perhaps without a peer among

Canadian novels."[32] Amid the general praise, however, one very neg-
ative review in the *Toronto Globe* hurt Wood all the more for its having
appeared in a Canadian periodical. In a letter to William Kirby
written on 6 December 1894, Wood says:

> I think you will be sorry to know that the single adverse critique my book
> has received (and it has been more widely noticed than I dared to hope) was
> given in the Toronto Globe, a *Canadian paper* – The article is so *very* savage
> and so *very* illogical & unjust that one might imagine it informed with
> personal spite – That I fancy is impossible – the sting lies in the fact of its
> being a *Canadian* paper – ... I only tell you this because I know you are
> Canadian enough to be sorry that a Canadian paper has been the only one
> to rend a Canadian work to pieces.[33]

The *Globe* review criticizes the novel primarily on the basis of what
it describes as its inaccuracy in presenting the treatment of the abandoned woman in contemporary society.[34] Against Wood's insistence
that this figure is ostracized and treated cruelly, the review claims
that she is in fact offered every assistance by all of society, particularly
women. The critic also condemns the excessive description in the
book, particularly the "analysis of soul struggles" and didactic reflections. However, she or he does find merit in the story, in its apt
parallels and images and its often skilful prose style. Its character
sketches of the "rustics" are also praised. The critic concludes quite
soundly that *The Untempered Wind* is a remarkable though not a great
book. Probably the rather excessive encomiums lavished on Wood's
first novel by the American periodicals invited the more critical
review in the *Globe*, and many of the points made therein are objec-
tively true. However, it does have a "savage" edge that may indicate
a quite predictable defensiveness against a novel set in Ontario
(although Wood never identifies the exact setting) and published in
the United States that presents rural Canada in a very dark light.

The favorable reception of her first novel and the financial success
met by her short stories allowed Wood to live and travel abroad as
she pursued her literary career. This was the first exciting period of
freedom of independent travel for women, a time when we see, for
example, Sara Jeannette Duncan, the successful Brantford, Ontario,
journalist and later novelist making a triumphant trip around the
world with another female journalist. An article in *Scribner's*, entitled
"Women Bachelors in New York," responded to the climate of the day
by describing the first "women's bachelor house" in New York, where
travelling and working women might rent rooms for a period of time.
It notes that in England women had clubs for this purpose.[35] A letter

to William Kirby, written on 6 December 1894, shows Wood to be on Mount Vernon Street in Boston, and invites the elderly Niagara novelist to visit her at her family home, "The Heights," where she would be spending the Christmas holiday.[36] She spent the winter of 1895 in Paris, and in 1896 she lived for a time in Philadelphia.[37]

The period after Wood's early success with *The Untempered Wind* in 1894 was not without sorrow, however. Her father died in 1896. As one of the youngest children and as an unmarried daughter, Wood must have felt pressure to keep her mother company at home. Before these family responsibilities closed in on her, however, she published a brief novel that moved dramatically away from the mode of her first work. There would be no more accurate portrayal of narrow village life, no more subtle analysis of treachery and deception. Instead, Wood jumped into a highly coloured romance of decadent life in New York and the American South, featuring wealthy characters and a plot reminiscent of Oscar Wilde's *Picture of Dorian Gray* (1891).

Wood's *A Martyr to Love* (1897)[38] is a highly sensational short (104 pages) novel. Its heroine is a woman of "bad blood," Laurine Tancred, a southern belle who, as the novel opens, is dramatically burning letters and laughing. These are love letters from her fiancé, a man of good character who genuinely loves her but whom Laurine is preparing to reject for a man of wholly unsuitable character, a rake and a roué. Laurine's history is revealed: she is the daughter of a woman who lived in California as a highly paid prostitute and married into the Southern gentry to give her daughter a good name. Unfortunately, the flaming letters set fire to Laurine's hair, and for several months she recuperates from burns that mar her appearance. Her fiancé receives the letter, written before the accident, breaking the engagement, and visits her to discover that she has been unfaithful. This he cannot forgive, and he insists that the engagement remain broken, though Laurine by this time is rather desperate to renew it. However, she extracts a vow of secrecy from him that he will not reveal the reason for the broken contract. His family, when it hears that the marriage is off, assumes Laurine to be the victim of a heartless man who jilted her in her hour of need, and he is banished from his home (a true gentleman of the South, he does not break his word to Laurine). Laurine vows that since he would not forgive her unfaithfulness and take her back, she will have revenge by making him fall in love with her again.

Laurine's beauty returns (although her hair inexplicably grows in dark rather than light!), and she steals away from her Southern home one night, leaving evidence of suicide and taking the gold that had been saved by her faithful old retainer, a maid who was in the employ of her mother in the bad old days of numerous "suitors" and riches. The maid dies when she discovers Laurine and the money missing.

Laurine goes to New York, where she adopts the name Amourette and lives much as her mother did, receiving jewels from her lovers, occupying a luxurious mansion, dining out in all the best restaurants, wearing splendid clothes, and travelling to France for holidays. The novel becomes very *fin de siècle* at this point, describing in detail the interiors of the fashionable French-style New York restaurants with their white walls and brass fans, and the cocktail hour where Laurine socializes with her wealthy, leisured, decadent bohemian friends. One day she is introduced to a famous and wealthy artist who has been worshipping her and wants to paint her portrait. He, of course, is the former Southern fiancé on whom Laurine wants to work her revenge. He does not recognize her, presumably because she was supposed to have committed suicide and also because her hair is a different colour. Another unexplained development is that she now falls in love with him, losing her former need for revenge, and for a time, as he paints her portrait, the two are happy. Laurine does have qualms about having the portrait done, however, because she has always believed that were she ever to have her portrait painted, she would die upon its completion.

Apparently because of the genuineness of her love, Laurine now undergoes a moral reformation, sells off her finery for charity, and lives in modest circumstances. The two plan to marry, but Laurine wants to wait until after the New York visit of her fiancé's pure, maidenly niece; she is concerned that if her true character were revealed to the niece, it might taint her. Just as it appears that the niece will marry and leave Laurine and her fiancé to their life together, an episode of confused identities leads the fiancé, who has completed her portrait, to believe that Laurine has been unfaithful and to kill her in a fit of jealousy. He discovers afterward that in fact Laurine was trying to protect the supposedly pure niece, who had been seeing a man of bad character (who is, remarkably enough, none other than the man for whom Laurine broke her original engagement). So Laurine pays belatedly for her waywardness; her fiancé is a broken man, and the portrait he has completed is sold to a New York beer hall, where it decorates the bar.

Clearly the sensationalism, coincidence, improbability, and total lack of any serious content, not even the redeeming rustics and local colour of the earlier novel, define *A Martyr to Love* as pure pulp. As melodrama and utter escapist popular entertainment it is quite good; as the narrator says, while one does not condone women of Laurine's character, one is interested in them. The novel, like her short fiction, would appear to be an example of Wood's willingness to write, at times, pot-boilers for the popular market. Yet there is a possible reading of *A Martyr to Love* that lends it some significance. In it Wood explores both the economic condition of women in the nineteenth century, prostitution being one of the few avenues of economic independence, and the dark side of male-female relations, particularly the link between women's beauty and their marriageability or economic well-being.

A Martyr to Love is not unlike several other Canadian romances of the day that exploit the decadent turn-of-the-century artistic world. However, *Martyr* does not do so as well as Maria Amelia Fytche's *Kerchiefs to Hunt Souls* (1895),[39] in which sensational bohemian scenes in the Paris art colony are wedded to serious social analysis of the condition of women vis-à-vis education and work. Nor does Wood do as well as Sara Jeannette Duncan, who locates *A Daughter of Today* (1894)[40] in both the Paris and the London art worlds to explore the character of a woman who uses her attraction for men to advance her career as a writer. The motif of the fatal painting certainly echoes Wilde's use of that motif in his *Picture of Dorian Gray*, but Wood does not begin to extract from her portrait the depth of symbolism achieved by Wilde. Both the fire that destroys Laurine's original beauty and the painting that threatens to represent her as she really is could have been used to heighten and explore her psyche. However, Wood opts instead for the easy route of reformation of character and moral retribution for past wrong.

Unlike *The Untempered Wind* and *A Martyr to Love*, Wood's next novel, *Judith Moore; or, Fashioning a Pipe* (1898) is not a tragedy. After her brief fling with exotic settings, Wood now returns to a local Canadian scene. Set in a small town named Ovid and presenting village and rural life realistically through its characters, incidents, and dialect, *Judith Moore* is a romance with a happy ending. In some ways it is an allegorical validation of the author's return from Europe to her own home.

Judith Moore is the story of Andrew Cutler, a Canadian farmer of Loyalist stock, who falls in love with Judith Moore, an opera singer of unnamed origin who has toured Europe to rave reviews and come to rural Ontario to try to gather her physical and emotional resources for her first American tour. At first the "rustic Antinous" and the "overtuned instrument" find their respective practical and artistic philosophies antithetical, and there are some tense moments of misunderstanding. But soon the relationship runs smoothly, as Andrew is enchanted by Judith's beauty of figure and voice and she is drawn to his strength and security. Their love grows and ripens through the Ontario spring and summer, but autumn brings Judith's cruel manager, who insists that she fulfil her contracts and takes her away to New York before she can talk to Andrew. The demands of the American tour drain Judith, and she collapses at a performance in the early spring of the following year. Andrew mystically hears her calling to him as he walks in the wilderness of his northern Muskoka property and rushes to her side, whereupon she recovers, then returns with him to Ovid and marriage.

While the plot of *Judith Moore* is certainly trite and improbable, there are qualities that make the novel quite fascinating. As details of the plot outline suggest, the novel demands an allegorical or mythical reading. The central characters, Andrew and Judith, while they are not wholly satisfactory in realistic terms, are archetypal: he, in his strength, manliness, and moral uprightness, of the young Canada; she, in her beauty and sensitivity, of art. Andrew embodies Canadian history in his Loyalist lineage and his eighteenth-century farm home with its fine old furniture and well-kept English gardens, modelled on the Augustan ideals of the first officer-settlers of the country. There is an intense, mystical relationship with the land that becomes apparent in his annual restorative visit to his northern property, where he walks the woods in tune with cold and wilderness; he is at one point described as carrying "the austerity and intensity" of the north in him.[41]

Andrew's honest, upright qualities are particularly apparent in contrast to the character of Judith's manager, who is grasping and manipulative, interested only in money and worldly acclaim. Andrew's rusticity suggests the infant state of Canada. Judith, with her nervous disposition, exquisite voice, and love of decorative dress, is the embodiment of art. We are never told Judith's country of origin. By bringing the two together, Wood suggests the potential of art to flourish in Canada. This was a theme common in post-Confederation literature, when the first generation to be raised as Canadians searched for a Canadian literature. Examples of the search appear in the essays of Charles G.D. Roberts, the *At the Mermaid Inn* columns of Archibald Lampman and his Ottawa colleagues, and in the journalism of Sara Jeannette Duncan, and many novels of the day attempt to define the Canadian national character.[42] The mythical qualities of Wood's novel reinforce the perception that art and the native spirit are not yet compatible in this country. The novel is a dream utopia in the tradition of William Morris[43] rather than a work of realism.

Several scenes in the novel involving Andrew and Judith have totally mythic qualities and cannot be taken seriously on any other level. Their meeting is such a one, in which Andrew, who has been sowing grain, hears Judith's voice singing in a nearby wood and runs towards her as if in a trance: "Andrew hardly seemed as if acting on his own volition. He had been summoned; he went ... Andrew's heart throbbed with something of that hushed tumult with which we approach some sacred shrine of feeling, or enter upon some new intense delight" (28). Their meeting is described as unconscious dream: "There are moments in real life, so exotic to lives into which they have entered that one hardly realizes the verity of them till long after, when the meaning of his own actions struggles through the mists and confronts him with their consequences. So it is in dreams, which reconcile with magnificent disregard of possibilities, the most wonderful conditions of person, place and time. 'I have come,' he said, half dreamily – stepping out of the shelter of the trees" (30–1).

The courtship includes scenes in which Andrew introduces Judith to his land by taking her on walks where he names the plants and animals, and Judith takes Andrew to undreamed-of emotional heights by her song. The path of love does not run smoothly at first, when Andrew criticizes the impracticality of Judith's attire and she finds the "frontier spirit" of Ovid to be stifling, but this friction quickly passes as the fundamental attraction of the two gains ascendancy. Judith is a revelation to Andrew, who until her arrival has had no one with whom he can discuss the literary books he hides beneath his bed at home. One cannot help but think of later novels (such as *As For Me and My House*, *The Mountain and the Valley*, and *Lives of Girls and Women*) in which Canadian characters, often potential artists, hide away to read or write or paint in fear that their uncomprehending society will catch them out. Canadian society traditionally, in keeping with the frontier spirit, has considered time spent on books (except, of course, the Bible) to be time wasted. Andrew's world is also a revelation for Judith. Its natural tranquillity has a medicinal, restorative effect after the demands and pressures of Europe. As she visits some of Andrew's favorite haunts, "enjoyment [is] so intense as to be almost painful" (102), and "for a moment, in Judith's mind dream and reality [become] confused" (103).

There are many signposts in the novel to guide the reader in a mythical reading. The name of the town itself, of course, reinforces the allusion to art, as does a long quotation that serves as introduction to the book from Elizabeth Barrett Browning's "Fashioning a Pipe," in which Pan draws a reed from the river and works it into an instrument of music. Wood makes the point, in introducing one of the "rustic" characters of the novel, that although art has not yet found a place in Ovid, there does seem to be potential: "It may be said here that throughout Ovid and its environs Susanna's proper name was a dead letter. She was 'Sam Symmons' Suse' to all and sundry. The Ovidian mind was not prone to poetry; still, this alliterative name seemed to have charms for it, and perhaps the poetical element in Ovid only required developing; and it may be that the sibilant triune name found favour because it chimed to some dormant vein of poesy, unsuspected in its possessors" (19).

In passages such as this one realizes Wood's intent to help to awaken her country to its artistic possibilities. One realizes it as well in the rather stylized, elevated, "artistic" language that characterizes the description of the land and the central characters of the book and in the seasonal, vegetational myths that underpin the novel's structure: Judith comes to Ovid and meets Andrew in the spring; their love develops and "ripens" in the summer; the manager separates them in the fall; Judith languishes in the winter; and Andrew returns to fetch her with apple blossoms in the early spring.

Wood's intent is also apparent in the description of Andrew's winter walks in the north, when he gains some summit and "pausing, looked far across the peaks of graduated hills, clad in sombre cedars weighted down with snow, white, silent yet instinct with that mystery which presses upon us pleading for elucidation" (57). Wood adopts the method already used by the Canada First proponents, that would be pursued by artists like the Group of Seven and modernist poets in the 1920s, of using the northern landscape to epitomize the spirit of the country. It is on his annual northern trek that Andrew mystically hears Judith calling to him from New York for help. This scene also sustains Wood's theme of the desirability of art in this country:

Far away from New York, in the silent spaces of a virgin forest, a man was lying on the snow, his gun beneath his arm ready for use. But he was keeping no lookout for game. His eyes were fixed upon an open space amid the tree tops, where a solitary star twinkled desolately. His face was thin, his eyes burned; the snows, the silence nor the solitude could calm that throbbing at his heart, could cool the fever of his veins ... Then ... there came to him, faint, aery, bodilessly, the words of a song – a song that ended in a plea, "Come. Come to me," and when it died away, Andrew Cutler sprang to his feet with a cry that echoed far between the icy tree trunks of the forest, "I come, I come." (227–9)

Andrew travels to Judith's New York hotel room in his faded velveteen work jacket and tweed work pants, carrying a large armful of Ovid crabapple blossoms. There, his wholesome presence and love are the instruments whereby Judith regains her health.

In presenting the wholesome Canadian prototype helping a tired and enervated art back to life, Wood suggests that the relationship between Canada and the arts is reciprocal – Canada has her role to play and her contribution to make to the world of the creative imagination. As in the slightly earlier stories by "Seranus," Canada is presented as a world far from the "madding crowd" where natural beauty and solitude provide the ingredients in which the creative spark may ignite and bring forth something memorable and lasting. At the end of the novel Andrew and Judith's love is described as a "poem": "They sometimes even dare to dream that their love will bestow upon them their own immortality – that through eternity they will be as they are now, together and happy" (240).

How does one explain the very different tone and theme of *Judith Moore* from those of *The Untempered Wind*, her other "serious" novel to date? The difference is, apparently, in the author's intent. In *The Untempered Wind* Wood was concerned about a social problem that she felt was pervasive in her time, that of society's intolerance of the abandoned woman. She adopted a tragic mode to heighten and dramatize that character and make her point. In *Judith Moore* she is concerned not so much with what is but what might be, not so much with a social problem but a cultural possibility. She adopts the mystical, dream-like mode to propose her passionately felt idea of her country as an Eden for the artist.

While there is a mythical structure to *Judith Moore*, the real charm and the enlivening ingredient of the novel is Wood's ability to re-create rural Ontario life. This is not the grim, rather gothic world of *The Untempered Wind* but one that has charm, beauty, and humour, although there certainly are limitations as well. Two homes in Ovid are the focal point of the novel, that of the Morrises, where Judith boards, and Andrew Cutler's home, presided over by his maiden aunt. Mrs Morris is a delightful humorous character and illustrates in a light manner the shortcomings of the local vision, particularly regarding art and literature. A thoroughly practical-minded person, she observes that Andrew Cutler has "a crank on books." A literal-minded Protestant, she dreads idolatry. When Judith describes the view from the Morris window on a particularly fine day as a "perfect idyll," Mrs Morris throws some stones she thinks Judith had been looking at down the cistern, confusing "idyll" and "idol." Although Wood treats Mrs Morris as a figure of some fun (as she did occasionally the matrons in *The Untempered Wind*), she also solicits strong compassion for her. All five of Mrs Morris's children die as infants, and beneath that rather rough and ignorant façade beats a warm and kind heart. In fact, all Ovid is seen with compassion by Judith, who thinks:

The pity of it! ... looking up at the miracle of the summer fields ... the upward aspiration of every blade of grass ... everything reaching toward the light. And these people surrounded by the strong silent stimulus of nature, going with their eyes fixed upon the clods, ... striving to grasp some puny self-glorification, letting the real gold of life run through their fingers like sand ...

When Judith heard one woman say to another, "She's a most terrible nice woman. She works like a horse," she did not feel as much like laughing at the narrowness of the vision ... as weeping, that life had ways which people trod wherein brutish physical exertion seemed the highest good.   (115–16)

Many of the townsfolk are portrayed as rather comic rustics, but not with malice. There are Hiram Green, who tries year after year as a member of the school board to hire single teachers with whom he might pair one of his five rather uncomely daughters, and the impish Tommy Slick, who administers purple stripes from his mother's dye to Mr Green's white horse, and Aikens, a home boy, raised like a slave on a local farm, who trades one kind of slavery for another when he marries a shrewish wife who keeps him on a very short lead. Village life is presented too in the superstitions and home remedies offered Sam Symons when his horse is in bad health. These include, as the locals sit in Sam's kitchen, Epsom salts, ginger, saltpetre, sweet spirits of nitre, rye, asafoetida, bleeding, bran mash, turpentine, salt, Black's Condition powder, and so on, as each of the male members of the community contributes his store of rustic knowledge. The remedies are brought to an end, however, when Sam returns from the barn to announce that the horse has died. Wood also has a remarkable ear for local pronunciation and phrases that capture the flavour of small-town Ontario better than any of her contemporaries. "'She does look gashly!' said Mrs. Morris. 'Whatever would I do if she was to be took! And this minute she looks fit for laying out'" (69).

Judith Moore did not receive the critical acclaim on its publication that had been accorded *The Untempered Wind*. It was not as widely noticed, nor was the praise so extravagant. Without doubt one impediment to recognition in the United States was that the novel was published in Canada. One is strongly tempted to speculate that the Canadian setting and theme further contributed to the diminished interest of American critics (although the setting of *The Untempered*

Wind can be recognized to be southern Ontario, it is never specified). *Judith Moore* did receive a short review in the *Nation* that rather tepidly pronounced that the novel "reminds one of a pale water color in a white frame with pink corners" and that "whatever its limitations, [it] has the merits of brevity and cleanliness."[44] The *Canadian Magazine* was kinder. In its review of *Judith Moore* it announced Wood to be one of Canada's foremost novelists, along with Charles G.D. Roberts and Gilbert Parker. It sums up the qualities of the book: "The great merit of the book lies ... in the charm of Miss Wood's descriptions, her faultless prose, her keen insight into motive, and her power for humorous characterization. She describes rural Ontario life with a charm never before found in any book. She sees the narrowness and meanness of village life, its pathos, its humour and its possibilities."[45]

Apparently the Ontario Publishing Company had great confidence in Wood as a novelist, no doubt largely because of the American success of her first book, because the same review noted that the publishers were said to have paid the highest price ever for a Canadian novel. It would seem that the publisher was satisfied with its Canadian reception, for a few months later the *Canadian Magazine* announced that *The Untempered Wind* and *Judith Moore* would be brought out in a special edition, "bound uniform."[46] Further evidence of Wood's financial success at this time is the prize of five hundred dollars she won for a short story, "The Mind of God," which appeared in the *Canadian Magazine*.[47]

After *The Untempered Wind* and *Judith Moore* Wood never again employed a Canadian setting in her novels. The reason likely lies in her desire for an international reputation and the lack of interest among American and British publishers in books that dealt seriously with Canadian concerns or used a setting of little interest to their audiences. The abandonment of the Canadian setting seems to have had an effect on her writing. Although her next two novels still display a strong ability to present village life and "rustics" with humour and interest, their themes become more sensational, romantic, and popularly entertaining. Gone are the serious social concern of *The Untempered Wind* and the idea of art in *Judith Moore*. What replaces them are more decadent, *fin de siècle* themes of evil, vampire-like women who lure men with their fatal beauty, sap their energy and goodness, and gain power and control over them. Both are rather melodramatic tragedies.

A Daughter of Witches (1900)[48] is set in a rural area of New England and draws on Wood's experience living in Boston after the publication of *The Untempered Wind*. It employs the current interest in hypnotism and the occult in the creation of its heroine, Vashti Lansing, who is, as the title suggests, the descendant of a woman burned at the stake for withcraft. Vashti is a dark, troubled character, driven to demonic acts when her love for her cousin, Lanty Lansing, is not returned. There is some suggestion that her powerful evil is responsible for Lanty's becoming an alcoholic after his marriage to his fair and good cousin Mabella, and she certainly does contribute to the deterioration of the couple's relationship by carrying false messages between them and doing little to support their character in the community.

In retaliation against Lanty and Mabella's marriage, Vashti marries Sidney Martin, a pale Bostonian aesthete who worships her dark beauty and whom she easily controls. Although he has no conventional religious faith (he is perhaps best described as a transcendentalist lover of nature and art), Vashti persuades him that if he loves her he will train for the ministry. She desires this because the parsonage is the finest home in Dole and the role of the parson's wife is the most prestigious. Sidney is also independently wealthy, which adds to his charms for the scheming Vashti. Her manipulation of Sidney after their marriage is increased by hypnotic treatment of the headaches that increasingly plague him. So great is her power that she eventually is able to control the content of his sermons, changing them from the loving and gentle ones of his early ministry to a dramatic fire and brimstone peroration near the climax of the novel in which she is able to vent all her pent-up venom and hatred towards a community she holds in contempt for not being as powerful as she. Vashti's wickedness is discovered, however, when she is caught "haunting" the terrified Mabella, who is alone in her home one night soon after the sermon. By chance Lanty discovers the caped and dark figure of Vashti at the window, and very quickly he and Mabella discover the author of their discontent. The novel concludes with happiness restored to Mabella and Lanty, Sidney a recluse in nature, and Vashti an invalid, paralysed by something like a stroke after her duplicity is discovered, and doomed to live the rest of her life passively and in the control of others.

Clearly, in its main plot *A Daughter of Witches* is a sensational novel. However, it features some marvellous "rustic" or rural characters, particularly the comic Temperance Trilby, the faithful servant in the Lansing home. In the presentation of Temperance, Wood displays once again a sharp eye and ear for life, unfortunately not in this case wedded to a satisfying overall idea or design. The novel is notable as well for its rather *fin de siècle* interest in the fatal woman, a character found in the poetry of Swinburne, whose writing Wood admired, and his "decadent" disciples. Perhaps of most interest, though, is speculation about the reason for Wood's interest in Vashti – the jealous or slighted woman. It is possible to see Vashti, in her rejection by the man she loves, as representative of the thwarted woman, her fear and insecurity as typical of women's consciousness in a society where love and marriage are the *raison d'être* and failure to find them is disastrous. Through Vashti, Wood may be expressing the frustration and anger of women in a world that gives them little outlet for their energy and ability. It is particularly significant that Vashti insists that her husband become a minister, a figure at the centre of the rural patriarchal order. By controlling her husband she controls the community, a retaliation against the power that was usurped from her when she was unsuccessful in attracting Lanty's affections. The dark images of evil that emanate from Vashti suitably capture the psychology of this figure. Of course Wood's novel has the traditional moral ending in which "good" is rewarded and "evil" punished. However, it is very much the case that Vashti is the most fascinating character in the novel, and that the others – the pretty Mabella, the muscular Lanty, and the weak Sidney – are pale indeed by comparison.

A Daughter of Witches was reviewed in England as popular fiction. The *Athenaeum* described it as having an original theme: "the influence of a strongly magnetic and forceful personality … over an ultra-refined and delicate soul, Sidney Martin, whom she marries."[49] It notes, however, that "most people will prefer to the 'problems' of the book a very excellent account of various specimens of American rusticity. Miss Temperance Trilby, the 'help' of the New England farmstead, is an excellent portrait." The *Spectator* declared that the book would have been charming "but for the blot of the unnaturally unadulterated wickedness of the heroine."[50] It liked Wood's "subsidiary characters [who] are drawn with delicate humour." After returning to the subject of the unrealistic heroine, the review noted that the book is "excellently written and can be heartily recommended." The *Canadian Magazine*, which first published *A Daughter of Witches* serially, was more favourably disposed to it. It approved of its "fresh humour, vivid insight into the feminine nature, and its real dramatic power."[51] It also approved of the heroine: "The study of Vashti – a woman whose passionate and undisciplined temperament is probably incomprehensible to commonplace minds – is one of the strongest pieces of work in recent fiction." It ended with the rather parochial remark that "*A Daughter of Witches* with some local colour in the Canadian country scenes, with which the authoress is so familiar, would have been even more successful."

Meanwhile, however, the author was seeking respite from the familiar Canadian scenery by frequent visits abroad. A portrait in the *Canadian Magazine* in 1901 informed the reader that she was back in Canada after a visit of several months to England.[52] She was presented at court that year in London. Morgan described her in *Types of Canadian Women Past and Present* (1903) as "even now away from home on a visit to England."[53]

Wood's next novel, *Farden Ha'* (1902),[54] reflects this hankering for scenes far from Queenston Heights and the Niagara farmland, and Wood's desire to participate in the larger literary life beyond Canada. *Farden Ha'* is a tragic romance in which the heroine, Marriotte Hamilton, who married only to escape a very unhappy family situation and whose marriage has never been consummated because her husband respects the fact that she does not love him, has a child by another man. She, the child, and her lover die in a mine shaft during an explosion, and her husband, in a rescue attempt, dies also, of gas fumes.

The novel is set in a coal-mining town, Trailfit, in Scotland, a town that very much resembles the Lanarkshire area in which Wood was born. Wood had visited Scotland on her European travels and draws on this experience for details of local landscape, dialect, and folkways. The novel focuses on the inhabitants of Farden Ha' (Farthing Hall), a partially restored fantastic old ruin, once a castle, of which the tower and quadrangle remain. Like their home, these people are fantastic and bizarre. The husband, David Hamilton, who has been disowned by his well-to-do family for making an unsuitable marriage, has lost his small funds on a farming venture and now works in the mines and lives with a wife whom he treats as a child. Marriotte (Hogg) Hamilton, his wife, married to escape a family cursed by "bad blood" and has her own bedroom. Little Davy, an orphan adopted by David Hamilton, is a hyper-sensitive and possessive (of David) child, a natural musical genius whose violin-playing in the tower mirrors and heightens the emotions below. The stranger, Harald Bowman, nephew of the mine owner, has come to manage the mine; he boards at Farden Ha' and falls in love with its mistress.

From the beginning the novel is filled with portents of the terrible doom that hangs over Farden Ha': rooks and magpies stir restively in the eaves of the hall as Harald Bowman comes to town; David Hamilton and Harald Bowman meet in the doorway to Farden Ha' as "Life and Death at the portals of Eternity"; Davy plays plaintively and heart-breakingly on the night of Bowman's arrival; the townspeople are uncomfortable at the look of Bowman and read the signs that disaster is immanent. Dark birds, feverish violin music, the dark hall, and the knowing stares of the townsfolk provide a tragic chorus throughout the novel, heightening the unhappy action. There is also a Cassandra figure in the character of old Betty of the Knocken, who knows that Marriotte is destined for tragedy. Atmosphere is provided by a violent storm and fallen meteor the night Bowman realizes that Marriotte and David do not live together as husband and wife. The natural landscape contains such folk superstitions as a "fairy well" and a "murderer's stone." As the attraction between Marriotte and Bowman develops, Marriotte sits Penelope-like in her home sewing fantastic designs in scarlet thread. In short, most of the ingredients of the gothic romance and of Scottish superstition are used to heighten this tale of illicit love.

The one quite fascinating feature of the novel is the building and fruition of the relationship between Marriotte and Bowman. Their attraction is primarily physical, Bowman bringing out all the "bad blood" and gypsy in the dark Marriotte, who is an exact opposite of Bowman's correct English fiancée, the fair and even-tempered Edith. The forbidden relationship builds with great tension as the two lovers go through the usual trite domestic motions under the watchful eyes of her husband, Bowman's host, and little Davy, who loves David and does not want to see him wronged. The culmination of the tension comes one day after Bowman has realized that Marriotte is a wife in name only. David is away and young Davy is in the tower playing tempestuous Hungarian gypsy music. Bowman chances to walk into Marriotte's room, where he discovers her dancing in a trance of passion to Davy's music, wrapped in her red-embroidered cloth:

The door was half opened, the uncurtained window let in a flood of glorious sunshine, and dancing in this radiance was a vision which half blinded him. A woman, with bare arms and neck, swathed about with yards and yards of gaily-broidered cloth, the floating ends of which she caught in delicate finger tips, and swayed in graceful arabesques so that she seemed surrounded by flashes of different lights – like a spark dancing in a flame. Her hair was unbound, and floated about her in a dark cloud ... This was no longer Marriotte Hamilton. It was a creature of flame. A *gitana* maddened by the music of Czardas – a Zingara knowing no law save those of her own passions, no fear save that her lover might withdraw his love ... The music grew wilder – the dance more wonderful – she began to croon to herself – her song was one name. He heard it – "Harald – Harald –"

He entered and shut the door.

She wheeled like a flash, her drapery like scarlet flame about her – she stood for a moment rigid – poised a-tiptoe like a slender Diana, her eyes glowing – her cheeks carmine – her lips like the buds of the Begonia they call "bleeding heart."

Then she was in his arms. (211–12)

At this point the author closes the door on the ensuing scene of passion; Wood had gone as far as she dared, and further than most women writers of her day ventured, in describing erotic and illicit love. Although she does protect herself and her characters by having them describe their love in subsequent scenes in elevated, spiritual terms and by heaping dire, fateful consequences on them, and although it is known all along that Marriotte was married in name only, yet she does in essence present a torrid, passionate, physical relationship. Once again, as with *A Daughter of Witches*, the reader can hardly help speculating that in her presentation of the woman who defies society's taboos and dares to act according to her own will, Wood is speaking to some need in the women of her day.

Wood dedicated this novel to her brother William, who had continued to act as her best critic: she seems to have relied on his judgment. The dedication reads as follows:

> To my brother,
> WILLIAM WOOD,
> I offer this story of the grand old land
> We both love so well.

William must have been proud of his sister's accomplishments, because he had her novels specially bound into one volume.

Farden Ha' was not as widely reviewed as *A Daughter of Witches*. Perhaps the *Athenaeum*[55] review is typical of the novel's reception. It says that the picture of Scottish rural life Wood presents is distinct and that the author's style is vigorous, though she is not yet "mistress of her craft"; she elaborates irrelevant matter and wanders off into general reflections. It does question the morality of the novel, which seems to suggest that a man should ignore the situation when another man comes into his home and gets his wife with child. It also accuses the author of lacking humour.

Farden Ha' does resemble Wood's own earlier novels, with the exception of *Judith Moore*, in that it once again shows her fascination with women who defy society's laws. These women allow passion rather than propriety to rule their lives; they are rebels who ally themselves with nature rather than society. With the exception of Myron Holder in *The Untempered Wind*, they use their "feminine arts" to gain ascendancy over men; they are of the "witch" or "vampire" breed. The novels may be seen as a response to the relative powerlessness of women in the late nineteenth century, a rebellious statement with the therapeutic function of releasing pent-up or thwarted energies and desires. The images of darkness, evil, and the supernatural all reflect that repressed, taboo, subterranean world of feeling and desire that had no easy outlet for women in Wood's time.

One other point may be made about Wood's philosophy or "ideas" in her novels. In *A Martyr to Love* the narrator postulates a theoretical question: what if all our moral laws are the result of some perversion of man?

How strange if all these restraints that we call moral laws were evolved from the moral deformity of some far back progenitor – some man in whom nature warped the free, true impulses, so that ever after he and his descendants were hived in cages of laws – well, it is hard to tell, and, at any rate, it would be madness to open the cages.[56]

This passage recalls the narrator's defence of Myron Holder in *The Untempered Wind* when she observes that the law Myron has broken is a social law, not divine. Wood does not go far with her exploration of the arbitrariness of Victorian moral and social codes, but she is quite remarkable among nineteenth-century Canadian women novelists for raising the matter at all. It would seem that her experience, perhaps in England not far from Swinburne and the Pre-Raphaelite circles, led her to doubt or at least to treat with some ambivalence the social laws that guided the vast majority of women of her day.

Those social laws – especially the conventions regarding the filial duty of an unmarried daughter – now beset the thirty-nine-year-old author. The farm at Queenston Heights, which had remained in the Wood family for ten years after the father's death, was sold in 1906. Joanna Wood and her mother moved to "The Knoll," at Front and Regent Streets in Niagara-on-the-Lake.[57] By this time Wood's literary career had fallen off, perhaps in part because of the claims of filial responsibility, perhaps because the type of writing she did no longer drew the kind of interest it once had. Other personal factors might account for the cessation of her writing. She is reported to have had a nervous breakdown, although it is not known when;[58] it or its symptoms may have interfered this early with her ability to write. While no reason has been given for her illness, one can speculate from her life and writing that the early success and high expectations followed by a later falling-off of her literary career, combined with the frustrations and tensions of being a single woman seriously pursuing a career in a world where the vast majority of women still married and had families, may well have been factors. Certainly life in Niagara-on-the-Lake in 1906 must have been anticlimactic after the excitement of her literary travels in the previous decade.

In addition to living with her elderly mother, Wood maintained a friendship in Niagara-on-the-Lake with another woman writer, Janet Carnochan, author of numerous articles and several books about the history of the Niagara region.[59] Like her friend, Wood presented occasional papers at the Niagara Historical Society meetings. The woman who had been hailed as one of Canada's best novelists and had her photograph taken by "Otto" in Paris and her portrait painted "by Lord Gwydyr's clever granddaughter" was now giving talks on "Impressions of Europe" (April 1908) and "Reminiscences of Queenston" (February 1908)[60] in what was virtually her home town. There must have been few compatible spirits indeed in Niagara in the early twentieth century for the woman who had enjoyed such early literary promise, lived in the most exciting cities of the world, known some of the prominent people of her day, and espoused enlightened ideas on writing.

In 1910 Wood's mother died. At some time not long after this she began the pattern she followed for the rest of her life, of living alternately with her sister, Mrs Jessie (Alex) Maxwell, in Detroit and her brother, William, in New York. She corresponded with Janet Carnochan of Niagara. A letter written to Carnochan in 1915 shows a glimmer of the old independent fire and the love for her country of the fifty-two-year-old expatriate living in Detroit. Wood describes attending a peace parade:

And oh my dear – there was a company of Canadians out to take part in the parade and I *wish* you had seen them – not a man of them under 6 foot. I was by the kerb & I raised by voice in what might be termed a yell. Canada – Canada – Canada For Ever – my dear, every man jack of them "faced" my way & the man in command saluted – Oh I was so elated – it was fun & I can assure you I was proud as a peacock – I suppose it was not *strictly* speaking ladylike – but oh my dear when I saw the maple leaf on their caps all the throng melted & I saw Niagara Common with the blue Lake on one side & the green ridge of the mountain on the other.[61]

In 1919 Wood sent Carnochan a poem that once again betrays emotion for her homeland, but this time it is that of sadness and loss:

Dear old Niagara I have come
Back to your doors again
And as I neared your shaded streets
I felt a thrill of pain –

But – A bird's note thrilled
From a high high tree –
And the sun gleamed through the rain –
My footsteps turned to where I hoped
A welcome stayed for me –
I reached the doors – the house was closed –
I said "Can these things be?"
"I've come to Fairview and behold
No latch string out for me?"
But close at hand
Within the shrine
Created for things past
I found my friend – I saw her smile
Was comforted at last!! –[62]

The poem suggests the sense of loneliness and isolation Wood must have felt in a world that seemed to have forgotten her.

No trace of Joanna Wood is extant from the period of this letter in 1919 until her death in Detroit at the home of her sister in 1927. Her death went unnoticed in Canadian periodicals of the time, except for obituaries in local papers. Indeed, so obscure had her life become that until a few years ago it was assumed in standard Canadian reference books that she died in 1919.[63] Miss Elsie Stevens of St Catharines is to be credited with correcting this error, through great scholarly persistence. It has thus been possible to discover the few obituaries that exist. Joanna Wood was buried in 1927 in the family plot at Fairview Cemetery, Niagara Falls. By then, though, her period of literary activity was long over; she had lived outside Canada for many years, and the modernists were fast leaving her generation behind.

From the brief portraits that appear in magazines of her day and from family communications it is possible to determine something of Joanna Wood's character. She was described as not being a "new woman" politically, as not being concerned about the suffrage question.[64] She was described too as enjoying feminine attire and decor, a taste that is certainly borne out by her photographs. We know nothing of Wood's romantic life. However, from the novels one surmises that she was a woman capable of understanding and feeling great passion. An undated poem by Wood in the possession of Miss Stevens suggests that Wood did at some time feel the power of love strongly:

I dreamed that Love was but a little child
A weakling thing to cherish and command –
And so held out my arms, and bid him in

To rest and shelter in my heart of hearts.
He took my heart, and taking it he wrought
With it as best him seemed – and soon I knew
That He – not I – did give command. And swift
Rebellion came, and against Love I fought
... [Ellipses are those of the poet]
I once thought Love a Child! But now I know
That Love's an angel, great and very strong –
So great I tremble and most greatly fear
And turn with fear to hide fear in his arms.

Wood did take her writing seriously and had definite ideas about writing and society. In her article on Swinburne she defends his controversial *Poems and Ballads* (published in 1866, the year before she was born) and insists on the right of the writer to describe the human body:

That we may not paint the beauty of the flesh in words when every day it is painted in pigments is one of those contradictory propositions which, to use a Scottish expression, "rouse the birse" of every artist who employs a pen instead of a brush. The anaemic art which affects to despise the body is essentially false and worm-eaten. To despise the bodily life as apart from the spiritual and mental is as who should despise the very precious vessel which contains the elixir of life; of bodily needs and passions is twisted that "silver cord" which binds body and soul together – let him who would ignore it beware, for if the "golden bowl" of the body is broken, the "silver cord" of its needs and longings loosed, our day's work is ended. Well! the chisel no longer usurps the right to confer immortality upon mortal beauty![65]

She was also liberal-minded in her attitude to society, particularly the poor or those who had transgressed against society's laws. She may have been the model for the character Miss Marshall, a good woman who takes in orphans to live on her farm, in the story "Betty and Bob" by the Niagara writer Ann Helena Woodruff.[66] Certainly her sympathetic treatment of the heroine who is "a mother but not a wife" in *The Untempered Wind* shows a strong concern for the abandoned woman in society. Wood was also a woman of ambition who, for the ten productive years of her literary career, pursued her writing in a professional way, travelling to and living in the settings of her novels (Boston for *A Daughter of Witches*, Scotland for *Farden Ha'*) in order to capture local atmosphere. Her novels, in their depiction of manners, attitudes, folkways, and dialect, demonstrate keen perception of regional characteristics.

Finally, Wood dared to be different. In her defence of the poetry of Swinburne, and in her fascination in almost all her novels with unorthodox women of passion and sensuality, she reveals a woman of independent thought. *A Martyr to Love* employs a heroine who is the daughter of a prostitute and chooses to follow in her mother's profession. In *A Daughter of Witches* her heroine marries in spite and bitterness a man whom she does not love, and brings all her powers of vengeance to play on the man whom she did love but who spurned her, and on his wife. In *Farden Ha'* a woman who is married to one man has a torrid affair with another. Her choice of such protagonists suggests that Wood had achieved some distance for herself from rigid Victorian standards.

What must be our final assessment of Joanna E. Wood? She was one of the earliest novelists to present rural Canadian life in realistic and critical terms. No nineteenth-century writer better presents the sound, smell, and feel of day-to-day village life in this country. She also had an admirable ability to create rural types, often with humour and affection. In most of her novels she raised questions about the role of women in society, exploring those who defied society's restrictions. Like other women novelists of the nineteenth century, she used the stylistic tools of the popular novel, sensation and romance, to present her subversive themes powerfully and effectively to her largely feminine readership. In her treatment of questions relating to women Wood is important to the development of feminist themes in Canadian literature. She is also significant, in her accurate and "felt" depiction of place, to the development of realism in the Canadian novel.

Conclusion

Sextet: six writers playing variations on the theme of creative energy, playing in spite of or perhaps because of the pressures of daily living, and adding the bittersweet tone of their sex. Each of the six novelists produced at least one novel well worth a reading by anyone interested in Canadian social history, in the status and accomplishments of women in the nineteenth century, and in the power of fiction to create its own place and time and people. Leprohon's *Manor House of de Villerai* (1859), Robertson's *Shenac's Work at Home: A Story of Canadian Life* (1868), Fleming's *Lost for a Woman* (1880), Wood's *Untempered Wind* (1894), Saunders' *Girl from Vermont* (1910), and Harrison's *Ringfield* (1914) all have fine qualities, even if we would hardly apply to any one of them the terms that novelist-critic Robert Barr applied to Harrison's *Forest of Bourg-Marie*: "a work of genius ... superb in character drawing, noble in diction, thrilling in incident."

The lives of the sextet span one hundred and twenty-four years, from 1823, birth date of Margaret Murray Robertson, to 1947, death date of Marshall Saunders. The regional sweep of their experience embraces California and Scotland, the slums of New York and the musical salons of Ottawa, the tradition-bound town of Niagara and the seigneury on the Richelieu bound by a different tradition.

In a time and a place tending towards conventionality, these six women writers emerge as unusually energetic and enterprising. Perhaps living as women in post-colonial Canada had something to do with their strength. As colonials, all Canadians had learned devious ways of circumventing the social and moral edicts of an imperial centre, just as women had developed ways of circumventing patri-archal edicts. Post-colonial Canadians faced a confusion of tastes and ideas imported not from one imperial centre but from three: Britain, the United States, and France; simultaneously, nineteenth-century women were bombarded by varieties of certainties about their status, needs, and duties – from religious groups, from art movements such as Pre-Raphaelitism, and from the suffragist rebels in all the "mother" countries. All these new developments encouraged a traditional fem-inine stance of quiet ironic acceptance of discrepancies between accepted ideals and actual practice.

Study of the lives and works of our six authors does more than add a Canadian footnote to books such as Ann Douglas's *Feminization of American Culture*. Taken together, this sextet of writers contribute significantly to our understanding of nineteenth-century preoccu-pations and dreams in Canada as well as the aspirations and devices of creative women in all times and places.

These people were not part of a literary school, not even part of a loose network of congenial colleagues. Each was barely aware of the existence and creations of the others. In fictional modes our sextet range from sophisticated sketch to melodrama, from society romance to sordid exposé. What they wrote appealed to a number of different audiences: each writer captured a feeling of life that a segment of her contemporaries chose to enjoy in recreational reading. Each cre-ated fictions that fitted into the desires and fears of many readers. Together they can be taken as indicative of popular taste in a suc-cession of nineteenth-century audiences.

Those audiences are gone now, but the fictional work of these six Canadian women writers has qualities that can still catch both our fancy and our intellectual concern. Each story is crafted with enough verve and colour to remain readable. From the ensemble of the fictions certain common strains sound, making us conscious of the subtle connections between women and fiction, gender and genre.

Fiction, it appears, has some sex-specific qualities. Women story-tellers shift the traditional elements of the story of the human quest, adjusting the tale of the "hero with a thousand faces" when that face has feminine lineaments. The six women in our group, in spite of their range in time, place, and audience, share some strategies in structuring conventional stories so as to allow for a female bias. Lifted out of their cultural and biographical contexts, the stories together constitute a noteworthy and surprising vision of women's life and values.

In this group of stories the development of the women characters in particular piques our interest and reminds us of changes in the self-image and desires of women readers. Women characters in these novels often change and develop to an extent and in ways not observable in other literatures. Thus, while courtship is often the ostensible concern, learning through experience or through pursuing a self-directed quest or *Bildung* is a major theme. In many of the fictions feminist remarks, made even by outwardly conventional protagonists, question women's education and opportunities. For example, an unmarried mother in one of Wood's novels and a woman artist in another both question the situation of women. With all these writers, minor characters are shown leading interesting lives – competent, self-assured, public-spirited – even when the protagonist is more conventional.

As we note the recurring development of contrasts between two women characters within a novel, we can speculate that these contrasts externalize the conflicts within the writer herself. Consciously or unconsciously she scripts her own story within that of her characters. Parts of herself that she may not dare admit to – ambition, jealousy, desire to conquer, aspects of her more passionate nature – may be ascribed to a woman character (often presented ostensibly as the villain of the piece). Sometimes, too, the woman character who is, at least on the surface, disapproved of is given the more intelligent, wittier lines. Leprohon foregrounds such a woman in *Florence; or, Wit and Wisdom*. Wood, in *A Daughter of Witches* and *Farden Ha'*, creates as protagonist an intelligent, passionate, evil woman – the sort of woman to whom an earlier writer such as Fleming might assign only a supporting role. Wood's women have the power to manipulate those around them, both male and female. Wood's strong evil protagonists are punished, of course – but only after the readers have been afforded a chance to identify briefly with female force and power. With the exception of Wood, women characters who are disapproved of are not usually destroyed, or at least not as violently as in novels by male authors.

It is interesting to speculate on the absence of mothers from most of these novels. In most cases the protagonist has no maternal guidance. Nor are children much in evidence, in spite of expectations based on the contemporary assumption that a woman's life centred on mothering. Women like Louisa in Leprohon's *Stepmother*, obviously criticized by the author for being superficial, mercenary, and manipulative, fail to win the hero – he is kept for the proper heroine – but the stepmother wins at least a second prize, a worldly, superficial man, a kind of mirror-image of herself.

Artists themselves, our novelists at times create artist protagonists. Wood's brilliant international opera star Judith Moore captivates her

Canadian farmer lover with her artistry. The union of the artist with the representative of the Canadian – the northern landscape – allegorizes the creative potential of late nineteenth-century Canada, at the same time giving the reader the expected resolution to a courtship story. Leprohon's artist protagonists are more problematic, however. Her lively Florence Fitz-Hardinge, whose creativity is reflected in her journal and sketch-book, is both too lively and too satirical. She loses her wealthy, aristocratic – and conventional – suitor to a gentle, submissive – and conventional – young cousin. This novel does not end, as most courtship novels do, with marriage, but concludes only when Florence's irrepressible tongue has caused her own physical collapse and serious injury to her husband. Docility rather than energy, humility rather than wit, Leprohon's readers may conclude, are the social attributes required of young women. But Leprohon, herself witty, creative, and quick, is surely encoding another theme, the injustice of such a verdict. At the time of writing Florence's story Leprohon was an unmarried nineteen-year-old, becoming much involved in Montreal society and no doubt beginning to see that for a young girl in a bourgeois provincial town it was dangerous to reveal too much liveliness, wit, and creative ability. The young author was aware that her own wit and cleverness must be masked in social situations. "Seranus" Harrison's Pauline, in *Ringfield*, completes the series of portraits of woman as artist. This powerful actress plays a fatal part in the fall of Joshua Ringfield. Such a vision of the artist's power is related to Seranus's passionate insistence on her own value as a writer, but it is also an absolute vision of the antagonism between artistry and the constraints of religious inhibitions.

Fleming comes close to completing the female quest with *Lost for a Woman*, in which her protagonist runs away from the conventional happy ending of sentimental romances – aristocratic marriage and wealth – to make her own way in the world. But the novel does not conclude here, with the hero now on her own and open to the variety of experiences that her independence suggests. The writer imposes closure: the protagonist leaves her contented, independent life for remarriage, this time to an artist figure. Such an ending, while less conventional than the earlier marriage, since it includes neither wealth nor title, nevertheless integrates the protagonist into conventional social structures. It thus lends credence to Rachel Blau Du Plessis's contention in *Writing beyond the Ending* that "*Bildung* and romance could not coexist and be integrated for the heroine at the resolution."[1]

The Canadian novelists we have examined can, to a point, be read as illustrations of some general themes about women's use of narrative structures. In Du Plessis's words, for women in nineteenth-century fiction, "usually quest or *Bildung* is set aside or repressed, whether by marriage or death" (3–4). Du Plessis points out the effect that the woman writer's dilemma has on the narrative structure of her novel: when the writer is faced with the decision between quest and marriage for her protagonist, there is "a disjunction between narrative discourse and resolutions ... a sense of contradiction between the plot and the character, where the female hero/heroine seems always to exceed the bound that the plot delineates" (7). Such a resolution, Du Plessis points out, while "obeying social and economic limits for middle class women as a group, is in conflict with the trajectory of the book as a whole" (70). One senses such a contradiction when Fleming's Dolores, in *Lost for a Woman*, leaves her independent home life for marriage, and when Leprohon's talkative, satirical Florence, rather than finding the happy, successful life such a clever, attractive young woman might be expected to enjoy, is shown to be causing her own destruction. These novels, it seems, are characterized by what Du Plessis describes as "the struggles between middle and ending, quest and love plots, female as hero and female as heroine" (7).

Yet although many of the Canadian sextet's books simply reinforce the conclusions of established critics such as Du Plessis, others among our examples offer something more – some unique working out of woman's lot. Thus Leprohon dared to be different in her creation of Blanche de Villerai, a young seigneuresse who asserts when she meets the handsome, charming young man to whom she has been affianced in childhood, "I will never marry him till I have learned to love him," and rejects him at the end of the novel with the words, "I hope, Gustave, you do not share the error, that an unmarried woman must necessarily be unhappy ... Though I may eventually marry, if I chance to meet one of your sex whom I may learn to love and respect, I certainly will never marry to please them, and to escape the dread appellation of old maid." Such an unconventional resolution to a courtship story is neverthelss in accord with the character of Blanche as perceived throughout the novel, and may be seen to be a natural evolution for the writer, too. Settled as a mature wife and mother, Leprohon was now able to give the reader a novel in which there is not a "struggle between middle and ending, female as hero and female as heroine."

Margaret Murray Robertson's Jean Dawson, in *The Twa Miss Dawsons*, whose lover drowns, is a rare instance of Robertson's concluding a novel with her protagonist unmarried; this is the one Robertson novel in which the protagonist is a successful businesswoman. But

Robertson's *Shenac* also offers us a strong, self-determining woman, one who with equal independence chooses to marry.

Saunders' Patty Green in *The Girl from Vermont*, a strong woman involved in many social causes, rejects her handsome young suitor for his widower father, a man with whom she can debate issues and for whom her love evolves through growing trust and friendship. Du Plessis offers the theory that strong women frequently marry such trustworthy older men, as in Jane Austen's *Emma*, as "a way of using and occupying otherwise superfluous female energy": "Rising up the imaginary ladder of maturity and class is a substitution for independent quest" (8). But on the contrary, with Saunders' Patty it is possible to see a successful conjoining of quest and marriage.

Fleming's Dolores in *Lost for a Woman* runs away from the sentimental novel's happiest of situations – and survives to make a second choice for herself. Leprohon's Antoinette in *Antoinette de Mirecourt* also reverses the conventions of sentimental fiction: she defies her father and society's strictures when she marries an alien, an Englishman, secretly; the novel does not stop there but goes on to show the dire results of such a union, and then on again to show her happy, self-directed second choice. Again, both Canadian writers have presented a more energetic and hopeful vision of the potential for self-determining women.

This tendency culminates in the work of Joanna Wood. Wood, more than the other writers considered in this book, foregrounds the driving or passionate woman, a character who appears frequently in Fleming's novels in a peripheral, usually antagonistic, role. Wood considerably alters the romance convention in *Daughter of Witches* and *Farden Ha'* by scripting into them elements of women's existence not usually revealed – a capacity for jealousy, anger, and intense passion. Her protagonists respond passionately to the relative powerlessness of women in the late nineteenth century, and they are made to suffer from their attempts to control their own destinies and the men in their lives – one dies with her lover and their child; the other survives paralysed.

In varying ways these writers were moving away from the story of the conventional woman's life as scripted by romance writers to write stories that did not end as did the traditional courtship story. Saunders' popular animal stories direct attention to animal rights, but she also shows concern for other social issues – sometimes feminist, more often humanitarian social concerns – poverty, slum housing, poor working conditions. Leprohon is often concerned with the alien and her disruptive effect on a family, sometimes as protagonist, at other times as catalyst in the affairs of others. Wood's Myron in *The Untempered Wind*, an unmarried mother, is shown bringing up her child in a small, harshly judgmental village.

For contemporary readers of these late nineteenth-century women writers, the messages about self, role, love, marriage, career, and power were probably exhilarating even though muffled. For modern readers the stories as a group reveal unsuspected currents of female desire. Novels by Leprohon, Fleming, Wood, and Saunders show rebellion against patriarchy, women's lack of power, and the ideology inherent in conventional courtship plots. As readers, whether considering Leprohon's Blanche de Villerai or Wood's Myron Holder or Saunders' Patty Green or Fleming's Dolores or Harrison's Pauline, we see protagonists who are heroes rather than heroines, women who in their lives question or clash with or reject traditional roles.

Reader-response theorists may question whether the writers intentionally or unintentionally encoded the feminist meanings that emerge for us and may have stirred women readers of earlier generations. Perhaps, in the words of Stanley Fish, "What utterers do is give hearers and readers the opportunity to make meanings (and texts) by inviting them to put into execution a set of strategies."[2] Perhaps, as Wolfgang Iser explains, readers as co-creators supply what is implied rather than written, filling in the gaps, finding what is "embryonically" in the text.[3] We can never know how our predecessors decoded these stories. But their vast popularity suggests that some response deeper than casual time-passing was at work.

After considering in their historical and social contexts the six life-stories with their interfacing fictional tales, we can return to the problem of this sextet's current exclusion from the literary canon. Are these novels indeed the work of writers who knuckled under in tough circumstances and dissipated their talents? Or are they the work of writers clever enough to embed still-powerful messages in formulaic stories and stereotypical characters? Did these works disappear because they lacked depth, or were they unfairly bypassed by a biased academy? Must we assume that they are inferior to the works that have been judged valuable by recent critics – the works of Mrs Moodie and Sara Jeannette Duncan, for instance? Have we here a case of non-survival of some of the fittest?

In answering this last question at least we can remember that by the end of the nineteenth century Mrs Moodie's fame had evaporated. Furthermore, even when in the 1960s a renewed interest in pioneering life revived *Roughing It in the Bush*, her other novels were not similarly resurrected. Sara Jeannette Duncan's political novel *The Imperialist* also returned from obscurity during the revival of literary nationalism in the 1970s, although it was not in fact very successful on publication in its own time; and despite the appearance of three recent book-length studies of Duncan as part of a resurgence of interest in women's writing, only two of her other novels have been reprinted. L.M. Montgomery and Nellie McClung have always maintained their hold, but as producers of paraliterature in the subgenres of children's fiction and social polemic. We must ask whether such writers have survived or been revived because of superior talents or because of unrelated circumstance; and as a corollary, whether Saunders, Fleming, and the others may enjoy a similar literary rebirth. The answer can only be given after the evidence is in, and the evidence appears in books now out of print and hard to find. We hope the present study will encourage a re-examination of the evidence and enable at least a partial revision of judgment.

We cannot dismiss these writers as naïve producers of formula fiction or as the Harlequin romancers of their day. Each exploits and explodes the formulas she uses. Fleming, for example, in her last novel parodied (as does Margaret Atwood in our own time) the conventions of the popular novel. She was never the victim of the conventions but was well aware that in a paradoxical way they set her free to invent her own diversions and subversions. Leprohon used the conventions of the sentimental novel to write historical fiction, and in fact made political use of the conventional romantic plot. Wood's fiction, which at times incorporates elements of the sensational, does much more. Her *The Untempered Wind* is a problem novel primarily concerned with the situation of unmarried mothers in small-town Canadian society – sensational stuff in a special sense – but it also incorporates a realistic and vivid picture of the unsensational minutiae of small-town life.

Wood and Leprohon, Saunders, Robertson, Harrison, and Fleming – each in a different way adds to our understanding of the power of popular fiction. As a group they also offer us a broad and richly detailed view of the literary activity and exchange of their times, the models and taste of their country and its regions, the channels of dissemination of entertainment and ideas, and the modes and pressures of critical reception. Besides performing all these solemn and honourable tasks, our sextet can still be counted on to provide all the ingredients of a good read – laughter, suspense, pathos, stimulating ideas, and vicarious thrills. We hope they will be taken seriously by future literary historians – but not so seriously as to undercut their primary function – to capture and captivate yet further generations of readers.

Notes

INTRODUCTION

1 Elaine Showalter, *A Literature of Their Own: British Women Authors from Brontë to Lessing* (Princeton, NJ: Princeton University Press 1977), 73.

2 May Agnes Fleming, *Lost for a Woman* (New York: Carleton 1880), 8.

3 Rosanna Leprohon, *The Manor House of de Villerai*, in *Family Herald* 1, no. 12 (1861): 93.

4 Joanna E. Wood, *Farden Ha'* (London: Hurst and Blackett 1902), 211.

5 Marshall Saunders, *The Girl from Vermont* (Boston: Griffith and Rowland 1910), 3.

6 Saunders, *Beautiful Joe's Paradise* (Boston: Page 1902), 320.

7 S.F. Harrison ("Seranus"), *Crowded Out and Other Sketches* (Ottawa: Ottawa Evening Journal 1886), 94.

8 Wood, *Judith Moore; or, Fashioning a Pipe* (Toronto: Ontario Publishing 1898), 69.

9 Wood, *A Martyr to Love* (New York: Town Topics 1903), 45.

10 *Lost for a Woman*, 10.

11 Sandra M. Gilbert and Susan Gubar, *The Madwoman in the Attic: The Woman Writer and the Nineteenth-Century Literary Imagination* (New Haven: Yale University Press 1979).

12 Mary Kelley, *Private Woman, Public Stage: Literary Domesticity in Nineteenth-Century America* (New York: Oxford University Press 1984).

13 "The Little Page," in *For the Other Boy's Sake* (Philadelphia: Banes 1896), 118.

14 Wood to Janet Carnochan, Elsie Stevens' scrapbook, St Catharines, Ont.

15 Carole Gerson, *A Purer Taste: The Writing and Reading of Fiction in English Nineteenth-Century Canada* (Toronto: University of Toronto Press 1989), ix.

16 Margaret Nancy Cutt, *Ministering Angels: A Study of Nineteenth-Century Evangelical Writing for Children* (Wormley: Five Owls Press 1979).

17 Jane Tompkins, *Sensational Designs: The Cultural Work of American Fiction 1790–1860* (New York: Oxford University Press 1985).

18 Mary Jacobus, ed. *Women Writing and Writing about Women* (New York: Barnes and Noble Books 1979).

19 Drusilla Modjeska, *Exiles at Home: Australian Women Writers, 1925–1945* (London: Sirius Books 1981).

20 Lorraine McMullen, ed. *Re(Dis)covering Our Foremothers: Nineteenth-Century Canadian Women Writers* (Ottawa: University of Ottawa Press 1990).

21 Barbara Godard, ed. *Gynocritics: Feminist Approaches to Canadian and Quebec Women's Writing* (Toronto: ECW Press 1987).

ROSANNA MULLINS LEPROHON

1 Since 1940 there have been reprint editions in English of two of her novels and a scholarly edition of one; three short stories have been included in anthologies; two articles and a set of factual notes have appeared, one doctoral thesis, and entries in the comprehensive series *Canadian Writers and Their Work* and in the *Dictionary of Canadian Biography* – a surprising paucity of attention considering current interest in Canadiana and Victoriana.

2 She later changed her middle name from Ellen to Eleanora, according to A.H. Deneau (Brother Adrian), "Life and Works of Mrs. Leprohon," MA, Université de Montréal 1949. Except where otherwise noted, biographical details are based on this thesis.

3 *Histoire de la Congrégation de Notre Dame: Annales de l'Institut* (Montreal: Maison Mère de la Congrégation de Notre Dame de Montréal, 1810–1941), pt 3, XIX siècle, *1840–1849*, vol. 8 (1941): 109–10.

4 Student Accounts List, Archives, Les Soeurs de la Congrégation de Notre Dame, Register of Students, 1839–1843.

5 Ibid.

6 *Annales de L'Institut*, 8:109–10.

7 See "A Touching Ceremony" and "Tribute to the Memory of the Reverend Sister of the Nativity, Foundress of the Convent of the Villa Maria," in *The Poetical Works of Mrs. Leprohon (Miss R.E. Mullins)* (Montreal: Lovell 1881), 91–2, 179–81.

8 J.C. Stockdale, "Mullins, Rosanna Eleanora (Leprohon)," *Dictionary of Canadian Biography* 10 (Toronto: University of Toronto Press 1972), 536–8.

9 *The Stepmother, Literary Garland* (12 Feb. 1847): 79.

10 Ibid. (Mar. 1847): 136.

11 Ibid. (Apr. 1847): 172.

12 *Ida Beresford; or, The Child of Fashion, Literary Garland* (Feb. 1848): 11.

13 Ibid. (May 1848): 325.

14 Margaret Atwood, *The Edible Woman* (Toronto: McClelland & Stewart 1969), 70.

15 *Ida Beresford, Literary Garland* (Apr. 1848): 172.

16 Ibid., 176.

17 Ibid. (May 1848): 235.

18 Ibid. (Sept. 1848): 410.

19 Susanna Moodie, "Editor's Table," *Victoria Magazine* 1 (June 1848): 240.

20 "Alice Sydenham's First Ball" was reprinted in *Nineteenth Century Canadian Stories*, ed. David Arnason (Toronto: Macmillan 1976), 96–127.

21 *Florence Fitz-Hardinge; or, Wit and Wisdom, Literary Garland* (Feb. 1849): 49.

22 Carole Gerson, "Three Writers of Victorian Canada," in *Canadian Writers and Their Works: Fiction*, ed. Robert Lecker, Jack David, Ellen Quigley (Toronto: ECW Press 1983), 195–241.

23 *Eva Huntingdon, Literary Garland* (Jan. 1850): 18.

24 *Clarence Fitz-Clarence; Passages from the Life of an Egoist, Literary Garland* (Jan. 1851): 21.

25 Ibid. (Apr. 1851): 201, 203.

26 See Henry Morgan, *Canadian Men and Women of the Time* (Toronto: Briggs 1898), 577–8; and Rev. J.D. Borthwick, *Montreal, Its History; To Which Is Added Biographical Sketches of Many of the Principal Citizens* (Montreal: Drysdale 1875), 87.

27 *Eveleen O'Donnell, Boston Pilot* (29 Jan. 1859): 2.

28 *Family Herald* 1, no. 1 (16 Nov. 1860).

29 See Kathleen O'Donnell, "The Characters of 'The Manor House of de Villerai,' by Rosanna Leprohon," *Canadian Notes & Queries* 35 (Spring 1986): 9.

30 Pictures of some of the seigneuries she knew appear in *Old Manors, Old Houses* (Quebec: Historic Monuments Commission of the Province of Quebec 1927). See the de Niverville House (72) and the Montarville seigneurial buildings (129).

31 *The Manor House of de Villerai, Family Herald* 1, no. 1 (16 Nov. 1860): 1.

32 Ibid., 1, no. 12 (Feb. 1861): 93.

33 Ibid.

34 Ibid., 1, no. 3 (30 Nov. 1860): 17.

35 Mrs J.L. Leprohon, "*The Manor House of de Villerai*: A Tale of Canada under the French Dominion," ed. John R. Sorfleet, *Journal of Canadian Fiction* 34 (1985).

36 *Antoinette de Mirecourt* (1864; rpr Toronto: McClelland & Stewart, New Canadian Library 1963), 36.
37 Ibid., 17. Leprohon's words are very close to those of her neighbour, D'Arcy McGee, in an address to the Montreal Literary Club, 4 Nov. 1867, titled "The Mental Outfit of the New Dominion."
38 Deneau, "Life and Works of Mrs. Leprohon," 14.
39 *Armand Durand* (Montreal: Lovell 1868).
40 Ibid., 15.
41 *Ada Dunmore; or, A Memorable Christmas Eve, Canadian Illustrated News* (25 Dec. 1859): 122.
42 "My Visit to Fairview Villa" is reprinted in *Literature in Canada*, vol. 1, ed. D.M. Daymond and L.G. Monkman (Toronto: Gage 1978), 200–20.
43 Henry Morgan, *Types of Canadian Women* (Toronto: Briggs 1903), 1:202. Deneau, however, notes that there are no articles signed by Leprohon in *Saturday Night* and *Hearthstone*, so these works remain without clear attribution at present.
44 "Clive Weston's Wedding Anniversary" was reprinted in *The Evolution of Canadian Literature in English*, vol. 1, *Beginnings to 1867*, ed. M.J. Edwards (Toronto: Holt, Rinehart and Winston 1973), 266–301.
45 See Roy Daniells' comments on the *Canadian Monthly* in *Literary History of Canada*, ed. C.F. Klinck (Toronto: University of Toronto Press 1964), 194–7 – an analysis that does not include any reference to Leprohon.

MAY AGNES FLEMING

1 "An Interview with Mrs. May Agnes Fleming," *World* (New York), 10 Dec. 1878, p 8, cols. 2,3.
2 Baptismal record, St Malachy's Parish, New Brunswick Provincial Archives, mcf F1445, p 410, records the baptism of Mary Agnes Early on 17 Nov. at the age of three days.
3 Baptismal records, St Malachy's Parish, New Brunswick Provincial Archives, record the baptism of Catherine, aged 4 days, on 8 Oct. 1844, mcf F 1445, p 349; of Joseph, aged 10 days, on 1 Jan. 1848, mcf F 1446, p 379; of Bernard, aged two weeks, on 21 Apr. 1848, mcf F 1446, p 506.
4 Petition of Mary Early, 27 Aug. 1875, New Brunswick Provincial Records, Probate Court Records, RS 71. This petition, following the death of Bernard Early without a will, notes the existence of one son, James Patrick, of Saint John and one daughter, Mary Agnes, wife of John Fleming of New York. A further entry, dated 20 Feb. 1879, notes James Patrick's age as twenty-four. May Agnes was thirty-eight at this time.
5 Advertisement, *Morning Freeman* (Saint John), 10 Aug. 1875, p 1.

6 Ts, extract from unnamed Saint John newspaper, June 1863, Provincial House of the Religious of the Sacred Heart, Montreal. Unfortunately many records of the Religious of the Sacred Heart were destroyed by fire, and no records of the Saint John school or its prize lists exist today. I am indebted to the Reverend Sister Sheila Conroy, RSCJ, archivist, Provincial House of the Religious of the Sacred Heart, for this ts.

7 Interview, *World*, 10 Dec. 1978, p 8.

8 Ibid.

9 Petition of Mary Early. This petition is signed by Mary Early with an x, and the notation made that the petition was "read over and explained to said Mary Early who seemed perfectly to understand the same."

10 That May Agnes Early taught school in her early years is reported in W.G. MacFarlane, *New Brunswick Bibliography: The Books and Writers of the Province* (Saint John: Sun Printing Co. 1895), 31, and *Dictionary of Canadian Biography*, vol. 10 (Toronto: University of Toronto Press 1972), 269. School records are not available to confirm this, but her teaching experience is recorded in M.A. Nannary, *Memoires of the Life of the Rev. E.J. Dunphy* (Saint John: *Weekly Herald* 1877), 40, 43.

11 A number of May Agnes's early novels were published by Beadle and Adams, one of the first successful publishers of the new cheap paperbooks. The Beadle brothers – Erastus, Irwin, and James – first worked for other printers before setting up Beadle and Brothers Stereotype Foundry in New York. In 1858 Erastus joined with Robert Adams in the magazine business, and in 1860 they began publishing dime novels. In 1862 they bought Irwin, who was operating as Beadle and Co., and the company, thereafter known as Beadle and Adams, became a great publishing success.

12 "The Last of the Mountjoys," rpr in *The Old Red House among the Mountains* (New York: Lupton 1901), 27–32. This volume consists of three stories, "The Old Red House among the Mountains," by Mary J. Holmes, 4–15, and "Autumn Leaves," by Charlotte M. Braeme, as well as Fleming's story.

13 *Sunday Mercury* (New York), 26 June 1859, p 3. In the *Sunday Mercury* May Agnes's pseudonym is Cousin May Carleton rather than the Cousin Mary Carleton used in the local paper.

14 *Married for Money and Other Stories* (New York: Ogilvie 1891).

15 *Sunday Mercury* (New York), 7 Oct. 1860, p 2, cols. 4,5,6.

16 MacFarlane, *New Brunswick Bibliography*, 32, notes the publication of *Sybil Campbell; or, The Queen of the Isle* in the *Mercury* in 1861. R.G. Moyles, *English-Canadian Literature to 1900* (Detroit: Gale 1976), 133, lists several publications in book form, of which the earliest is New York: Beadle and Adams 1861.

17 *A Wife's Tragedy* (New York: Brady 1864), 38. Subsequent references are to this edition and appear in the text.

18 (New York: Criterion Books 1960). See, for examples, chaps. 6, 7.

19 Kay Mussell, *Women's Gothic and Romantic Fiction: A Reference Guide* (Westport, Conn.: Greenwood Press 1981), xi.

20 Saint John Marriage Register, New Brunswick Museum, Saint John, vol. G, 1863 to 1871, p 18.

21 MacFarlane, *New Brunswick Bibliography*, 32. DCB 10, 269.

22 See Frank Luther Mott, *A History of American Magazines* (Cambridge: Harvard University Press 1938), vol. 2.

23 "The Secret of Her Life," *New York World*, April 1889, rpr *Daily Sun* (Saint John), 5 Oct. 1903. Ganong Scrapbook no. 3, New Brunswick Museum, Saint John.

24 "The Secret of Her Life."

25 *Saturday Night* (Philadelphia), 1 Aug. 1868, p 4.

26 Ibid., 19 Sept. 1865, p 4.

27 *Baronet's Bride; or, A Woman's Vengeance* (Chicago: Donahue, n.d.), 231. Subsequent references are to this edition and appear in the text.

28 Interview, *World* (New York), 10 Dec. 1878, p 8.

29 Ibid.

30 See R.E. Murch, *The Development of the Detective Novel* (Port Washington, NY: Kenneket Press 1968).

31 See Lorraine McMullen, "The Divided Self," *Atlantis* 2 (Spring 1980): 52–67, which looks at early Canadian women writers who, "since they were creative and observant, could not help but perceive the disparity between the power and freedom of their male colleagues and the complete lack of power of their own sex and the limited experience open to them ... they consciously or unconsciously reflected their own dilemma, personifying in two women characters the conventional and unconventional aspects of their own personalities, and their own ambivalent response to their society and the role it sought to impose upon them" (66).

32 Sandra M. Gilbert and Susan Gubar, *The Madwoman in the Attic: The Woman Writer and the Nineteenth-Century Literary Imagination* (New Haven: Yale University Press 1979), 77–8.

33 Sydney McMillen Conyer, "The Reconstruction of the Gothic Feminine Ideal in Emily Brontë's *Wuthering Heights*," in *The Female Gothic*, ed. Juliann E. Fleenor (Montreal: Eden Press 1983), 95–6.

34 Interview, *World*, 10 Dec. 1878, p 8.

35 "The Sister's Crime; or, the Heiress of Ravensdale" appeared in the *London Journal and Weekly Record of Literature, Science and Art*, 15 May to 1 Sept. 1869. The author is unnamed.

36 "The Secret of Her Life," *World*, Apr. 1889.

37 Interview, *World*, 10 Dec. 1878, p 8.

38 "The Secret of Her Life," *World*, Apr. 1889.

39 *DCB* 10, 269.

40 Helen Waite Papashvily, *All the Happy Endings: A Study of the Domestic Novel in America, the Women Who Wrote It, the Women Who Read It, in the Nineteenth Century* (1956; rpr Port Washington, NY: Kennekat Press 1972), 181.

41 *The National Cyclopoedia of American Biography* (Clifton, NJ: James T. White 1931), 21:218.

42 Mott, *History of American Magazines*, 2.

43 Mary Kelley, *Private Woman, Public World* (New York: Oxford University Press 1984), 47.

44 James Derby, *Fifty Years among Authors, Books, and Publishers* (New York: G.W. Carleton 1884), 243.

45 Brooklyn City Register, reel 1198, p 9, Brooklyn Municipal Building.

46 Will 584, pp 41–2, King's County Surrogate's Court, Brooklyn.

47 See "Mrs. May Agnes Fleming," *World*, 25 Mar. 1880, p 5, col. 1; "Mrs. Fleming, the Novelist," *Daily Advertiser* (Boston), 6 Apr. 1880, p 1, col. 7; Papashvily, *All the Happy Endings*, 181.

48 "Mrs. Fleming the Novelist," *Daily Advertiser*, 6 Apr. 1880, p 1, col. 7.

49 "The Secret of Her Life," *World*, Apr. 1889.

50 Brooklyn City Register, reel 1557, pp 57–62.

51 Interview, *World*, 10 Dec. 1878, p 8.

52 "Mrs. Fleming, the Novelist," *Daily Advertiser*, 6 Apr. 1880, p 1, col. 7.

53 Interview, *World*, 10 Dec. 1878, p 8.

54 *Lost for a Woman* (New York: G.W. Carleton 1880), 8. Subsequent references are to this edition and appear in the text.

55 *New York Telegram*, 26 Mar. 1880, rpr *Saint John Daily News*, 30 Mar. 1880, p 2.

56 *New York Herald*, 27 Mar. 1880, rpr *Saint John Globe*, 30 Mar. 1880.

57 *New York Telegram*, 26 Mar. 1880.

58 Ibid.

59 Papashvily, *All the Happy Endings*, 181.

60 Interview, *World*, 10 Dec. 1878.

61 After her death, Fleming's husband tried to take control of the children but was unsuccessful. See "The Secret of Her Life," *World*, Apr. 1889. Also, Fleming's executors had some difficulty taking possession of some property she owned in the centre of Saint John, at the corner of Duke and Charlotte Streets. According to records in the Land Registration Information Office, Saint John, NB, May Agnes Fleming's executors, Francis S. Smith and Patrick Meade, attempted to gain possession of this property in 1880. Defendants in the case were Margaret McGoldrick and John W. Fleming. In July 1881 the property was

awarded to Smith and Meade by the New Brunswick Supreme Court (deed registered in bk 16, pp 302–4, doc. 56329).

MARGARET MURRAY ROBERTSON

1 "The Late Miss Margaret Murray Robertson," *Montreal Daily Witness*, 20 Feb. 1897, p 15.
2 See Harry Escott, *A History of Scottish Congregationalism* (Glasgow: Congregational Union of Scotland 1960), 254.
3 Ibid., 257–8.
4 "Death of Rev. Mr. Robertson," *Sherbrooke Gazette*, 14 Sept. 1861, 2.
5 New Register House, Edinburgh; Church of the Latter Day Saints, mcf E0045, p 15, 706.
6 See *Andrew Murray and His Message: One of God's Choice Saints* (London, Edinburgh: Oliphants 1926).
7 "The Late Miss Margaret Murray Robertson."
8 New Register House, Edinburgh; Old Parish Register, mcf 228, vol. 4.
9 Joseph G. Robertson, *Sketch of the Formation of the Congregational Church at Sherbrooke and Lennoxville* (Sherbrooke: Moorhouse 1890; CIHM 12755), 2. See also Rev. J. Douglas Borthwick, *History and Biographical Gazetteer of Montreal to the Year 1892* (Montreal: Lovell 1892), 139.
10 Borthwick, *Gazetteer of Montreal*, 139.
11 *Tenth Annual Catalogue of the Mount Holyoke Female Seminary in South Hadley, Mass. 1846–47* (Amherst: J.S. & C. Adams 1847), 5, lists Mary Robertson as a student in the senior class.
12 Ralph Connor (pseudonym of Charles W. Gordon), *Postscript to Adventure: The Autobiography of Ralph Connor* (New York: Farrar and Rinehart 1938), 8. "Mary R. Robertson," a biographical sketch of Mary Robertson prepared for the fiftieth year of the class of 1847 by Miss L.T. Guilford (11 June 1897, ts, Mount Holyoke College Archives), notes that Mary was a brilliant student, passed all her entrance examinations for the first two years, including geometry, which she had never studied, and graduated first in her class.
13 *Eleventh Annual Catalogue of the Mount Holyoke Female Seminary in South Hadley, Mass. 1847–48* (Amherst: J.S. & C. Adams 1848), 6, lists Margaret Robertson as a student in the middle class. Emily Dickinson also is listed in that class.

In a late novel, *Eunice* (1890), Robertson returns to her Mount Holyoke experience to write of two sisters, the younger of whom graduates from Mount Holyoke having completed the three years in two, while the elder has to leave the school after only one year. Of *Eunice*, the *Week* (Toronto) notes "the simplicity, clearness and thorough earnestness of purpose of this novel in which scenes and people are presented with charming naturalness and no little skill" (24 Jan. 1890, 124).

This late recollection of schoolgirl experiences recalls Marshall Saunders' use of her Scottish boarding-school experience as the basis for her last novel, *Esther de Warren* (New York: Doran 1927).

14 Mary Lyon, "Female Education: Tendencies of the Principles Embraced and the System Adopted in the Mount Holyoke Seminary" (1839, Mount Holyoke College Archives).

I am indebted to Patricia J. Allbright, College History/Archives Librarian, Mount Holyoke College, for copies of the 1846–47 and 1847–48 catalogues, the "Mary R. Robertson" ts, and Mary Lyon's "Female Education."

15 See *Eleventh Annual Catalogue of the Mount Holyoke Seminary*, 10–16, which outlines the course of study.

16 Connor, *Postscript*, 8. The biographical sketch of Mary R. Robertson also refers to this invitation to Mary Robertson to become principal of Mount Holyoke after the death of Mary Lyon.

17 "The Late Miss Margaret Murray Robertson."

18 *An Essay on Common School Education* (The Galt Prize Essay), Sherbrooke: J.S. Walton, Gazette Office 1865, 26 pp.

19 *Sherbrooke Gazette*, 18 Sept. 1861, p 2, and also Joseph G. Robertson, *Sketch of the Formation*, 2.

20 Borthwick, *Gazetteer of Montreal*, 139.

21 *Sherbrooke Gazette*, 3 Dec. 1864, p 4.

22 *Sherbrooke Gazette*, 17 Dec. 1864, p 1.

23 Montreal census, 1871, St Antoine, mcf 10046, p 93, no. 340.

24 "The Late Miss Margaret Murray Robertson."

25 Ibid.

26 Jennie's death is reported in the "Mary R. Robertson" ts.

27 "The Late Miss Margaret Murray Robertson."

28 Ibid.

29 Patricia Demers, "Robertson, Margaret Murray," *The Oxford Companion to Canadian Literature*, ed. William Toye (Toronto: Oxford University Press 1983), 712.

30 "The Late Miss Margaret Murray Robertson."

31 Philadelphia: American Sunday School Union c1866; also published later as *Shenac: The Story of a Highland Family in Canada* (London, Edinburgh, New York: Thomas Nelson 1889).

32 Connor, *Postscript*, 24.

33 See Royce MacGillivray, "Novelists and the Glengary Pioneer," *Ontario History* 65, no. 2 (June 1973): 64–5.

34 Ibid., 61–8.

35 Connor, *Postscript*, 8.
36 MacGillivray and Ross, *A History of Glengarry* (Belleville, Ont.: Mika 1979), 79–81, 85–6, 93–4, 118.
37 *Shenac*, 75–6.
38 Connor, *The Man from Glengarry* (Toronto: Fleming H. Revell Co. 1901), 121.
39 *Shenac*, 10.
40 Connor, *Man from Glengarry*, 15.
41 *Shenac*, 133.
42 Connor, *Man from Glengarry*, 266.
43 *The Inglises; or, How the Way Was Opened* (London: James Nisbet 1872).
44 *The Twa Miss Dawsons* (London: Hotter and Stoughton 1880), 11.
45 Borthwick, *Gazetteer of Montreal*, 392.
46 "The Late Miss Margaret Murray Robertson."
47 Ibid.
48 See Elizabeth Waterston, "Canadian Cabbage, Canadian Rose," in *Twentieth Century Essays on Confederation Essays*, ed. Lorraine McMullen (Ottawa: Tecumseh Press 1976), 93–101.
49 "The Late Miss Margaret Murray Robertson."

SUSAN FRANCES HARRISON

1 Harrison to Clarence Stedman, 10 May 1895, Stedman Collection, Butler Library, Columbia University, New York City.
2 Marjory Willison, "Mrs. J.W.F. Harrison – Seranus," *Canadian Bookman* 14, no. 7 (July–Aug. 1932): 80–1.
3 "S. Frances Harrison (Seranus)," in John W. Garvin, ed., *Canadian Poets* (Toronto: McClelland, Goodchild and Stewart 1916), 124.
4 Willison, "Mrs. Harrison," 80–1.
5 A. Ethelwyn Wetherald, "Some Canadian Literary Women – I. Seranus," *Week* 5 (22 Mar. 1888): 267–8.
6 "Murray, John Clark," in Henry James Morgan, ed., *The Canadian Men and Women of the Time* (Toronto: Briggs 1912), 841. Morgan incorrectly states that Dr Murray went to McGill in 1892. In fact he did so in 1872; see W. Stewart Wallace, ed., *The Macmillan Dictionary of Canadian Biography* (Toronto: Macmillan 1978), 608.
7 Willison, "Mrs. Harrison," 80.
8 Wetherald, "Some Canadian Literary Women," 267.
9 Willison, "Mrs. Harrison," 80.
10 "Harrison, John W.F.," in Morgan, *Canadian Men and Women*, 507.
11 Wetherald, "Some Canadian Literary Women," 267.
12 Ibid.
13 Morgan, *Canadian Men and Women*, 507.

14 Wetherald, "Some Canadian Literary Women," 267.
15 Willison, "Mrs. Harrison," 80.
16 This trip is referred to in Wetherald's 1888 article, 267. Wetherald refers to Harrison's having been in England "six years ago."
17 Harrison to Stedman, 16 May 1895, Stedman Collection.
18 For a discussion of the significance of Quebec in English Canadian fiction in the nineteenth century, see Carole Gerson, *A Purer Taste: The Writing and Reading of Fiction in English in Nineteenth-Century Canada* (Toronto: University of Toronto Press 1989).
19 Henry James's influential *Daily Miller*, which defined the American type in relation to the European, had been published in 1878.
20 See Gerson, *A Purer Taste*, for an analysis of the taste of the reading public in nineteenth-century Canada.
21 One of the most useful studies on the subject is Jane Tompkins, *Sensational Designs: The Cultural Work of American Fiction 1790–1860* (New York: Oxford 1985).
22 *Crowded Out and Other Sketches* (Ottawa: *Ottawa Evening Journal* 1886), 94. Subsequent references to the stories are from this edition and appear in the text.
23 Wetherald, "Some Canadian Literary Women," 267.
24 Ibid.
25 Toronto Conservatory of Music Papers, Thomas Fisher Rare Book Library, University of Toronto.
26 Morgan, *Canadian Men and Women*, 507.
27 Willison, "Mrs. Harrison," 80.
28 *The Canadian Birthday Book*, comp. Seranus (Toronto: Blackett Robinson 1887).
29 *Pine, Rose and Fleur de Lis* (Toronto: Hart 1891).
30 Edmund Clarence Stedman, ed., *A Victorian Anthology 1837–1895* (Boston and New York: Houghton Mifflin 1895). Pages 633 to 678 are devoted to poets of the Dominion of Canada.
31 Garvin, *Canadian Poets*, 123.
32 Wetherald, "Some Canadian Literary Women," 267.
33 Advertisement in *Week* (29 Sept. 1893), 1051.
34 A brochure describing her program and containing excerpts of reviews is in the H.J. Morgan Papers, vol. 10, National Library, Ottawa.
35 This excerpt is quoted in ibid.
36 An undated letter to Henry Morgan states that she is "looking after my literary interests" in New York. As the letter contains a brochure on her 1896–97 program, it is likely that she was in that city in 1897 or 1898. Morgan Papers, vol. 10, National Library, Ottawa.
37 Letter to W. Campbell, 20 Apr. 1899, Lorne Pierce Collection, Douglas Library, Queen's University Archives, Kingston.

38 Sophie Almon-Hensley, "Canadian Writers in New York," in the *Dominion Illustrated Monthly* 2, no. 4 (May 1893): 195–204.
39 *The Forest of Bourg-Marie* (London: Arnold 1898), 4. Subsequent references are to this edition and appear in the text.
40 "Recent Novels," *Nation* 68, no. 1757 (2 Mar. 1899): 166–8.
41 "Literature in Canada," *Canadian Magazine* 14 (Dec. 1899): 135.
42 Willison, "Mrs. Harrison," 80.
43 "Harrison, Mrs. Susie Frances," in Morgan, *Canadian Men and Women*, 508.
44 Ibid.
45 Letter to Dr? (name erased), 14 Sept. 1904, in Henry Sproatt Collection, Thomas Fisher Rare Book Library, University of Toronto.
46 Willison, "Mrs. Harrison," 80.
47 See n 43.
48 Pauline does not marry Crabbe, as implied in Gerson's discussion of *Ringfield* in her *Purer Taste*, 129.
49 Review of *Ringfield* in *Bookman* (London) 47, no. 280 (Jan. 1915): 134.
50 Harrison to Hathaway, 19 Feb. 1916, in the Thomas Fisher Rare Book Library, University of Toronto.
51 Harrison to Hathaway, 23 Feb. 1916, in the Thomas Fisher Rare Book Library, University of Toronto.
52 Garvin, *Canadian Poets*, 123–32.
53 Letters from Harrison to Lorne Pierce, 2 Oct. 1929, and 1932(?), Lorne Pierce Collection, Queen's University Archives, Kingston.
54 Ibid., 12 Nov. 1928.
55 Willison, "Mrs. Harrison," 80.
56 Harrison to Pierce, 2 Oct. 1929, 12 Apr. 1930, and 20 May 1930, Lorne Pierce Collection.
57 "Isabella Valancy Crawford," *Week* 4 (27 Feb. 1887): 203.
58 Elsie Pomeroy, *Sir Charles G.D. Roberts* (Toronto: Ryerson 1943).
59 Pomeroy to Pierce, 26 Jan. 1939, Lorne Pierce Collection.
60 "Victorian Poets," *Week* 4 (24 Nov. 1887): 838.
61 "To Marshall Saunders," in the Marshall Saunders Birthday Book, Lorne Pierce Collection.
62 Harrison to Stedman, 16 May 1895, Stedman Papers.

MARGARET MARSHALL SAUNDERS

1 "The Story of My Life," *Ontario Library Review* 2, no. 2 (1927): 42.
2 The diary ms is in the Saunders Papers, Acadia University Library Archives, Wolfville, NS. A ts copy of letters home is in the Lorne Pierce Papers, Queen's University Archives, Kingston.
3 30 Sept. 1876.

4 Quoted in a letter to Lorne Pierce, 11 Dec. 1935.

5 Diary, 22. A full account of Saunders' last year in school and its relation to her later work is given in Lorraine McMullen, "Marshall Saunders' Mid-Victorian Cinderella; or, the Mating Game in Victorian Scotland," *Canadian Children's Literature* 34 (1984): 31–40.

6 "The Story of My Life," 43.

7 Marshall Saunders, "How I Began to Write," ts for a speech, in the Pomeroy Collection, Mount Allison University, Sackville, NB.

8 Ibid., 2.

9 See Bruno Bettelheim, *The Uses of Enchantment* (New York: Knopf 1976), for a hypothesis about the way such legends serve to allay fears of sexuality.

10 *My Spanish Sailor* (London: Ward 1889), 62.

11 Thomas Raddall, writing fifty years later in *The Nymph and The Lamp* (Boston: Little Brown 1950) of another overwrought Nova Scotia girl married to an older stranger, uses a similar set of shipboard details to convey the sense of hysteria. Raddall's wife was Saunders' cousin; Raddall may have read and remembered the late Victorian novel dealing with a theme like his own. More probably he simply used, as Saunders did, a familiar setting for a complicated nervous effect.

12 Karen M. Saunders, "Margaret Marshall Saunders: Children's Literature as an Expression of Early 20th Century Reform," MA, Acadia University 1978.

13 In 1888 Sara Jeannette Duncan made a similar choice, publishing as "Garth Grafton." In 1895 Lucy Maud Montgomery dropped her feminine nom-de-plume, "Maud Cavendish," and began publishing under the neutral name L.M. Montgomery.

14 F.L. Mott, *History of American Magazines* (Cambridge: Harvard University Press 1968).

15 Letter from Charles Banes, 24 June 1895, Saunders Papers.

16 *Beautiful Joe* (Toronto: Standard 1894), i.

17 "How I Began to Write," 2.

18 Letter from Banes, 24 June 1895.

19 There is a reference to "your friend Roberts" in a letter from Banes, 10 May 1895.

20 *Beautiful Joe's Paradise* (Boston: Page 1902), 36. Subsequent references are to this edition and appear in the text.

21 See Margaret Atwood, *Survival* (Toronto: Anansi 1972).

22 *The Story of the Graveleys* (Boston: Page 1902), 114.

23 There was a pigeon named Princess Sukey in Saunders' aviary at this time. See *My Pets: Real Happenings in My Aviary* (Philadelphia: Griffith & Rowland 1908), 60.

24 K.M. Saunders, "Margaret Marshall Saunders," 1.

25 *"Boy": The Wandering Dog* (New York: Grosset 1916), 1. Subsequent references are to this edition and appear in the text.
26 *Beautiful Joe* (Toronto: McClelland, Goodchild and Stewart 1918), author's copy in the Osborne Collection, Boys and Girls House, Toronto Metropolitan Library.
27 Phyllis Blakeley, "Margaret Marshall Saunders: The Author of 'Beautiful Joe,'" *The Nova Scotia Historical Quarterly* 1, no. 1 (Sept. 1971): 225–39.
28 L.M. Montgomery, *The Selected Journals of L.M. Montgomery*, II, ed. M. Rubio and E. Waterston (Toronto: Oxford University Press 1987), 28 Oct. 1915, 350.
29 Ibid., 17 Oct. 1916, 348.
30 *Bonnie Prince Fetlar* (Toronto: McClelland & Stewart 1920), 189.
31 *Jimmy Gold-Coast* (Toronto: McClelland & Stewart 1924), 64.
32 McMullen, "Marshall Saunders' Mid-Victorian Cinderella," 31–40.
33 Letter to Lorne Pierce, 11 Dec. 1935, Lorne Pierce Papers.

JOANNA E. WOOD

1 "Judith Moore," *Canadian Magazine* 10, no. 5 (Mar. 1898): 460.
2 Joanna E. Wood, *The Untempered Wind* (New York: Tait 1894).
3 "An Inheritance of Dishonor: A Child's Sorrow," *Current Literature* 16 (Oct. 1894): 378.
4 "Literary and Personal," *Week* 11, no. 46 (12 Oct. 1894): 1073.
5 "Books and Authors," *Canadian Magazine* 11, no. 3 (July 1898): 180.
6 Joanna E. Wood, *A Daughter of Witches* (Toronto: Gage 1900).
7 "Literary Notes," *Canadian Magazine* 16, no. 4 (Feb. 1901): 388.
8 The author is greatly indebted to Miss Elsie Stevens, St Catharines, Ontario, for an interview in August 1985, in which Miss Stevens shared the results of her research into the life of Joanna E. Wood. The full product of Miss Stevens' work may be found in a scrapbook she has assembled on Wood, copies of which are deposited in the St Catharines and Niagara Falls public libraries, the Brock University library, and the Niagara Historical Museum.
   Much of Miss Stevens' information was obtained from a niece of Joanna E. Wood, Mrs Eckler of Webster, New York, who has since died. It is from Mrs Eckler that Miss Stevens obtained information of the Swinburne connection and through her that she saw the locket. In fact Mrs Eckler stated that Wood had been engaged to Swinburne. This does not seem likely, as there is no evidence of a romantic attachment in Swinburne's life at this time (the two would likely have met in the late 1880s, when Wood made her first travels to Europe and is said by Mrs Eckler to have met the Swinburne sisters); there was a great age difference (Swinburne was then in his fifties, Wood a girl of around

twenty), and what we know of Swinburne's "confirmed bachelor" life-style does not make a marriage proposal likely. It is worth noting, how-ever, that Theodore Watts-Dunton, or Watts as he then was, with whom Swinburne lived at The Pine, Putney, made a May-December marriage when he married in 1905, at the age of seventy-three, Clara Reich, who was then twenty-one.

It is not all unlikely that Wood may have made a "literary pilgrimage" to The Pines, or that she might have met Swinburne on one of his visits to his sisters. Wood listed Swinburne as one of her favourite poets in 1896 ("Joanna E. Wood," *Buffalo Illustrated Express*, 27 Dec. 1896, p 7) and an article on Swinburne by Wood appeared in the *Canadian Magazine* 16, no. 1 (May 1901): 3–10. The article is the only one by Wood on a fellow writer. It also suggests a more than passing acquain-tance with the author in the photographs, and includes a copy of a page of manuscript printed "by special permission" and Wood's state-ment that "she knows as a matter of fact that his translation of them [Victor Hugo's verses, *The Children of the Poor*] was as spontaneous as though he were voicing the inspiration of his own brain" (7).

Two other clues reinforce the Swinburne connection. Mrs Eckler informed Miss Stevens that the Swinburne sisters sponsored Wood's presentation at court. An article by Wood in the *Canadian Magazine*, "Presentation at Court" (17, no. 6 [Oct. 1901]: 506–10), suggests that Wood was indeed intimately familiar with that ritual and likely was presented. Finally, Henry J. Morgan, in *Types of Canadian Women Past and Present* (1903) reveals that Wood had her "portrait painted by Miss Sermonda Burrell, Lord Gwydyr's [sic] clever granddaughter." There was a distant kinship between Lord Gwydir and Swinburne; the former is listed as one of those who attended the poet's funeral in 1909 (Philip Henderson, *Swinburne: The Portrait of A Poet* [London: Routledge and Kegan Paul 1974], 282). Moreover, letters to "Dear cousin Sermonda" are included in *The Swinburne Letters*, ed. Cecil Y. Lang (New Haven: Yale University Press 1962), vol. 6: "Born in 1876, Sermonda Burrell was the daughter and heir to the 5th Baron Gwydir. She married John Henniker Heaton ... in 1902" (171).

9 Personal communication, Miss Stevens. Also see preceding note for article by Wood, "Presentation at Court."

10 Henry J. Morgan, *Types of Canadian Women Past and Present* (Toronto: Briggs 1903), 1:353.

11 Ibid., and "Literary Notes," *Canadian Magazine* 16 no. 4 (Feb. 1901): 389.

12 R.E. Watters, in *A Checklist of Canadian Literature 1628–1960* (Toronto: University of Toronto Press 1959), 420–1, lists three more titles: *The Lynchpin Sensation*, which has not been found; "Unto the Third Genera-tion," in *All the Year Round* 67 (1890): 395–404; and "Where Waters

Beckon," in *Tales from Town Topics*, no. 45 (1902): 1–112. I am indebted to Carole Gerson's entry on Wood in the *Dictionary of Literary Biography* for the latter two sources. Other short fiction by Wood appeared in the *New England Magazine*, the *Christmas Globe* and the *Canadian Magazine*.

13 Of the several recent articles on this subject, one of the best is Nina Baym's "Melodramas of Beset Manhood: How Theories of American Fiction Exclude Women Authors," in *American Quarterly* 33, no. 2 (1981): 123–39, which argues that American critics have tended to define American experience and culture in male terms, thus excluding women's experience and culture (writing) from the canon. Also, Carole Gerson, in her "Anthologies and the Canon of Early Canadian Women Writers," in Lorraine McMullen, ed., *Re(Dis)covering Our Foremothers* (Ottawa: University of Ottawa Press 1990), has provided a detailed study of how Canadian women were dropped from Canadian literary anthologies in the late nineteenth and early twentieth centuries.

14 E.K. Brown, in his article "The Problem of a Canadian Literature," first published in 1943 (in E.K. Brown, *Responses and Evaluations: Essays on Canada*, ed. David Staines [Toronto: McClelland and Stewart 1977], 1–23), cites that colonial mentality, the frontier spirit, and puritanism as the central obstructions to the writing and appreciation of literature in Canada. For more contemporary discussions of the problem, see Carl Ballstadt, ed., *The Search for English-Canadian Literature* (Toronto: University of Toronto Press 1975). Of particular interest are articles by Sara Jeannette Duncan and G. Mercer Adam that attempt to counter just the impedimenta defined by E.K. Brown over half a century later.

15 Statistics obtained at the Scottish Record Office, Edinburgh.

16 Personal communication, Miss Elsie Stevens. Also, Miss Stevens showed me a funeral notice, 1 Aug. 1854, which had been in the Wood family, concerning the Rev. James George Wood, whose mother had died in Slamanon. It is preserved in the Wood scrapbook.

17 Miss Stevens shared with me all information on the Wood property. Her scrapbook contains a picture of the Wood house.

18 "Joanna E. Wood," *Buffalo Illustrated Express*, 27 Dec. 1896, p 7.

19 Ibid.

20 Miss Stevens obtained this information from Mrs Eckler.

21 Ibid. See also n 8.

22 *Canadian Magazine* 17, no. 1 (May 1901): 3–10.

23 "General Gossip of Authors and Writers," *Current Literature* 16 (Oct. 1894): 289; 17 (Jan. 1895): 13.

24 Desmond Pacey, "Fiction (1920–1940)," in Carl F. Klinck, ed., *Literary History of Canada* (Toronto: University of Toronto Press 1965), 667.

25 Jane Tompkins, *Sensational Designs: The Critical Work of American Fiction 1760–1860* (New York: Oxford 1985).

26 Wood, *The Untempered Wind* (Toronto: Ontario Publishing Co. 1898), 6, 7. All subsequent references are to this edition and appear in the text.

27 Maria Amelia Fytche, *Kerchiefs to Hunt Souls* (Boston: Arena 1895; rpr Sackville: Mount Allison University, R.P. Bell Library 1980, with an introduction by Carrie MacMillan).

28 See *Buffalo Illustrated Express*, 27 Dec. 1896, p 7.

29 "Literary and Personal," *Week* 11, no. 46 (Oct. 1894): 1073.

30 "General Gossip of Authors and Writers," *Current Literature* 16 (Oct. 1894): 298.

31 Ibid., 17 (Jan. 1895): 13.

32 "Books and Authors," *Canadian Magazine* 11, no. 3 (July 1898): 270.

33 Joanna E. Wood to William Kirby, in the William Kirby Collection, Ontario Provincial Archives, Toronto, Miscellaneous Correspondence, box 6.

34 "Of the Making of Books There Is No End," *Globe*, 10 Nov. 1894, p 9.

35 "Women Bachelors in New York," *Scribner's* 20, no. 5 (Nov. 1896): 626–36.

36 Wood to Kirby, 6 Dec. 1894, in the Kirby Collection, box 6.

37 Miss Stevens from Mrs Eckler.

38 Wood, *A Martyr to Love*, in *Tales from Town Topics*, no. 23 (1897): 7–104 (rpr New York: Town Topics 1903).

39 See n 27.

40 Sara Jeannette Duncan, *A Daughter of Today* (New York: Appleton 1894).

41 *Judith Moore; or, Fashioning a Pipe* (Toronto: Ontario Publishing Company 1898), 59. All further references are to this edition and appear in the text.

42 See also Carl Ballstadt, *The Search for English-Canadian Literature* (Toronto: University of Toronto Press 1975).

43 William Morris's *A Dream of John Ball* (1888) or *News from Nowhere* (1891) are examples of the genre.

44 "Recent Novels," *Nation* 67, no. 1736 (Oct. 1898): 264.

45 "Judith Moore," *Canadian Magazine* 10, no. 5 (Mar. 1898): 461.

46 "Books and Authors," *Canadian Magazine* 11, no. 2 (June 1898): 180.

47 "The Mind of God," *Canadian Magazine* 10 (Apr. 1898): 536.

48 Wood, *A Daughter of Witches* (Toronto: Gage 1900). The novel was first published serially in the *Canadian Magazine* in 1899.

49 "New Novels," *Athenaeum*, no. 3801 (1 Sept. 1900): 276.

50 "Recent Novels," *Spectator* 85, no. 3 (3 Sept. 1900): 309.

51 "Book Reviews," *Canadian Magazine* 16, no. 1 (Nov. 1900): 91.

52 "Literary Notes," *Canadian Magazine* 16, no. 4 (Feb. 1901): 388.

53 Morgan, *Types of Canadian Women Past and Present* (Toronto: William Briggs 1903), 1:353.

54 Joanna E. Wood, *Farden Ha'* (London: Hurst and Blackett 1902). Further references are to this edition and appear in the text.

55 "New Novels," *Athenaeum*, no. 3874 (25 Jan. 1902): 110.

56 Joanna E. Wood, *A Martyr to Love* (New York: Town Topics 1903), 45.

57 Miss Stevens from Mrs Eckler.

58 *Niagara Falls Review*, 2 May 1927, obituary.

59 Janet Carnochan's major work was *History of Niagara* (Toronto: Briggs 1914).

60 I am indebted to Miss Stevens for bringing these to my attention.

61 A copy of this letter may be found in Miss Stevens' scrapbook.

62 This poem is included in a letter to Carnochan, a copy of which is in the Stevens scrapbook.

63 See Watters, *A Checklist*, 420, and my article on Wood in William Toye, ed., *The Oxford Companion to Canadian Literature* (Toronto: Oxford University Press 1983), 835.

64 "General Gossip of Authors and Writers," *Current Literature* 17 (Jan. 1895): 13.

65 "Algernon Charles Swinburne: An Appreciation," *Canadian Magazine* 17, no. 1 (May 1901): 8.

66 This is surmised by Elsie Stevens, as the story is set in the Niagara area, contains a character like Mrs Deans in *The Untempered Wind*, contains a farm that resembles the Wood farm, employs a social theme similar to that of *The Untempered Wind*, and the Woods and the Woodruffs were friends. Personal communication, Stevens to MacMillan, July 1984.

CONCLUSION

1 Rachel Blau Du Plessis, *Writing beyond the Ending: Narrative Strategies of Twentieth-Century Women Writers* (Bloomington: Indiana University Press 1985), 3.

2 Stanley E. Fish, "Interpreting the *Variorum*," in Jane P. Tompkins, ed., *Reader-Response: From Formalism to Post-Structuralism* (Baltimore: Johns Hopkins University Press 1980), 183.

3 In Tompkins, ed., *Reader-Response*, xv.